THE EXPERT WITNESS

THE EXPERT WITNESS

My Life at the Top of Scientology

by Jesse Prince

Copyright © 2018 by Jesse Prince

Prince Publishing
Las Vegas, Nevada

All rights reserved. No part of this book may be reproduced or transmitted in any form or by any means, electronic or mechanical, including photocopying, recording, or by any information storage or retrieval system, without permission in writing from the copyright owner.

ISBN-10: 1725992639
ISBN-13: 978-1725992634

Library of Congress Control Number: 2018909484

Printed in the United States of America

Acknowledgements

Although this memoir is about the life of one person, many others have helped me along the way to get this book born and I am very grateful to them. I thank Nancy Many who gave so much of herself to make this work happen. Without her love and care this work would not exist. I'd like to thank my friends in Chicago who helped me come back to life when it looked like my life was over. I'm talking about my brother Ron Prince and my daughter Cleopatra Joy. I'd also like to thank my two grandchildren for coming so many times to check on me while I was convalescing. I am grateful for my great granddaughter Kloe, who was also there with me through my tribulation, she truly makes my heart sing. I want to thank others who stood vigil over me in one way or another when I was helpless: Torry Smith, Kenneth George, Levette Haynes and her whole family, Jesse Wilson, Chuckaluck, my Dezi, my Jill Blue , Eva Savage, my Sheila Sandoz and others who took the time to care for me when I needed it most. I acknowledge the love and healing I received from the sacred Divine Spirit and the miracle of Norman, who kept me alive and going financially for as long as he could while I got better. I thank Tez, Freddie and Jeff

Hawkins for helping me get this book across the finish line. Finally, I'd like to thank David Miscavige for approving and choosing me, so I could tell this story to the world.

Contents

	Foreword	i
	Introduction	1
1	The Last Expert Testimony 2010	13
2	Entering the Dragon	25
3	The Upgrade	39
4	Over the Rainbow 1982	59
5	The Chosen One 1982	71
6	The Real L. Ron Hubbard	83
7	The Purge 1983	91
8	Scientology Above the Law 1983	99
9	Missions Without Mercy	113
10	Rise of the Independents	125
11	The War Begins 1984	133
12	The War Gets Vicious	151
13	Miscavige Caught in the Crossfire 1984	159
14	Traveling Man 1985	181
15	The Portland Crusade	195
16	The End of the Independents	199
17	The King is Dead 1986	209
18	WTF L. Ron?	223
19	Mary Sue Hubbard is Taken Out	235
20	Post L. Ron, Fraud on Parade	241
21	Power Play at the Top	247

22	I Have to Choose	253
23	Showdown	259
24	Time for Leaving	265
25	Finding My Way Back to Humanity	279
26	Stacy Brooks and Bob Minton, Death of Lisa McPherson 1998	287
27	Facing the Fear	295
28	Dirty Tricks	303
29	The Expert Speaks Out	309
30	The Campaign to Destroy the LMT	315
31	Switching Sides	327
32	Doing Scientology's Bidding	339
33	Reawakening	349
34	The Scientology Trap	353
35	Scientology Lies, Marty and Black Dianetics	361
36	What About Me?	371
	Appendix 1: Lisa McPherson Affidavit	377
	Appendix 2: MSH Affidavit	399

Foreword

THIS WORK TOOK LONGER than it could have to get done, however timing is everything. In my life, I've never prayed for "Things," I've never prayed for possessions beyond what I could carry. I am a praying person because I was raised by my mom to be that way. When I pray, I have always prayed for patience. Like every mother that raises a child, after an infant is weaned the next learning curve is learning to control one's emotions and desires. After that a parent teaches a child manner and morals. Al least that is the way it was in my household for a while. There was a time in the not too distant past it was inconceivable for me to have the support of friends from my past that have helped me share this story. In the beginning, it was a lonely task trying to wake my Scientology friends to the truth about Scientology. I was shunned and feared by the very people I'd spent a good part of my life living with. That was a painful and lonely experience, but I knew I had to carry on in the hopes that one day we would all understand better. That day is here right now.

The substance of this forward is not written by me, but by two old friends I've known for decades. I'll let them explain further:

The Expert Witness

Book Review by Terri Gillham Gamboa

Wow, wow and wow !!

This is a revealing and gritty, nail-biting page turner, up all night spell-binding saga that will hold you in complete suspense.....

This book is what we've all been waiting for - the real underlying sneaky, deceiving and criminal activities of the "Church" of Scientology and David Miscavige finally exposed for the world to see.

This filled in the gaps for me - what Miscavige had been up to behind closed doors with only his top aides by his side and on a "need to know" basis, this is like something out of a spy movie where heads roll and people suffer to keep the vicious and dirty past hidden…

Now we can see the true fraud, lies and deceit started by Hubbard and continued by David Miscavige and what he has done to cover the eyes of the world, the celebrities and his trusted followers who honestly have NO CLUE of the depths of this man's deceit and deception, his continuing destruction of other human lives while claiming to be the champion of "saving mankind."

A few of the key subjects revealed here:
- Fraud and lies to the IRS and FBI, Scientology as a religion only for tax purposes
- Shredding evidence & Judge tampering to hide their crimes
- David Miscavige's mother-in-law "commits suicide" in extremely suspicious circumstances where he is directly involved

Foreword

- Shredding evidence & condemning the key witness in the Lisa McPherson death in order to hide Miscavige's direct involvement and causation of her death
- Fraud and lies by Miscavige to all staff and followers about Hubbard's death and OT powers in order to continue the scam
- The fraud and scam of OT 8, a level one reaches only after spending hundreds of thousands of dollars in the "church"
- Blackmail, Brainwashing and torment of the staff & public, and Miscavige using the Scientology public as his troups to Fair Game against those that have left and are speaking out, the whistleblowers
- Conning and stealing money from the followers even resulting in suicides and failure
- Lying to the Scientology celebrities, staff and public to keep the scam going and the use of Disconnection and Fair Game for this same purpose
- Hubbard's and Miscavige's deplorable and inhumane handling of "psychotics" and "psychotic breaks" that end up driving people more insane and literally causing death
- The ousting and illegal removal of Mary Sue Hubbard

Mary Sue even stated way back then that she did not trust David Miscavige, she felt he was destructive to Scientology and that he was a deceptive power-hungry person bent on taking over everything.

She was right.

He then went on to oust every top exec in Scientology until he had achieved a major coup, had literally shanghaied the "church" to be his own tool and powerhouse against others who got in the way of his total control and personal benefit, he has since led a path of destruction for 30+ years....

Jesse describes in his book a scene from "Night of the Living Dead" where church members were calling his group "Religious Bigots" for exposing the inner secrets of the church. Miscavige keeps the members secluded from any outside information so they truly believe those speaking out are liars and bigots. They literally live in a controlled bubble, controlled by Miscavige who is the sole and only Dictator of this multi-billion dollar destructive organization cleverly camouflaged as a "church".

The details go on and on and paint a very clear picture of the nasty inner workings of Miscavige's "church".

This book will rock the world of David Miscavige and the "Church" of Scientology as well as the thousands that have fled.

Finally - the real Dirty Deeds, details and facts are exposed, the World of Scientology's inner secrets and most damaging fraud and crimes perpetrated on the International public and staff but hidden behind the brilliantly clever smoke and mirrors orchestrated first by Hubbard and then and now by David Miscavige.

Miscavige's reign of terror will finally come to an end with the revelation of these facts along with the other ongoing public exposures by hundreds of people who have left. Miscavige and "his church" can only call hundreds of people liars for so long before it comes crashing to an end and that end is near with the revelations in this book.

Foreword

We have all prayed for this day, for truth and justice for the many who have been wronged and robbed by this ongoing scam, people who have lost their loved ones, their life savings and their sanity.

Jesse says it so well in his book - what we have all experienced – what people are now crying out everywhere:

"....I realized it was what I'd experienced during those last four years of L. Ron Hubbard's life that convinced me; Scientology was a dead end and evil. Scientology makes perfect sense until the very end. When is the end? The end comes when Scientology has extracted all that it can from you, with your consent. The minute a Scientologist or Sea Org member ceases to be useful or no longer obeys; their end with the subject comes swiftly."

I have known Jesse Prince for almost 40 years and he is one of the most humorous, charismatic and likeable people you will ever meet and a true friend throughout all these years. Jesse was always a hard working Sea Org member who worked his way up to the very top level of Scientology in RTC (Religious Technology Center) – the group responsible for protecting the Technology of Scientology & Dianetics. Jesse was the right hand man to David Miscavige during Miscavige's beginning days of power and deceit. He saw and heard a lot of things that made him later speak out all over the world against the church until the church viciously took him down and he almost died as a result. This is who Jesse is though, he will not quit, he will persevere and make the truth known in any way he can. Jesse has love and compassion for his fellow man and I have always seen that in him and it shines through in this book and his determination.

Miscavige was the person taking church reports to Hubbard via Pat Broker at secret rendez-vous and then returning with Hubbard's thousands of orders and advices to the church and ASI - secret because Hubbard was in hiding and not supposed to be managing the church personally. Miscavige had the power and control of the secret boxes and was able to re-write any reports he wished in order to communicate and manipulate to attain his own goals. Self appointed as Chairman of the Board for ASI as well as Chairman of the Board for RTC and Scientology he basically took control and power of it all and ousted any that crossed his path until he gained complete authority over every top level of the church, control of all finances, bank accounts and held signed resignations for every corporate position so he could implement them if that person did not obey his wishes.

This mixture of both secular and non-secular control violated IRS rules & regulations and continues to this day. In 1993 when Miscavige threatened the IRS with thousands of law suits and even civil suits against the IRS staff personally they succumbed and gave the "church" their tax exempt status.

To this day Miscavige champions this as his greatest achievement with the event "The War is Over" that he has his followers watch repeatedly.

Little did the IRS know that Miscavige had spent millions in Private Investigators, attorneys and a large Public Relations firm to get me out of the country so the IRS could not question me as I was a Lifetime

Trustee of the top level of the church – Church of Spiritual Technology – appointed by Hubbard personally but this was not known by me as Miscavige was able to hide these corporate documents. My name as one of only 3 Lifetime Trustees was on the documents submitted to the IRS for their tax exempt status yet I had left the church forever in 1990, 3 years prior. So Miscavige knowingly submitted fraudulent documents to the IRS and paid to have a company ensure I was out of the country and in Australia for 2 years so the IRS could not question me and find the fraud he had committed.

The other 2 Lifetime Trustees were Marion Pouw & Greg Wilhere who also probably do not know of their true corporate power. They have not been seen for many years now so could well be locked away and under guard 24/7, just like Miscavige's wife, in a secret location.

Following in Aleister Crowley's footsteps – Hubbard's mentor - Hubbard and Miscavige had no respect for the law, were above the law and did not have to abide by anybody's rules. They had their own. They would simply find ways around the law or lie, cheat and steal to cover up. They became masters at it.

Miscavige then spent millions having us followed and kept track of for 28 years after leaving so that he could ensure I did not become a threat to his power and lies. Unfortunately I didn't know enough details to oppose him, information while we were in the "church" was always on a "need to know" basis - until now - with Jesse filling in the holes with this book.

The Expert Witness

Jesse is exposing here for the world to see the fraud and scam started by Hubbard and perpetrated by Miscavige since the early 1980's, conning his peers, fellow Scientologists and Sea Org members and then viciously attacking them if they dare to leave and speak out.

Miscavige has even led the Scientology staff and public to believe that he is the "chosen one" chosen by Hubbard to take over and run the "church" yet this is NOT the case at all, he stole the position from the many others personally appointed by Hubbard and used his powers to squash anyone who would say otherwise. Yet the Scientology websites state loud and clear that Miscavige was personally chosen by Hubbard to take over. Hubbard had no idea Miscavige was taking over. Many of us know that for a fact. In 1984 and 1985, right before Hubbard's death, Miscavige had managed to lose 30 million of Hubbard's personal money by investing it in oil wells that failed, the largest single loss in the history of Scientology by about 30 times. Others had been RPF'd for years for losing just 1 million. If Hubbard knew about this he would ensure Miscavige never had an executive position again, he would have been assigned to the RPF (Rehabilitation Project Force) for years or even offloaded. But Hubbard never found out as he died after this happened and Miscavige made sure it was not in any of the reports that went to Hubbard. Years later he started claiming he was the "chosen one".

Jesse also worked closely with Marty Rathbun (both in the church and then on the outside). Marty also tried to expose Miscavige but after years of harassment and life threatening activities by the

Foreword

"church" Rathbun finally succumbed in order to survive and protect his family. Leah Remini and Mike Rinder have spent many years carrying that torch which Jesse has now also picked up and taken to a whole knew level of exposure and at great risk to his own person.

I have enough personal knowledge of some of the facts that Jesse is revealing here to know that all of this makes complete sense and fills in the holes of why Miscavige later beat people up, locked up all the top execs in a trailer home under 24 hour guard at the secret International HQ's and kept them separated from their families, introverted and intimidated so they would never leave or speak out against him and so he could continue to lie to the staff about the whistleblowers and "SP's" on the outside (whom he calls "liars" and "bigots").

This is also why he had to lock his wife away at one of the secret bases, because she started saying that he was going "nuts". Same thing Hubbard's first two wives said about him.

It's obvious once you read this book why the church has tried to stop it and it has taken the author 20 years to complete and almost died doing so….. The Fair Game tactics by Scientology (a multi-billion dollar "church") and orchestrated directly by Miscavige have been horrendous and debilitating to the point of near death but Jesse has hung onto life and persevered with determination to finally release these important facts and details about the inner workings, orders and vicious demands of Miscavige and how he cleverly and relentlessly manipulates the truth to cover his Dirty Deeds against thousands of people.

THE EXPERT WITNESS

Jesse spent years as an expert witness for the "Church" of Scientology and then spent many years as an expert witness against them, exposing their evil deeds all over the world until they threatened his family and Fair Gamed him to stop.

Hence this book…. "The Expert Witness".

Jesse was an expert witness against the "Church" of Scientology in many court rooms and many different countries.

I am overwhelmed with Jesse's resolve to get these facts out to the public so that people can learn the true nature of Miscavige and his "church" that carries out his every whim in the name of "saving mankind" and leaves a path of chaos, death and destruction.

Miscavige has no compassion or care for his fellow man, I observed that when I worked for him and this is what finally made me leave. His only intent is money and power and it always has been. I worked directly with Hubbard for 22 years and with Miscavige for 10 years. I saw and witnessed their true characters which ties in with everything Jesse is saying in this book. We were not privy to all of this but heard or saw enough snippets to know something like this must have been happening. Now it is revealed.

Any group that must use "Disconnection" and "Fair Game" on it's departed followers and whistleblowers, (especially the higher up you were and the more you knew…..) obviously has to be a scam and not a "church".

Watch Miscavige as he now tries to quickly discredit and destroy Jesse Prince and myself for these words, he will claim this book is "all lies" by "bigots" and "haters", the same patter they've used for 30+

Foreword

years whenever someone speaks out. Hiding behind "religion" is their ONLY protection.

The trouble is there are now over 20 books written by different people and an endless stream of internet information and with Leah Remini and Mike Rinder's brilliant "Scientology and the Aftermath" TV series of true and documented stories by those that have been viciously harmed and damaged by Miscavige and his "church", the weight against Miscavige is now astronomical and picking up speed daily.

This book will peel one of the thickest layers of the onion that shields the "Church" of Scientology and David Miscavige and may they never be the same again.

May the Attorney General, the FBI and the IRS step in and do their job of shutting down one of the largest scams known to mankind cloaked as a "religion."

Terri Gillham Gamboa

Born into Scientology by parents Peter Gillham & Yvonne Gillham Jentzsch - both extremely well known and well loved by thousands of Scientologists worldwide, they were an example of what we all thought Scientology was supposed to be.

A Scientologist from 1954-1990 and long term Sea Org Veteran 1968-1990.

One of the original 4 Commodore's Messengers on the Apollo 1968-1975.

Commanding Officer of the Commodore's Messenger Organization (CMO) for many years and set up the original CMO to manage Scientology 1972 through 1980.

Top executive who worked directly for Hubbard for 22 years.

Worked with Miscavige for 10 years.

Executive Director of ASI "Author Services Inc" - L. Ron Hubbard's publishing company and business management company from early 1980's to 1990 while Miscavige reigned over as "Chairman of the Board" with the duplicate position of "Chairman of the Board" for Scientology management mixing both secular and non-secular roles thus violating IRS rules & regulations.

One of only 6 most top trusted Senior Executives assigned the "Diamond Star" pin by Hubbard personally for every year that it was in existence in the 1980's.

Lifetime Trustee of the top church echelon - Church of Spiritual Technology, personally assigned by Hubbard - unknown that it was a Lifetime assignment as Miscavige (overseeing the implementation) locked these corporate documents away when he took over the church and it was only found out many years later what he had done.

Foreword

About Jesse Prince's "The Expert Witness" by Rob Williamson, Writer and Ex-Sea Organization Member

I met Jesse Prince in Clearwater, Florida, late 1970s. We happened to be in the famous Ft. Harrison Hotel there, where he had me laughing so hard I couldn't see through the tears and my gut hurt so bad I couldn't stand or walk. He thoroughly enjoyed "getting to me" and prolonged and worked that pleasurable pain as long as he could until I absolutely couldn't take no more. Never forget it. Never forget him.

Now it's 2018 and to this day, he welcomes me with that grand, Aunt Jemima grin, and if I'm lucky, I'll get one of his big belly laughs. That's Jesse. That's his Spirit. It's contagious. I think it's important to recognize Jesse Prince is Black. I know he'll chuckle at my use of adjectives here. No disrespect. On the contrary.

So now we segue into a particular reality that needs to be known - L. Ron Hubbard was prejudice against Blacks and all loyal Sea Org Members copied the Commodore.

Jesse was the only Black I knew in the SO. He said he came in touch with one other. They were an extreme minority. This is significant because it made Jesses' trip through his tenure a tad harder than most. Like his life. It was tough.

This is something to think about. How did he climb from a position of complete ignorance of Hubbard and what he created, to become one of a handful of people who studied everything L. Ron ever wrote or said and master it to such an extent of becoming an Inspector General for all of Scientology, all over the world, in less than 10 years, despite the black genes. He rose to possess more authority than everyone else but a few, besides Hubbard himself, over the whole movement. He was # 3.

Well, I suppose it had to be his genes. After all, he won over and accomplished most everything he set his mind to, beginning at his roots in the streets of the Southside of Chicago, to, giving you this book. I'm certain there's more to come. That's Jesse.

It's an important book and let me tell you why.

"Shore Story" was a vital protocol for L. Ron and the Sea Organization. It's been that way since the very beginning. A Shore Story is an acceptable truth the Sea Org will tell anyone it wants to keep secrets from, and that's from just about everyone. Like back in the early days we told everyone that our ships and sailors were "Operation and Transport Corporation/ O.T.C." Everything Sea Org, Hubbard and Scientology were secret. "O.T.C." was put out front as a blinder. A misdirector. Shore Story.

That we were "United Churches" when the Apollo and its staff became landlubbers in '75 is another example. Shore Story.

Needless to say, "Scientology's a Religion"; a Shore Story to camouflage a secret truth, that it's not a Religion. That Shore Story supports a con.

What's really aboard that ship you see sailing into your harbor? The answer to that question is surely a Shore Story.

Even inside Scientology and especially The Sea Organization, strip away all the Shore Stories, the mysteries, the secrets, the lies and what do you get? Jesse does this in his book.

"Over The Rainbow", was another Shore Story, this one for Scientologists. In a very early age in Jesses' SO career, he went there. He was picked to go there by people from there. They shanghaied him. He was selected to be an integral part of L. Ron's International Headquarters. That was soon after I met him in the late '70s.

That's why this book is so vitally important. It traipses over the Shore Stories from earlier on and it talks about what went on behind closed doors. It tells the truth — time, place, form and event. It speaks of stuff no one knows but those who were, and some who are, under the rainbow now.

Jesse was there right after Hubbard died. That he dropped his body and was off to do OT research without it is just another Shore Story; a crazy one. The truth is, L. Ron was an alcoholic, always drunk on high dollar liquor, demented, drugged and degraded, incapable of communication with his ass full of track marks from being injected with more narcotics than a human body could stand. And he was delusional. At first he believed he was Buddha reincarnated, then The Messiah in His Second Coming, and Lucifer in the end. How does one become a True Believer of that?

There's a strange relief that ensues from being told the truth, even though that truth is some kind of terrible and horrible. It can still set you free. I began having nightmares again when I read this book. It described such moments that made me squirm, get upset; if you can only imagine. But I for one would rather know the truth. Scientology is not what it's trumped up to be. Another Shore Story? Something L. Ron made up for some reason?

Why should you go through this? The reading it… the finding out? Mainly, because it's still going on in pretty much the same format of lies? Just maybe, this truth, this book will help set the World free of Scientology. Jesse tells this truth. He's an expert witness. He was there and back.

And now here, out of this insane group, Jesse wins out as an author. It's a page turner. It's a tell all. And Jess tells it like it is, in such a way, like you're rapping with him over a few drinks, so to speak, and he's telling you where he's been and how it was, then and now. It's an important story because, it's about Jesses' life and the manipulations behind Scientology; an insidious, evil cult.

INTRODUCTION

THIS STORY IS OF MY TIME as a member of the Church of Scientology. I joined the movement in the summer of 1976 in San Francisco, California, and walked out for the last time in the fall of 1992.

Recently, Scientology has made headlines internationally due to a wave of high profile celebrities that have left the movement on bad terms and made this known to the media. Actor Jason Beghe, Film Writer/Director Paul Haggis, Singer Lisa Marie Presley and Actress Leah Remini have all publicly retreated from Scientology. Before that, there was a wave of people who were corporate executives within the top levels of Scientology who had defected from the movement. They were telling horror stories of the abuse and degradation that happened routinely within Scientology, behind closed doors, out of sight to the print and news media.

Without revealing my experiences with Scientology, I've sat with people who had little to no prior knowledge of what Scientology is, to view programs about Scientology. In the end, there are always those lingering questions: Why do people of above average intelligence get caught up in Scientology in the first place? Why do people like Tom Cruise, John Travolta, and Kirstie Alley give money to Scientology? From the outside, Scientology clearly makes no sense at all to most people with an average intelligence or street smarts, so how are they recruiting these people?

The answer is Scientology Technology or "Tech" for short. Some people swear by it and say it changed them for the better, while others say it ruined them financially, ruined their families, businesses, and relationships. What's the difference, and why is there a difference? The simple answer will surprise you. The answer is *time*.

Scientology Technology is a series of repetitive processes that induce a trance-like hypnotic state of mind so that L Ron's ideology can be downloaded into a person's mind. The more Scientology Technology a person gets, the more they want. I'm sharing my knowledge and experiences with Scientology in all its many forms with the intent that you, the reader, will learn enough to protect yourself and others. Seemingly, there is a segment of the population that appear to be impervious to Scientology's strange ways and smooth-talking recruiters. This segment of people is easy to identify. They share a common trait which is they don't have enough money or assets for Scientology to be bothered.

I was a member of Scientology for 16 years and rose to its highest ranks. I completed many, if not all of the Scientology training courses, and every one of its auditing/counseling levels. Of all the training and counseling certificates I'd accumulated in my 16-year association with Scientology, the single most important title I earned is that of *Expert witness*. I was authorized by Scientology Church Management to

Introduction

represent the interest of Scientology in a civil court of law as an expert on the Technology of Scientology and the trademarks associated with the movement. Yes, there have been other ex-members who have been accepted by various judges as expert witnesses based on their training and experience within Scientology, but this happened after they had renounced Scientology.

I became an expert witness while serving as a corporate director of the Religious Technology Center (RTC). RTC is a Scientology corporation that holds the rights to the trademarks owned and registered internationally by corporate Scientology. I also earned a wall full of certifications representing completion of certified training levels and internships that are peculiar to Scientology only. I'll talk a little about that later.

Here are a couple of definitions for Expert witness. From *The People's Law Dictionary*:

Expert witness n. A person who is a specialist in a subject, often technical, who may present his/her expert opinion without having been a witness to any occurrence relating to the lawsuit or criminal case. It is an exception to the rule against giving an opinion at trial, provided that the expert is qualified by evidence of his/her expertise, training, and special knowledge. If the expertise is challenged, the attorney for the party calling the "expert" must make a showing of the necessary background through questions in court, and the trial judge has discretion to qualify the witness or rule he/she is not an expert or is an expert on limited subjects. Experts are usually paid handsomely for their services and may be asked by the opposition the amount they are receiving for their work on the case.

In most jurisdictions, both sides must exchange the names and addresses of proposed experts to allow pre-trial depositions.

And from Wikipedia:

> *An expert witness, professional witness or judicial expert is a witness, who by virtue of education, training, skill, or experience, is believed to have expertise and specialized knowledge in a particular subject beyond that of the average person, sufficient that others may officially and legally rely upon the witness's specialized (scientific, technical or other) opinion about an evidence or fact issue within the scope of his expertise, referred to as the expert opinion, as an assistance to the fact-finder. Expert witnesses may also deliver expert evidence about facts from the domain of their expertise. At times, their testimony may be rebutted with a learned treatise, sometimes to the detriment of their reputations...*
>
> *In Scots Law, Davie v Magistrates of Edinburgh (1953) provides authority that where a witness has particular knowledge or skills in an area being examined by the court, and has been called to court in order to elaborate on that area for the benefit of the court, that witness may give evidence of his opinion on that area.*

In the past, I'd been hired by attorneys as a Scientology expert, to assists lawyers who represented people that had filed civil lawsuits against Scientology. So far, in every courtroom I've appeared in, the presiding judge in the case has allowed my testimony despite the extreme protest of the high-priced lawyers Scientology hires to defend itself. This is also true for the one time I represented Scientology's interest as an expert witness in civil court.

Introduction

The information and accounts contained in this memoir are of my personal memories of incidents I recalled.

So what is Scientology all about? *Scientologist* is the name the Church of Scientology uses to designate its members, who practice and submit to the doctrines of Scientology and Dianetics as authored by L. Ron Hubbard, the god of Scientology.

In the United States, the Church of Scientology is recognized as a religious institution and has been granted tax-exempt status.

The *Sea Organization* is a paramilitary organization created by L Ron Hubbard to help him manage and exercise authority in any Scientology or Dianetics organization. Members of the Sea Organization wear uniforms similar to those worn by members of the United States Navy. The Sea Organization also has a rank and rating system nearly identical to that of the United States Navy. They also wear the same or similar insignia as people who are in US Navy to distinguish themselves among one another. The Sea Organization is staffed by the most dedicated Scientologists, who have signed a written contract to dedicate the next billion years of their existence in servitude to L Ron Hubbard and his personal goals for all humankind. You can find Sea Organization installations in Los Angeles, New York City, and Clearwater, Florida. There are also Sea Organization facilities in East Grinstead, Sussex England; Copenhagen, Denmark; Mexico City, Mexico and Sydney, Australia.

L Ron Hubbard created his own "Navy" to protect himself and enforce his orders within the confines of his newly created religious institutions known as Dianetics and Scientology. Similar to the US Navy, L Ron created a formidable intelligence department to protect his newly created movements: Dianetics and Scientology. Corporate Scientology spares no expense to hire the most powerful and influential law firms for representation. These professionals are paid handsomely to protect Scientology and obey its demands.

The Church of Scientology has been featured in national news stories because whistleblowers who were once at the very top of its elite Sea Organization are disclosing stories of torture, enslavement, corruption and physical abuse. Despite all the controversy, the Church of Scientology continues to count among its members some of the most talented known and unknown Hollywood celebrities.

I was officially in servitude to the Church of Scientology for sixteen years. After a protracted leaving process, I was allowed to leave the Sea Organization on Halloween, 1992.

This story covers the history and formation of the conglomerate known as the Church of Scientology today. The subjects discussed and documented here include the technology ("Tech") of Scientology.

Scientology Tech is the written word describing the reasoning and ritual application of the ideologies known as Dianetics and Scientology. The Tech is also the written codified record of instructions on how to perform the rituals and practices of Scientology. For a Scientologist, the importance of having and knowing the correct Technology cannot be overstated.

In a Christian Bible, the words of Jesus Christ are usually printed in red ink. Scientology Technology, which is solely the writings of L Ron Hubbard, is also

Introduction

printed in red ink. These writings are bound in dark, blood red colored reference books known as the Technology Volumes. These volumes have a symbol of a single large gold-embossed pyramid with three horizontal lines drawn through the pyramid indicating levels. Other symbols on these volumes include conjoined triangles with the letter S imposed over the triangles. These symbols are also embossed in gold. The Technology is the single basis for the existence of Dianetics and Scientology; it represents the lifeblood of the movement and is what it uses to gouge its staff and parishioners for huge sums of money.

The Technology of Scientology is highly valued and sought after by Scientologists. Similar to the Christian, Jewish, Muslim and Mormon Bibles; it claims to offer total salvation through the teachings of its god, L Ron Hubbard.

Another historical aspect I share is my relationship with the god of Scientology, L Ron Hubbard and those who served him. L Ron died in 1986, and he left a secret message for his faithful followers. He also promised he would return at a future date as a world leader or politician.

Just before his death in 1986, L Ron made biblical predictions of his self-proclaimed role in the "End of Days" sequence for planet Earth as given in the Bible Book of Revelations, King James Version. L Ron left a secret biblical prophesy that the great majority of Scientologists don't even know exists. This information is kept secret from the Scientology flock. Part of my story will include details of what I know about L Ron's secret message.

There are some excellent previously published books about the Church of Scientology that expose its underbelly. Each story provides personal accounts of the daily life and routines inside Scientology. They describe the disappointment of finding out they were deceived, abused and taken advantage of.

This story of Scientology is different than most that have come before, because it deals with the sacred doctrine of Hubbard's philosophy referred to as the Technology and how it seems to affect people. Again, every other aspect of the Church of Scientology exists solely to support the Technology. The Technology seems to attract high-powered Hollywood celebrities and executives like flies to ...candy.

The Tech is purported to be able to give individuals god-like powers over matter, energy, space and time through the study of occult wisdom as rendered exclusively by L Ron Hubbard. There is historical precedence of celebrity attraction to the occult. The reason for this may be simple economics. It's expensive to participate in the occult, especially if you're talking about Scientology – but I'm getting ahead of the story here.

I'll also describe the process of moving up the magic levels within Scientology. I guess a "higher-up" in any aspect of life has its privilege. I became a "higher-up" in the inner circle of L Ron's Sea Organization.

L Ron Hubbard was an active, hands-on kind of god for his created religion. He created and named all the staff positions and titles for his church organizations.

In 1982, L Ron Hubbard created what would be the final technical staff position he'd create to preserve his precious Scientology Technology. Ron

INTRODUCTION

commanded his personal staff to find the most qualified and skilled teacher (called a Supervisor in Scientology) from his advanced-level Churches to fill the technical position. Once found, he wanted the person brought to his secret facility near Hemet, California, which is the international management headquarters for Dianetics and Scientology. The cover name for this location is "Golden Era Productions," or "Gold Base." The idea was to bring the qualified person where L Ron intended to live. The person was needed to help him correct and train an international management team he was forming to take over his job of running the day-to-day operations of Scientology.

The new technical position was "Inspector General Cramming Officer." In forming its new corporate structure, an Inspector General Network was created as the "eye at top of the pyramid" of all Scientology and Dianetics corporations. This corporate model is similar to Freemasonry hierarchy, with Inspectors General at the top of the pyramid. Inspectors General in the Freemasonic organizations are at the very top of the pyramid at levels 30-33. Most Scientologists and Sea Org members don't understand the correlation between Scientology and Freemasonry because this is hidden from them. The man who referred to himself as "The Beast," Alistair Crowley, was an early mentor to L Ron Hubbard. Besides being an avowed Satanist, Crowley was also known to be a high-level Freemason Inspector General.

The current leader of Scientology, David Miscavige, was charged with the duty of finding the right candidate for the new tech position and helper to L Ron, and he did. That person ended up being me.

Mercifully, this only lasted for about five years from 1982-1987. These years gave me an insight into L Ron and Scientology that I would have never gotten any other way, so I guess I should be grateful for that.

Much later, I would come to understand it is impossible to learn what Scientology really is while being a part of it. Scientologists are strictly forbidden to read about or associate with any person or organization that contravenes its doctrines and tenets. For members, violators are subject to imprisonment in Scientology work camps. Individuals and organizations who oppose or question the authority and doctrine of Dianetics or Scientology are investigated by the Sea Organization's "Secret Service" department.

Part of this narrative is about my association with Scientology's Intelligence networks in their various forms. I spent some years in Scientology learning the game of espionage and counter-espionage. I learned tactics to eliminate enemy targets using legal and illegal means. I was a trusted participant in the inner circle of the Sea Organization "higher-ups."

I'll also discuss what I know about the origins of a cultural phenomenon known for aggressively fighting against nameless oppressors with their own nameless faces. The phenomenon refers to itself as Anonymous.

As I write these chapters I promise to make every effort *not* use Scientology terminology. When I use a Scientology term I will define it, but not necessarily right away, because it would make this writing boring

Introduction

and overly redundant, so please bear with me on that issue. Terms that I don't immediately define or explain will be defined and explained later in the text.

This story begins with a conference held by a special commission within the government of Hamburg Germany, in the spring of 2010, long after I had departed Scientology.

1

THE LAST EXPERT TESTIMONY
2010

EARLY DECEMBER 2010 I remember feeling hopeful and excited about the coming New Year. *I guess ignorance really is bliss.*

I am primarily known by most of my Facebook friends for my involvement in, and subsequent activism against, various Scientology corporations. I have written extensively about my experiences as a Scientologist and Sea Org member.

I left Scientology in 1992. By 2003, with a few minor exceptions, I'd pretty much disassociated myself from the subject of Scientology, for reasons we'll get into later, but the time off gave me a peace I felt I deserved. Then, sometime during the month of January 2010, I received the following invitation from my good friend Ursula Caberta, who at the time was a German politician and former State of Hamburg government official. Her official title was Commissioner for the Scientology Task Force of the Hamburg Interior Authority.

Dear Jesse,

We are organizing an informative event on the subject of Scientology for March 26, 27 and 28, 2010. I would be delighted if you would agree to be one of our speakers.

The current program sis as follows:

Speakers arrive on March 24, 2010. On March 25 there will be a preliminary meeting at our offices to cover the final arrangements for talks and papers to be presented, as well as the program for the event. We can leave the return flight open at this stage. The plan would be for speakers to fly back on Monday, March 29, 2010. However, if you would like to use this opportunity to enjoy our beautiful city of Hamburg a little longer, we could book a return flight for you at a later date.

The Office of Domestic Affairs (Innenbehörde) will pay for the flight and hotel accommodation from March 24 to 29, 2010. We can pay a fee of € 500.00. The Office of Domestic Affairs will look after security, as it usually does for these events.

I very much hope you are able to accept this invitation. We can then start planning the details. Of course, all of this depends on all those I would really like to see in Hamburg being able to join us.

Kind regards from a snow-covered Hamburg
Ursula Caberta

PS: The enclosed document contains more information about the planned contents of this event.

Of course, I accepted this great invite, which marked my first public appearance exposing Scientology to a new generation of recent defectors and a new group who went by the name Anonymous. At the time, I had no idea how this gathering would ultimately affect the course of my life. In my mind, at best I was just making a "cameo" appearance for history's sake.

Ursula and I have rich history together and I won't get in to all of that right now. Suffice to say we have had our own extreme experiences together dealing with the Scientology phenomenon and our friendship has survived the test of time.

When I arrived in Hamburg, she picked me up at the airport. We chatted about the trials and tribulations of our mutual experiences on the way to the hotel. I can't deny my affection for Ursula because she is such a strong and loving woman. There is a long list of ex-Scientologist that will tell you Ursula helped them separate and recover from Scientology when no one else could or would.

There was a basic program for the conference and it changed and evolved slightly, but here is a basic copy of the program that I was able to retain:

Ursula Caberta
Head of Working Group Scientology,
Office for Domestic Affairs, Hamburg
Scientology: The people without rights
under L. Ron Hubbard's system

In the Federal Republic of Germany Scientology is regarded as an anti-constitutional organization. The organization is based on the ideological principles of its founder, L. Ron Hubbard. He died in 1986. His successor, David Miscavige, has been the target of serious accusations brought by former high-ranking colleagues. He is said to have turned Scientology into what it is today, an inhumane system.

What is the evidence for this assumption? Is Miscavige responsible for the current state of affairs or is the current boss's conduct in fact founded in Mr. Hubbard's ideology? All the same, this David Miscavige was brought into the world of Scientology when he was just a child. How did the Scientology system develop? The ideology of L. Ron Hubbard and its application to people. David Miscavige – the perpetrator?

The example of Scientology and the role of the current international leadership (previously Hubbard, subsequently Miscavige) are to be used to illustrate the following issues:

- *How is a system created that takes away people's rights? What rules does it follow?*
- *What makes people become involved in such a system and obey it blindly?*
- *Are any changes discernible in the Scientology system due to David Miscavige assumption of power after Hubbard's death, or does he apply and implement Hubbard's guidelines in a different way?*

These are questions that need to be pursued.

On the one hand there are reports about the inner workings at the organization's headquarters; on the other hand there are the conclusions to be drawn from the outside world. The policy for dealing with ideologies that violate human rights is derived from a consolidation of these findings.

Comparisons are opposite and necessary. Are there parallels that can be drawn between the Stasi system of the former German Democratic Republic (GDR) and the ethical system of the Scientology organization?

The concealment of the system's inner workings from the outside world – did the GDR system employ methods comparable to those of Scientology? What is the role played by celebrities involved in these systems? Can comparisons be drawn with the GDR? What is the role of child rearing and education? The former GDR had forced adoption, Scientology has forced abortion. Influence through schooling.

Dr. Müller-Enbergs, Research Associate with the Federal Commissioner for Documents of the State Security Service of the former German Democratic Republic (GDR), in close co-operation with the Head of Working Group Scientology, Office for Domestic Affairs, Hamburg, and with support from former high-ranking members of Scientology and their related experiences, will be looking for and finding answers to these questions.

This discussion is designed as a basis for the representatives of other European countries to consider the way in which their respective countries handle evolving totalitarian systems with a claim to political power. Representatives from France, Belgium, the UK and Australia will be invited to attend. The reconcilability of Hubbard's ideology with the constitution of the United States of America will also be a topic for discussion.

The exact program will be arranged once the speakers have been finalized.

When I arrived at the conference I met up with Los Angeles attorney Graham Berry. We also have history working together to expose Scientology. Also present were Hana Eltringham, Amy Scobee and Marc Headley, former Scientologists and Sea Org members I had known at Scientology's International Base. Both Marc and Amy had written books about their experiences.

Seeing Amy again was a pleasant surprise. I've known her since the early 1980's. She was a young blonde beauty and worked as a messenger for L Ron in Clearwater, FL. She encouraged me to write a book, but my argument was I didn't know what to say that hadn't already been said. I remember telling her I didn't think I'd write a book, but I would figure something out.

I'd also met "face-to-mask," then later face-to-face, with some members of Anonymous, and I really enjoyed that. The Anonymous members were invited guests, along with representatives of police, security and intelligence communities from Belgium, France and the United Kingdom. This was an unusual mixture of people for sure. All were there to get answers and exchange information about Scientology.

At the time I had no idea who or what Anonymous was or what it stood for. We got on well and they were interested in what I had to say. I marveled at the fact that some who identified as Anonymous had even read some of the things I'd written about Scientology and published on the internet. Some had seen videos of me along with others peacefully protesting in front of various Scientology Church organizations. I learned they had been doing some Scientology protesting of their own in grand style. Most, if not all of the Anonymous people had been involved with peacefully picketing various Scientology churches internationally. The intent of the picket was to inform current members and the general public of the alleged beatings David Miscavige was being accused of as well as other human rights violations

The Last Expert Testimony

Other European government representatives also attended the conference, from France, Belgium, and others I don't recall. I met with representatives of police agencies from various European countries as part of the second-day conference. All of the invited guests spoke from a podium and took questions afterwards. Most of the actual conference was later posted on the Internet. This turned out to be a long day and a very long night of discussions and interviews with the invited speakers.

During the evening of the Hamburg conference, after all the events of the day were concluded, we all sat down for our dinner together. There was laughter and loud talking through the night.

As the party started to break up into smaller groups and such, Amy Scobee and I had our parting conversation. I asked her why she was doing what she was doing. By that she understood I meant why was she speaking out about her experiences in Scientology? Did she not understand how dangerous this could be to her personally, and her family?

Paraphrased, Amy said she understood there was a risk involved, but she didn't care. She said she didn't think the Sea Org had the same ability to be destructive to ex-members as they had in the past due to the amount of people leaving the movement. She felt there were few competent people left in the higher and lower levels of the Sea Org to get the criminal activity accomplished like they used to. She no longer had any use for L Ron's tech, and she decided just to tell the truth, as she knew it. I smiled as she asked me the same question. Why do I bother doing it at all?

The Expert Witness

I was prepared for the question. During my hiatus from Scientology, I'd had time to reconcile that issue fully, so my answer was clear. I told Amy on the journey of life there are many roads. During my journey down the roads of life, I fell into a deep hole. It took some time for me to get out of that hole so that I could continue my journey. I realized after getting out of that hole, the least I could do for my fellow travelers is to post a warning or danger sign pointing to the hole, so that's why I do it. Hell, I'd even be involved in rescue efforts to pull as many people out of the hole as I could. Most of the people I helped get out of the hole took off running once they could see the light of day again. As a result, for too long, far too few were involved in the rescue effort at all. I found myself extending my hand back into that hole to grab anyone out that I could. The more people I pulled out, the less help I had. People just got out and ran the hell away!

I wondered, what did Amy mean when she said she didn't think the Sea Org had the same ability to be destructive to ex-members as they had in the past due to the amount of people leaving the movement?

On the and third final day, we ended the conference in the early afternoon, and the invited guests spent the rest of the day on a sightseeing tour of Hamburg's beautiful architecture and popular places. We all took pictures of each other and promised to stay in touch. The next day we went home.

When I got back home to Chicago, I felt like writing something relevant about the conference itself and an overview of my opinions.

Here is an excerpt from a short article I wrote shortly after the conference. It was published on an Internet newsgroup called Ex-Sea Org message board. I don't remember exactly how I got mixed up with that group, but I sure was happy to be in contact with people I didn't think I'd ever hear from again. It was like a homecoming of sorts, and I was feeling somewhat excited and rejuvenated by the contact.

In the article, I refer to two men, Marty Rathbun and Mike Rinder, who I had worked with at the upper echelons of Scientology management. Marty had been the Inspector General for Ethics in RTC - the second-in-command of all of Scientology - and Mike had been the international spokesman for the Church of Scientology, and also the head of the Church's intelligence arm, the Office of Special Affairs. I had butted heads with both of these men, when I first started speaking out, and they were still in Scientology. Both men have since left Scientology and, like me, were speaking out against its abuses.

Here is the article:

New Soldiers!

I don't know the exact chronology of the resistance against the ideology called Scientology, but it sure preceded my entrance into the fray. Fortunately, I documented the moment when I no longer felt so threatened by the movement and found the courage to fight back. This would be my way of releasing myself from the grip of my past involvement in the movement. In essence, this is when I began to write my story.

By September of 1998, I'd begin talking with lawyers who represented former Scientology adherents. It was at this point that I began to report my story.

THE EXPERT WITNESS

I traveled to Denmark, Sweden and Germany to speak with European Press and in some instances spoke with Secret Service agents who were in the employ of one of the countries above.

From the very beginning, during courtroom or deposition hearings against Scientology when I would see Marty [who was still in Scientology at the time], I began to ask him to leave the Scientology movement. We would see each other in the many courtroom proceedings we were involved in. I would say, "Marty, just walk away, you'll be taken care of I promise. Just leave, walk away." I have to admit my wanting Marty to leave the movement was not entirely rooted in just trying to save a fellow human being. Marty and I have had monster battles in courtrooms and on the street by proxy. Marty, along with Mike Rinder and the backing of the conglomerate league of high priced lawyers owned by Scientology proved to be more adversary than I could handle.

Since Marty left the Sea Organization, we have talked. I thanked him for leaving and having the courage to speak out the way he is. The rage that ex-Sea Org members express against Miscavige seems to be common among all who know him. I look at my writings about Miscavige when I first got out and see the parallels between what Marty is writing about now in 2010, with what I had written about 12 years earlier.

Mike Rinder was the corporate face of Scientology for many years. That he is no longer in the Sea Org and starting to speak the truth about his experiences is a step in the right direction for him.

A video of Mike Rinder trying to visit with his son whom he just found out has cancer was posted on YouTube. According to the Sea Org people on site, Mike's son refused to visit with him. These guys have some guts to stand on what was once sacred ground for them, in defiance of disconnection, the very practice they vigorously defended not so long ago.

Mark Headley is another new high-profile soldier now involved in the struggle. We met on the other side of our previous Sea Org involvement as free men for the first time in Hamburg, Germany at the 2010 Hamburg Conference.

Amy Scobee was a Senior Executive of an organization within the inner circle of the Sea Organization called "The Watch Dog Committee." The Watch Dog Committee is the top echelon of management for the Sea Organization.

Amy has given inside information that reveals the mentality and modus operandi of the Sea Organization at its highest levels. The Scientology Sea Organization seemingly knows no limits to its calculated deception of others.

There are many more who have spoken out: Bruce Hines, Shelly Corrias, Sinar Parman, Jeff Hawkins... the list of people who have left the inner circle of Scientology's Sea Organization is long.

There is more awareness on an International level of the problems within Scientology and the Sea Organization because of the testimony of those coming out. The only other time I was aware of strong international attention on Scientology and the Sea Organization was back in 1977 when the US Government raided its corporate headquarters and handed prison sentences to some of its leaders.

The 2010 Hamburg Conference was a turning point for me. I began to see the formation of a real resistance to Scientology, led by those who had experienced its abuses first-hand. Scientology exists in secrecy, its inner workings hidden even from its members. Now at last those inner workings were being revealed.

It had been a long road from my first involvement in Scientology in 1976, through my departure in 1992, and my own efforts, which I will describe later, to expose Scientology. Now many others were joining the battle.

But let's begin at the beginning.

2

ENTERING THE DRAGON

1976, I WAS 22 YEARS OLD when I first contacted Scientology in San Francisco, CA. I'd recently arrived in California with my brother Ron and our mutual friend Jethro. We'd driven from Decatur, IL in April of 1976 headed for Sea Side, CA. None of us had ever been to California before and we were having an adventure. We were invited to visit Sea Side, CA by my father's girlfriend Pearl. We called her aunt Pearl. My father's younger sister Geraldine and her husband Bill lived at Fort Ord military base in Sea Side as well and we planned on visiting them. Jethro and I had recently received our IRS income tax checks, and we could afford the journey if we put our money together. We were bringing my younger brother Ron along for the ride.

I hugged Teresa, the mother of my first-born child, kissed my baby Cleo and got in the car with Jethro and Ron. We headed out in Jethro's late model Ford LTD and never looked back. We drove to Kansas and stopped for a night. The next day we drove all the way to Denver, Colorado. I remember stopping at some disco like place in or near Denver. There was plenty of parking in the attached lot. When we arrived, there were a good number of people already there and more were coming. The venue had a tall celling with a large dance floor area. I asked a beautiful dark hair Latina woman to dance and we danced disco style. There were many beautiful women in the club but not like her. She stood out from the rest and was being heavily perused by the disco flamboyant men wanting to dance with her next. My new beauty had a friend with her who was nice as well and she was also being perused by the men.

We all enjoyed ourselves at the disco but now we were tired and needed to sleep. We found a cheap hotel to spend the night. Ron and Jethro got a room together. Me and the pretty Latina lady got a room together and watched Godzilla on the TV among other things. That was the first time I'd ever had sex out of state, it was fantastic!

The next day we drove to Utah and spent the night at a mission somewhere near the downtown area of Salt Lake City. Big scary ass church buildings with gothic devil status were everywhere, and it was so quiet. The whole town felt strange like I'd somehow found my way into an episode of the Twilight Zone. White people were everywhere! I'd never been around that many before. I didn't feel safe. Some of them just stared at me like I was from the moon or something. No one attacked or called us names, so I quickly became comfortable with the situation. I had no plans to check out the night life while in Salt Lake City. My new girlfriend had warned me there was no night life in Salt Lake City that I'd be interested in. She told me about a mission shelter in the Salt Lake City area that we could go to sleep for free if I didn't mind going to church the next morning. My head was in the clouds with her and I couldn't believe my run of good luck! It seemed like going to California was going to be good for me - sure pal.

Driving to California was an adventure for sure and I could go on about it but that is not what this book is about.

After visiting with aunt Pearl, aunt Geraldine and uncle Bill in Seaside, CA we drove to San Francisco which is where my Scientology experience began. When we ran out of money, both Jethro and my brother Ron fled San Francisco, heading back to Decatur, IL. I decided not to go back. I decided to see what I could do there to become employed and find a place to live. I was able to get a couple of part time jobs to take care of myself and rent a room in an apartment from this nice older black man. He didn't live there, and he never asked for rent again after my first payment. When I look back on it now, that old man was like a father to me and the other young men who lived at the apartment. We were a group of strays from anyplace but California. There was a white guy named Steve, there was a Latino guy (Don't remember his name) and me. We were all young men around the same age far from home trying to work out what to do with our lives.

At 22 years old, I knew it was time to decide on a life career. I was considering pursuing a career in the Navy. Two of my cousins had gone to the Navy. Both were doing fine with enough money to support a family. My roommate Steve had already talked to a Navy recruiter and recommended I go down and talk to a recruiter. I went down to see a Navy recruiter. We filled out some paperwork and scheduled a fitness exam. I'm not exactly sure how long I had to wait for the exam, it may have been a week out. I never made it to the exam, Scientology got me instead.

I had just gotten off from a job and was headed home. As I walked through the Union Square area of San Francisco, a very attractive woman with long dark red hair casually strolled up to me and asked would I like to know more about myself? I was always on a search to learn more about being human, so I was interested. I was instantly attracted to her. This lady had the whole package going on and I was not shy about my attraction to her. I told her, I wasn't interested in knowing more about myself, but I would certainly like to know more about her. She looked at me and smiled and we began to make small talk as she walked me to the Scientology organization. In those days, the Scientology buildings were called organizations not churches. As we strolled toward the Scientology organization we chatted about having out of body experiences. I told her I'd had multiple out of body (OOB) experiences and I was interested in learning more about that. She told me Scientology had all the answers concerning the OOB phenomena and we were headed to the right place.

She walked me to the receptionist area and asked me to wait. I was asked to wait because the staff were changing shifts. The night shift known as Foundation Staff, were coming on. There were lots of people coming and going, all seemingly in a hurry. I took the time to give myself a tour of the place. During my solo tour, I discovered two items of interest. The first item was called a Grade Chart. This was a large paper classification chart that listed each training and processing level (Auditing) Scientology had for sale. There was specific pricing for each service Scientology had to offer. I read what was written about the higher levels of processing. Some were about the OOB phenomena I'd just been talking about with the redhead that brought me in. This is also the first time I ever saw super powers for sale. By laying down a large amount of cash I could have psychic and telekinesis abilities.

The other item I saw that interested me was the Now Hiring sign. I could always use another part time job for cash in San Francisco. Eventually someone sat me down and gave me the introductory talk about Scientology. I quickly got the point and asked if there were any part-time employment positions open for evening work. Of course, there was!

That very night I signed a 5-year staff contract to work as a Foundation Staff member for Scientology near downtown San Francisco. I was told the pay was not that great, but the training was free for staff members. The next day I started the Scientology Communications Course. Over the next few months, I would complete several basic courses which at the time were fun to do. The courses were designed to be a gentle but effective approach to learning what it means to be human and human potential. By being human, I mean each living individual person has three basic attributes in common. These attributes are the body, the mind and the spirit. Scientology uses training courses and psycho analysis to individually address these aspects of life to improve the condition of each.

The Expert Witness

Even though the pay was horrible, approx. $30.00 a week, the organization was a fun place to work. The place was full of people all the time with new people joining daily. My job was called Body Router. The name describes the task. It was my job to bring people off the street into the organization and sell them something like a book or a basic course.

One day a group of people arrived wearing Naval Officer uniforms. I thought this was odd that the Navy would be involved with Scientology. Come to find out these people dressed like Navy officers weren't in the Navy at all. They referred to themselves as an elite class of Scientologist known as Sea Organization Members. The lead person of the Sea Org group was a guy named Gary Epstein. Gary was tall and slender in stature. He also wore a beard and wire framed glasses. When he spoke, I recognized he was probably a nice Jewish guy from New York, which turned out to be true. Gary gave a speech to the staff and paying public about the Sea Organization. Gary said the Sea Organization was a group of the most ethical and competent individuals on planet earth. He explained the Sea Org was charged with the duty of guiding mankind in a better direction than it was headed. Gary spoke well and convincingly. As he talked I remember thinking how I would like to try the Sea Organization as a career. It seemed sort of like the Navy which I thought was a missed opportunity for me at that point.

After Gary gave his speech and the event ended, I went over to talk with him about the Sea Organization. He told me about the origins of the Sea Org and many other things which I didn't really understand but he said something that got my total attention. Gary told me he was the Commanding Officer of the Scientology Organization that delivered the upper level courses having to do with OOB and other paranormal phenomena. Gary told me he was working on his upper levels and he was beginning to develop quasi superhuman abilities. He told me I could learn these skills if joined the Sea Org and became a member. He pumped me up and said only the best of the best are accepted. I would have to start out by signing up for the Sea Organization for no less than one billion years! Gary told me this was merely a symbolic gesture of the commitment and dedication required to be a member of the Sea Organization. I felt like I was signing up for the Navy Seal Team or some elite Marine unit - but I wasn't. Signing a symbolic contract in exchange for a chance to learn super human abilities seemed like a good idea at the time. Famous last words, right?

I signed the Sea Org contract that night. I signed on the condition I would be a staff member of the advanced organization that my recruiter, Gary was the head of. Within two weeks I was flown to Los Angles where I began my Introduction to the Sea Organization indoctrination. The Sea Org facility was in an old manor formally owned by the famous actor Charlie Chaplin at 1629 Park Ave near Echo Park in Los Angeles. The house had been converted into a training and living facility for at least 30 young men and women. I think there may have only been one shower for all of us. Our schedule was up at 7am out of bed, face washed, and bed made by 7:15am. Then 20-30mins to eat breakfast which was always muesli, sometimes powdered eggs and sausage with toast. After breakfast we were required to do cleaning and renovation work around the property where we lived along with other nearby properties owned by Scientology. After work we showered then had dinner. After dinner we were required to study 5 hours a night. When study was over it was bed time. There was no time to do anything but what we were told to do. It was the 70's and America was having a love fest to go along with the Hippie movement. In my new environment things were sexual among the new arrivals however that behavior was discouraged by our overseer's.

From the fall of 1976 until the Spring of 1977 I studied the basic training courses to become a trained Sea Org adept and worked to renovate Scientology owned properties nearby. My plan was to finish my basic training, then report to the Advance Organization to have access to the secret knowledge. The final course required to graduate the training program I was on was called Mission School. Sea Org members are required to execute missions into its organizations worldwide. To go on mission means two to three Sea Org members go to a Scientology organization that is having problems and temporarily take over the day to day operation of the organization. This action is done under the direction of the Sea Organization which is the management operation for all Scientology organizations worldwide. The day I finished the mission training course, I was sent on my first mission.

In the spring of 1977, Scientology purchased the old Cedars of Lebanon Hospital at 4833 Fountain Ave in Hollywood, CA. The property contained at least 7 separate buildings located on two city blocks. The property was purchased to centrally locate all

Scientology organizations scattered around Los Angeles. At that time the complex was surrounded by a 7-8ft chain-link fence with barb-wire along the top. There was also a trained German Shepard dog that patrolled the perimeter of the fence. My mission was to convert a single wing of hospital rooms into bedrooms for executive Sea Organization staff members. These staff members were on mission to design and renovate the complex.

Even though I had very little experience doing any type of construction, I was selected for a mission to renovate a small office space, as well as a partial hospital wing formally used as in-patient bedrooms. I was given access to a small army of people for 5 hours a day to get the job done. There were approximately sixty, white men and women between the ages of 20-60. There were a few Hispanic people sprinkled in but NO black people! I was told these people were part of a group known by the acronym "RPF" which means Rehabilitation Project Force. They all wore black boiler suits like a uniform. Some had a goldenrod color arm band worn on the right arm. Others had a dingy white arm band also worn on the right arm. They were an odd bunch in that they ran where ever they went and they addressed everyone they spoke to as Sir, men and women alike.

I was sent on mission to complete an exact renovation project with step by step targets to execute the assignment. The mission seemed very official but also felt like a role play game. I was expected to report on the progress of my assignment a couple times a day. The person I reported to was called a mission operator. I forget what that person's name was, however I don't think I'll ever forget his explanation of what the RPF was and what it was for. He told me these people were on their way out the door, being kick out of Scientology. They had severely violated Scientology and Sea Organization policy but Instead of being kicked out, these people were being given a chance to redeem themselves through the application of L Ron's Dianetics and Scientology technology. I was told these people were on the program of their own free will even though they worked more than 12 hours a day, were fed leftover food and paid $4.30 per week. I remember thinking I like Scientology, but I don't think I like it like that. In other words, I couldn't see the value in becoming someone's willing slave. I didn't like what I was seeing at all but there was no way for me to avoid the people on the RPF because they were my assigned work crew.

After a few days, I was told by my mission supervisor my mission was falling behind target. I was not getting my targets done fast enough and this was beginning to cause heavy stress. The only way to get ahead was to work more which meant little to no time to sleep. After some days of little to no sleep the happy me began to fade. I began to fell numb and detached. I knew I had to go somewhere and get some sleep or bad things would happen. Despite the emergencies and heavy demand for production, I just walked off the job, found a bed and went to sleep.

After only a few hours, someone found me and told me my presence was being demanded by someone who worked for L Ron and he was not happy! I went ahead and got up even though I was still very exhausted, but I had a new-found spark of energy. I got out of bed and followed the messengers all the way to the person that demanded my company.

The person who demanded I get out of bed was Commander Wayne Marple. Emissary of the Commodore, L Ron himself. At this point I was stalking like a cat. The people leading me to Wayne were ignorant of my intent which was to kick somebody's ass very soon. Chicago born Jesse, the street fighter was out and in control.

I was led to Wayne, who was pudgy and short in stature. When I saw he was a little person my fury was dialed back to the point I didn't slap the shit out of him right away. Wayne stood there proudly wearing a Naval Officer uniform. He had more stars and campaign bars than commander Mc Bragg from the Rocky and Bullwinkle show. He also had stripes on the sleeve of his little Navy jacket. I was strangely impressed and momentarily disarmed by his glamor spectacle of authority. He began to speak and immediately let me know he was a representative of L Ron come to check out the progress of my mission. He said he was not impressed with the work that had been done so far but he demanded that I get out of bed that instant and get back to work. I used the last of my restraint reserves and told him the next thing I was going to do was get some sleep. After that I would work again. That was not the right answer for Wayne, and we locked eyes. I'm not sure what he thought he was going to say but he seemed to change his tune and toned down. Maybe because I stepped forward and closer to him. Wayne said I was disrespectful to a Sea Organization officer which was a high crime. My instant sentence for my crime was assignment to the RPF or leave the Sea Organization. I told Wayne the choice was simple, I was out, Mr. Gone, bye bye!

Wayne told me it wasn't that simple. I had to leave by way of the RPF. He reminded me that I was under a billion-year contract to L Ron and the Sea Organization. I told him I was done with the Sea Organization and Scientology as well. I didn't need it. In the back of my mind I was hoping the Navy would still take me. I was only twenty-two years old. Next it was my turn to be surprised by the unexpected. As if on cue, the male RPF members encircled me, physically laid hands on me and guided me to a room. I was told if I wanted to leave, there was a routing form I needed to follow but at this point they needed to isolate me because I was upsetting the other members.

Being surrounded by hostile white people had only happened to me one time before and that was not a happy time. I'll tell you what happened as briefly as possible. I was either 12 or 13 years old, living in Chicago when me and a group of friends rode our bikes into the wrong neighborhood. We knew we were in an all-white neighborhood but foolishly thought us kids were enough to have safety in numbers. Me and three other kids of the same age watched as a group of young white men from across the street began to point at us and yell to one another. I watched in horror as they quickly gathered and began to pick up wooden boards from a home that was being torn down. The next thing you know, about fifteen of them came running towards us!

My friends turned tail and road off as fast as they could. I tried to do the same, but the chain slipped off the sprocket on my bike and I wasn't going anywhere. They caught me and used a piece of rope they found at the construction site to tie my hands behind my back. I was surrounded by angry white men screaming at me saying they were about to hang me. I was lead to a tree with tall overhead branches to be hung. A white woman screamed from her window at the men and told them to leave that child alone. She said she was calling the police on them right now. The men shouted, "Fuck you lady" and managed to get the rope over one of the tall branches above me. They made a noose and put it around my neck, then jerked it so it was tight around my neck. One guy who acted as the leader told the others, to hang this nigger proper, one of them was going to have to let me stand on their back while the others pulled the rope. An argument ensued because none of the white men present wanted a nigger standing anywhere on them. In the meantime, that white lady come out on the porch with the phone in her hand at the end of the line. She is yelling to someone about what she is seeing.

I can only guess the apparent leader of the group figured this incident was turning out to be way more trouble that he wanted. He asked me a question. He said, "Look Nigger, if we let you go what are you going to do?" I told him "I'm going back to Africa!" He asked me if that was where I lived. I told him no. He said why would you go back to Africa if you don't live there? You don't have to go back to Africa, just stay the fuck out of this neighborhood! I told him okay, they let me go. I put the chain back on my bike and road away. As soon as I got a safe distance away I told those white people what I really thought about them. During this incident, only one of the friends I'd come with came back to help me, that was Paul Johnson, my forever childhood friend. They were going to hang him as well after he gave himself up so that I was not facing these crazy people alone.

Now here I am again in 1977, surrounded by aggressive white people but this time I don't have any friends to help.

I was taken to a room where I was confined until I completed my leaving routing form which no one would give me a copy of. I wasn't allowed to even see it until after I'd been confined to that room all day for days on end. The routing form seemed endless. So many steps to complete that involved plenty of subjective analyzing by my captors. I was constantly being reminded of the contract I'd signed and my lack of ethics and integrity for not wanting to honor my commitment. Different people who were also in the RPF would talk to me about the personal "wins" they were having all the time. Every person that was sent to talk to me told me their personal stories of "winning" from doing the RPF program. I was told all I had to do was learn how to correctly apply Scientology technology on another and let someone apply it to me. If I still wanted to leave after that I could go. They argued this is the reason I joined and signed the contract in the first place. I may as well stay to see what all the fuss was about. I began to associate learning Scientology tech with surviving what this was I'd gotten myself into. I still didn't understand what "crimes" I'd committed to warrant this last chance opportunity. After a while, I gave in and decided to try it out. I'd come there to learn something, and this was the opportunity for me to learn or leave. I only wanted to learn the secret, upper level training they offered.

3

The Upgrade

AFTER I AGREED TO TRY the program I was given a little more freedom. I still had at least one personal guard keeping an eye on me all the time, but I could come out of the room I'd been in. I was given a used black boiler suit to wear. I had no idea it would be a long time before I'd wear regular street clothes again. After putting in a day's work as a worker on the project that was once my mission, I started my initiation into the mystery technology of L Ron. My first lesson was all about controlling and being controlled. Learning the mechanics of control was vital if I was ever to learn how to control people, machines or objects properly. The first tech I learned was a process called Operating Procedure by Duplication. The procedure required two tables placed a short distance opposite of each other, one medium sized hardback book and a soda bottle. The book and bottle were each placed separately on the tables. The process is for two people and the procedure goes like this: Two people stand together at one of the tables. One of them is the operator, the other is the person being controlled. The operator directs the other to look at the object on the opposite table which is the book. The person who asked can gently grab the persons chin to direct their line of sight to see the book. Once the operator is satisfied the person has seen the book he thanks the person. The operator then directs the person to walk over to the book. He then tells the person to pick the book up. When the person has picked the book up the operator will ask What is its color? What is its weight? What is its temperature? Then he tells the person to put the book down in the exact same place where it was. Next the operator will tell the person to look at the bottle. Walk over to it. Pick it up. The ask the same series of questions for the bottle. In the end the operator tells the person to put the bottle down in the exact same place and they start all over again. This goes on for a minimum of 25 hrs. The roles are reversed for another 25 hr minimum. This went on for an average of 4-5 hours a day until complete. Important to note, the rule was once you start you finish. If the person doesn't want to do it anymore you gently or not so gently physically force the person to execute the command you give them. After I completed this process I was much easier to control. I also somehow felt emotionally detached from my prison like environment.

 The next technology I learned was called Dianetics. Dianetics is a procedure to help people "erase" bad memories. After about six months of Dianetics, I had erased who I'd been. To this day I have a difficult time remembering some parts of my life before Scientology because it was erased. That's what Dianetics is supposed to do. I was like a sponge absorbing and practicing the techniques of L Ron. I was curious and hopeful L Ron's technology would uncover abilities and power I had hidden in me waiting to be developed. I was hardly alone in my quest for power and abilities. There were one hundred twenty others on the program with me. All of the other people were white. There was only one other person who was not white and was browner than me, his name was Andre Tabayoyan.

Andre was the leader of all the people doing the program and everyone answered to him. I became one his deputies. For the next 18 months, I was on the program renovating the entire old Cedars Sinai into the Scientology complex it still is to this day. There is much I could say about my time on the RPF program but that's not what this book is for or about. There were some highlights that I will briefly cover.

After it was obvious I was no longer a threat because I'd asked to leave I kind of blended in somehow. I quietly put my head down and studied as much as I could and didn't cause any trouble. I don't remember how, but I was promoted to Deputy Bosun for Stewards and Supplies. That is strange title for a not so strange function. I became responsible for making sure I coordinated with staff not on the RPF to ensure people on the RPF had food to eat. I was also responsible to make sure everyone had the black or dark blue boiler suit, a bed and bedding, study supplies etc. Out of the one hundred and twenty people on the RPF there was one regular celebrity connection that was always interesting to see. There were two recent additions to the program from the Scientology Celebrity organization. A nice lady named

Cathy Wasserman and another named Tracy Lewis. Tracy was married to a semi famous Hollywood B actor named Jeffery Lewis who had played a villain role with Clint Eastwood in some spaghetti westerns among other things.

When a person was put on the RPF program, they would be required to abandon all parental contact with their children unless supervised for very limited time periods like once a day. The children of Sea Organization members assigned to the RPF were for the most part on their own. When Tracy was assigned to the program, she was the step mother of an infant named Juliette Lewis. The parentless children were held in a child care facility known as the Melrose. The building was overrun with cockroaches that could not be exterminated because the poison would affect the children, so they had lots of roaches instead. It was my responsibility to pick up the children of the people in the RPF program so the children could visit their parents for 30 minutes a day. I drove a large cargo van that had the seats removed. When I would go to pick up the babies who lived on Melrose St. in LA, they would be accompanied by one or two adults who also sat on the floor with the babies laid out on the floor as I drove them across town to Hollywood. Juliette was one of the babies I would drive. The year was 1977 and there were no seatbelts or child seats. It's a miracle no child was ever hurt in an accident while we mindlessly drove them around.

On July 8th, 1977 I lay asleep in the predawn hours on a mattress that's on a bare floor in the basement of the Scientology complex on La Bra Ave in LA. I was sleeping deeply from working to exhaustion the day before. I was in the room with at least 8 other people who were also on mattresses on the floor. There was no electricity and the room were completely dark. Suddenly there was a loud crash of the door to the room being smashed against the inside wall. As I struggled to wake up all I could see were bright lights winging around the darkness. I also saw black lines swinging around in time with the bright lights. Next, I hear a strange voice say What the fuck is this? What are you guys doing? Stand up and put your hands up! Everyone in the room stood up and put their hands up and followed the lights out of the room. Once outside as my vision cleared I could see the bright lights were large flashlights and the black lines I'd seen, those were single and double-barreled shot guns pointed at us all. The people pointing the guns were U.S. FBI Agents.

We all stood there, smut faced and slack jawed looking like coal miners! No one from my group spoke. Scientology staff member Ken Holden came dressed up like a Catholic priest soon appeared in the basement where we were being held by the FBI. Ken began to explain to the FBI Agents that we were voluntarily doing some type of monk monastery program and had taken a vow of poverty. That's why we looked the way we did. He went on to explain that we were on a grueling program of self-discipline of our own choosing. He cautioned the agents not to upset us or violate our constitutional religious beliefs and practices.

I remember thinking, what a load a shit, where'd he get that from? I would have never thought of saying that, but it seemed to work. The agent told us we could put our hands down and we were free to do whatever it was we did. Ken walked us to the horseshoe area of the building where FBI Agents with guns drawn lined the streets. Two agents passed by carrying a chainsaw that they promptly took to a door. The area the FBI was breaking into in Scientology was called B 1. B 1 stands for Bureau One. This was the unit that housed the Intelligence data and activity files. This is when the United States Government found out Scientology Intelligence Agents had broken into Government Offices and stolen confidential Government files under its nose. All hell broke loose, and several Scientologist ended up going to prison but that's not the amazing part of this story. What blows my mind to this day about that incident is not one of the one hundred and twenty people on the RPF program asked anyone from the FBI to help them get out of there!

    For the duration of my time on the RPF program the primary technology we used on each other was Dianetics. For five hours a day, I would attempt to erase aspects of my life by going over and over it until it erased, or I was lead to some earlier incident that was from my imagination or a past life. These incidents were meaningless to me and did not have the same power as actual incidents I'd experienced in my current life. We were required to go along with these procedures to become Clear. In Scientology, the state of Clear means the person is free of the effects of emotional trauma from their past. The definition of Clear has changed over the years. A person in Scientology achieves the state of Clear when they realize they were just making up those incidents in the first place. Once the person says they are just making up incidents in Scientology procedures, they can go on to the next level. If this makes no sense to you than know you are okay and have not been infected with L Ron's nonsense.

I spent nearly two years erasing my previous life in the RPF program. During that time, I realized sometimes, I was just making stuff up to have something to talk about during my Scientology procedures. I proclaimed to my Scientology technical consultant that I had achieved the coveted mental state of Clear. I was no longer a homo sapiens. When a person has achieved the state of Clear they become Homo Novus, the next level of evolution beyond Homo Sapiens! That happened towards the end of my RPF program. I was finally let out of the program in 1978 fully ready to receive the Scientology secret upper level doctrine to give me the super powers I so badly wanted.

I immediately started the course Scientology sells called Operating Thetan Courses One. This is the beginning course for learning the promised super powers. In those days, Scientology proudly proclaimed as fact it was manufacturing ultra-humans with a step by step process like a factory. I saw with my own eyes, people standing in front of the staff and paying public of the organization proclaiming they now had para-normal abilities! There was a Scientology magazine produced by the Scientology Advanced Organization appropriately titled "Advance". It featured success stories written by people who had recently completed courses which caused them to have paranormal abilities. I'd suffered the tortures of the dammed on the RPF program for the privilege of being invited to be ultra-human at no further cost to me. People who are not staff members paid tens of thousands of dollars for every

Scientology procedure on the way to becoming a super human. My twenty-three-year-old logic and high school education told me I made a right decision giving Scientology a try. At the time, it seemed like a worthy sacrifice of my time to live the rest of my life in comfort and power, a no brainer, right? Finally, I was about to learn if the end really justified the means. I wanted to know where and how far this thing I'd gotten into could go. I was all in. I didn't know exactly what for, but I was open to options. Enticed by the promise of occult knowledge, I was at the front door of magic in Hollywood, California. The door was mine to open and I did.

I started the OT 1 advance course and read the information. In all honesty I was ambivalent at best with the results. From what I remember, the instructions for this level were to go out among people at a train station and people watch. There was also the added activity, we had to imagine putting an intention into the people we observed then notice any response. The purpose of this level was to extrovert a person's attention after a long period of introspection processes (Dianetics). There was such a low expectation of achievement for this first level most people finished within a day or two.

I completed the OT 1 course. The only notable difference I noticed was this time it was me standing in front of the staff and public claiming new abilities that were not entirely true. The whole act was more of a show for the others. There was an unspoken agreement among us newly produced ultra-humans that we would not demonstrate our abilities in front of others because that would be a gross display of power and an unethical act.

We all quickly learned to perpetrate the unspoken deception of nonexistent, newly acquired paranormal abilities for the benefit of those who were yet to have their own personal experience. To be fair, some people would go on and on about their newly acquired super powers, however at no time, past or present did I ever see anyone demonstrate any act that I considered to be of paranormal origin. Talking on and on, about doing paranormal acts and odd synchronicities was the normal conversation people were having while participating in the secret levels.

The next level advance level was the OT 2 course. This course was about traumatic incidents that supposedly happened to all people of Earth many millions of years ago. These incidents were outside of my natural experience for many reasons. I was only in my twenties so had no idea what specifically happened hundreds of thousands of years ago that was influencing me today. Each person attempting to complete this level "imagined" the incidents if they didn't come to you naturally. Next, I followed the instructions to erase the ill effects of these traumatic incidents. This is a simplified explanation of what this level is supposed to be all about, the material is much more complicated to understand. I went through the materials and followed all instructions exactly. As I performed the given instructions for the procedure my whole body began to feel hot as if I were standing in direct sunlight on a hot day. Amazingly, this was noted as a side effect from doing the process in the instructions. As I imagined the incident, I got warmer and warmer to the point I began to sweat. I could feel my heart beating and I became alarmed. I didn't know or understand what was happening to me. The process required that I do it alone in a locked room for privacy. It was only me in there with whatever phenomena I had conjured. I remember feeling exhausted from all the heating and waves of energy flowing through me. My skin felt like I had a sunburn which was not possible because I'd been inside a closed room the whole time. This all proved to be a bit too much for me, so I ended the procedure and crawled into bed for a nap.

I woke up a short time later and immediately noticed how disoriented I felt. My size felt different. I don't know exactly how to explain it, but somehow, I felt larger in size than I had before. The feeling lasted for some days until I felt normal. I went to the Scientology examiner and explained what had happened to me. The next thing you know, I was given permission to advance to the next level. This was the first time something extraordinary altered my reality from doing Scientology procedures. I couldn't explain exactly what it was, but it felt good, like a temporary euphoria and I wanted more. I remember thinking, I'm on my way to the magic and I'm glad I had the patience to wait for it.

After taking a short break to enjoy my new advanced self, I enrolled for the next advance course OT 3. Prior to starting the actual procedure of the course there was a hand-written note by L Ron, the author of the course that came with dire warnings. L Ron stressed the importance of following the procedure exactly or one could become violently ill and die! The information after the warning was a story of space aliens 75 million years ago. The story is about an evil galactic overlord named Xenu who solved over population on his planet by telling everyone to report in to file their income tax. When the people showed up to pay their taxes they were taken in and had false memories implanted into their spirits. The story goes on to tell how all the spirits were bundled up and flown on an airplane to earth where they were dropped on volcano's which then exploded. After the explosions, ribbons flew up in the sky and captured the Spirts and took them to see a movie that went on for 36 days. L Ron wrote the movie implanted ideas about religion. L Ron wrote disparagingly of the Christian faith proclaiming Jesus Christ was also a false memory. At the end of the movie, the pilot whom it's assumed is driving the airplane tells the viewer they are just making this whole thing up. L Ron wrote these spirits are everywhere all over one's body. The idea was to start a dialog with these spirits and erase in their minds, that 36-day movie they saw long ago using a form of Dianetics. If the spirits didn't leave after that, the person doing the level had to get the spirit to start at the beginning of the universe, four quadrillion years ago to observe cherubs flying about making loud snapping noises. This level is super-secret and highly touted as the super human maker! My exact reaction after reading this science fiction nonsense was to close the course book and leave. I was in a bit of a shock. Could this really be the coveted secret to life as discovered by L Ron? I remember feeling nervous and agitated over the two and a half year's I'd wasted chasing a science fiction story. My enthusiasm for my quest of attaining super human abilities was rapidly fading. I started thinking about what I would have to do to go back home and start my life over again.

The Expert Witness

I didn't return to the course for some days until I was sent for by the course supervisor. The course supervisor assigned to take care of staff was a black man named Harold. He was the only other black person I'd seen so far involved in the game of making ultra-humans. Harold asked me what was going on and I sort of told him the truth. I told him I was disappointed with the material I was studying, and it didn't meet my expectation. Harold just looked at me and smiled. He explained to me that almost everyone said the same thing after reading the materials for the first time. He told me that I was in the danger zone because I'd been exposed but had not started the procedure. He talked to me about his personal experience when he first started the level. He mentioned that he like me felt like he'd hit a brick wall but that was partly the reason the level was also referred to as the Wall of Fire. Harold patiently handled all my concerns. He explained it was possible I could compete the level as fast as I wanted. The materials for the course stated the activity was like digging a ditch. Harold assured me I'd feel much better once I'd gotten myself through the level. Before you know, I was back on the course hunting these spirits referred to as Body Thetans or BT's for short. L Ron also referred to these spirits as fleas and they could swarm into clusters. The spirits would manifest as a pressure or dark area on one's body. The basic procedure was to start a conversation with these entities, do the procedure and get their agreement to leave.

I started having conversations with entities in a room alone doing the procedures as instructed. This went on for nearly 3 months. One day I wrote in my course report that I couldn't find any more entities. I wrote there were no more BT's and I was just making it up. That marked the end of the level. After that I was instructed to go to the Scientology examiner to declare my completion of the level. I stood in front of many people and told them how powerful I felt. Everyone clapped like seals at an ice cube party. On to the next level!

I can't really recall the details of the OT 4 and OT 5 advanced courses. The only thing that mattered is neither course involved looking for and starting conversations with spirits. I had a bad experience calling up spirits and it was not my favorite activity but a necessary evil at times. These levels involved spotting spots in and around the body. Some of the procedures involved walking as well as more people watching. I completed these two levels without incident.

In 1979, there were only seven advanced secret levels being sold by Scientology. I had completed six of the advanced levels and I was about the begin the final level. The final level was called OT 6. I had completed OT 7 out of sequence when I completed OT 3. Doing OT 7 out of sequence was standard procedure at the time.

OT 6 was the level where a person would become more than human. This level required you to demonstrate and prove your new abilities by passing a final test. This level was the most unusual I'd ever attempted. The information and procedures outlined for this level were not wholly unfamiliar to me. I had studied similar instruction from other practices like Buddhism, Tao and other books before Scientology. This level involved the new adept learning how to separate the spirit from the body. The procedure involved laying quietly in a bed alone with your head pointed toward magnetic north by the compass. After getting in the correct position, the next step was to quite the mind, no voice or monkey mind chatter. When the mind quiets, one would then will the spirit to separate from the body to achieve the out of body state. This was something that took practice. There were instructions to travel to different areas of earth observing people. The idea was to put an intention into unsuspecting people to cause them to do something that was not something they thought to do on their own. The procedure was like attempting to temporary "possess" another's body. To complete this level, it was required the person separate spirit from flesh, travel to a different country and make a stranger write you a letter and mail it to your mailing address. I never completed this level. No one I knew had completed the level.

   An evaluation was done to determine why people were not completing the OT 6 level. This evaluation was called "Ridge on the Bridge". L Ron authored the evaluation. He wrote the reason why people were not able to complete the OT 6 level was due to a missing step in the Scientology advanced level courses. I didn't get very far with the OT 6 level. I only got to the part of laying in the bed in the correct position. After some practice I could occasionally separate my spirit from the flesh by vibrating out! After getting out I would get anxiety and panic if I went too far or lost sight of my physical form. That usually resulted in having to start the separation process again another day. The instructions on the course were lacking in my opinion. There wasn't enough information for how to stabilize after achieving separation. While on the advance OT 6 course the course levels for OT 4-7 were officially retired from all Scientology advanced organizations and was being replaced by a new Scientology procedure specifically designed to solve the problem of the ridge on the bridge. This new procedure was the answer Scientology organizations needed to get on the with business of making ultra-humans. This newly discovered missing step was called New Era of Dianetics for Operating Thetans (Ultra Humans).

The problem I was having with this new missing step is it was not yet available in the Los Angeles area. The only Scientology Organization authorized to train people for the new course was in Clearwater, Florida at a place called the Flag Land Base. Flag was and still is the top organization for learning Scientology doctrine. Flag was also known as the Mecca of Scientology Technology. People from all over the world who practice Scientology came to buy the best service and courses it had to offer. As far as achievement was concerned, I was considered a rising star in the Scientology LA area. I'd only joined the organization in 1976 and was almost immediately put in its penal camp for 18 months. By the Summer of 1979, I had completed all but one (OT 6) advanced course Scientology had to offer. I knew many others who had been around the movement for much longer than I had and were nowhere near the advanced levels I'd already completed. Since graduating from the RPF program I never held a regular job in any one Scientology organization. I was always used for special projects that were not very visible compared to other jobs. The projects were always temporary and always required my limited technical skills I'd learned during my Scientology jail time. There was also a status and recognition bestowed on those who had completed advance courses. I was beginning to get used to my new-found status, however I didn't join the group to play organization or follow the leader. I was specifically there for the magic, nothing else interested me. Soon it became clear I had to get to Flag if I was going to continue my progress studying magic. I was curious about the new fix L Ron worked out. Things had begun to get interesting for me when the previous advance courses were recalled and no longer sold or taught at any price. The special projects that I worked on while at the Los Angeles area often resulted in me working with people who were responsible for managing the week to week operations of the Scientology organizations located in the in the western United States. These were the people who wore the Navy uniforms and insignia of which I had no attraction yet found myself often being pulled in for special projects involving management activity. I began to learn Scientology management policy used to manage its organizations. There is an equal demand for management staff to know and apply the administrative policies exactly as written by L Ron. The rule was L Ron wrote the rules, simple as that. L Ron wrote he had transcended your average human in intelligence and ability. L Ron was the creator and master of the ultra-humans that were being created to eventually overtake the earth. All the earth people would be forced to submit to L Ron and his mighty organizations.

    I made a friend while on the RPF program who went by the name Spike. When he completed the program, he was transferred to the Flag Land Base. Spike told me there was a need for a person to become a course supervisor for the new advance level program and I should ask for the position. I met the qualifications for the position but didn't want to go through all the paperwork to initiate the process. I don't remember who, but someone recommended I write a letter to the wife of L Ron and ask to be transferred as the quickest way to get to Flag. I followed that advice and Mary Sue granted my request. Before long I was a course supervisor at the International Training Organization which was part of the Flag Land Base in Clearwater, Florida.

For my first course, I was retained and certified as a Flag Trained Course Supervisor. I also retained and got certified for all previous technical practitioner training I'd completed before. While I was being trained, all Scientology procedures I'd received before were studied and verified for completeness. I also received security clearance to proceed to the new advance levels. I short order, I was involved with training staff from Scientology Advanced Organizations from the United Kingdom, Copenhagen, Denmark and California who would administer the new advanced levels to qualified paying customers at a high price. At the time, this new advance level had to be accomplished with person known as a technically trained practitioner or Auditor for short.

Students from European countries were multilingual, English was not their first or primary language. I personally learned about life working with people from other cultures and I was fascinated with that. There were up to fifty students in the process of learning when I joined Flag. I had French students, German students, Danish students, Italian students, Russian students, Hispanic students and South African students. As most of my students graduated the course, they were required to complete an internship course. I was transferred to the position of Intern Supervisor and mentored these same students through the internship. After completing the internship, the students worked as Auditors in the technical division administering the new advanced levels to paying public. There were plenty of paying public. I remember when the organization started making over a million dollars each week for months then it jumped to 2 million a week. The auditors were heavily monitored for quality control. I ended up following them to become a quality control and correction person known as a Cramming Officer in Scientology organizations. I sat in this position for some years and learned from the best individuals involved with the administration of the advance levels in Scientology. I became an expert at my job and was well thought of by my peers. The only person I hadn't worked with at that point concerning Scientology advanced levels was L Ron. That was about to change.

This is a picture of me and my family before I left for a vacation to California. On my knee is my first born Cleopatra Joy and her mother Teresa Diviner circa 1976

This picture is from 1978, I was 24 years old and had been recently released from the RPF thanks to Terrie Gamboa.

This was taken at my rehearsal dinner for Sandra's marriage to James 1977 or 78 at Rene Duke's home. Starting on the far left is Joyce and Doug Fiandica, Jesse Prince, Barbara Yarborough, Cheryl Herzer, Larry Anderson my minister, Sara Reyes Santarsaro Bellin Johnny Schlesinger, me, Anthony or Nicholas Eckelberry, James, Steven Eckelberry, mom Carla Kent, friend Barbara, Karen, my brother and Rene Duke. These are some of my new friends who I was on the Rehabilitation Project Force with in Los Angeles.

4

OVER THE RAINBOW
1982

IN 1982, I BECAME A PART of the staff who were committed to always be at L Ron Hubbard's personal beck and call. This small group of individuals were constantly subjected to his incredible ferocious temper and his tendency to speak and write what can now only be described as nonsense.

This is what I witnessed and was a part of during the last four years of L Ron's life. I can't speak about the type of person he was before because I had only thought I knew who he was. There are many others who were with L Ron during other times in his life, and they can speak to such, I can't. What I can do is give you my memories and perspective of the last four years of L Ron's life starting with the year 1982.

I was twenty-eight years old, and I had been living at the Flag Land Base in Clearwater, Florida for about three years. The Flag Land Base was Scientology's "Mecca," the place where the most advanced Scientology levels were delivered. The central building at the Flag Land Base was the Fort Harrison Hotel, where most of the action took place in those days.

I'd become part of a team of technical individuals who were considered to be the best in the world at the application of what Scientology had to offer as far as it's "Technology" is concerned. The Senior Case Supervisor International, David Mayo, headed the team. The other senior technical staff were Jeff Walker, Jill Gleason, Dennis Erlich, Ron Norton, Ray Marquat, David ("Spike") Bush, Ray Mithoff, David Ziff and a fellow named Glenn whose last name I don't remember. Maintaining a high quality of delivery of Flag services was our job, and everyone played the game well. The division we all worked in was titled Qualifications or Qual for short. There was also the Technical Division, and this is where the top trained Auditors and Case Supervisors worked.

We were all Sea Organization members. I think on average we were paid $50.00 a week. For extra money, sometimes, after hours, I worked in what was called "The Canteen." I found this nice definition of the word *canteen*: "a type of food service location within an institution in which there is little or no waiting staff table service." My co-worker and friend Spike also worked at the Canteen. Some nights we would make over $100.00 each in tips for maybe 3 hours of work. Instead of serving liquor and beer, we sold huge milkshakes and hot greasy hamburgers with cheese and onions fresh off the grill. This was our little secret, but there was one other person in on the deal, named Sven Peterson Sven Peterson. He was responsible for getting food supplies for the Canteen, as well as the two restaurants at the entrance of the Fort Harrison hotel.

Money was meaningless to me then. I had all that I needed plus some to buy my wife a happy surprise occasionally. I used most of the extra money to support my secret alter-ego lifestyle. A few of us from the Technical and Qualifications Divisions had motorcycles. I'd owned a few motorcycles, but in 1982, I had my most prized possession, a black 1978 Kawasaki 1000 series. When I got on that thing, I felt like I turned into Ghost Rider or something.

There are some very long straight roads in Clearwater. One road in particular I'd regularly race down was Highway 19. My other favorite long straight road was between Clearwater and the Tampa Bay airport. This road is known as the Causeway, and it turns into Highway 19 as it approaches Clearwater. I've gone in excess of 140 Mph down these roads more than once on different motorcycles. I don't advocate this type of behavior because I've seen the grease spots some riders get turned into after a fatal accident. Those speeds were what my odometer said anyway.

I can't imagine what I was thinking, but it was exhilarating to roll on two wheels at those speeds. I could feel the whole experience in every fiber of my body as I became one with my machine. Once me and a few renegade staff: Spike, Rick Sheehy, and Ray Marquat got into a race on Highway 19 with some of the local riders. The police got involved, and we ended up out-driving the police and got away. I received my fair share of traffic tickets for doing stunts on the beach streets in Clearwater.

The primary Scientology facility that delivered high-priced services to the Scientology elite was the Flag Service Organization, located in the Fort

Harrison Hotel at 210 S. Fort Harrison Boulevard in Clearwater. I lived less than a mile away with my wife in a renovated roadside motel called "The Heart of Clearwater." We called it HOC for short.

At the rear of the Ft. Harrison Hotel was a large size swimming pool that looked like a mini-tropical paradise. Affluent people from Europe and elsewhere would spend the day sunbathing around the pool while waiting to start or continue with services they'd paid for. Life was simple and almost ordinary, in that it was predictable. The only person screaming and yelling at the staff was Dennis Erlich, who was the Senior Cramming Officer in the Qualifications Division. He was known for having anger management issues.

I remember the day Dennis came back to the Qual area and told some of the staff he had been at a meeting that was held at the Sand Castle, a waterfront beach hotel facility, also owned by Scientology, located within a mile of the Fort Harrison Hotel. He told us it looked like the Scientology Mission Holders were going to take over the management of the Church! I wouldn't understand the significance of what he was talking about until months later. It appeared that a major conflict was starting to brew between the very top of Scientology's Church Management and the very bottom of its organizational hierarchy known as the Mission network.

Mission Holders were ordinary "field" Scientologists who were licensed by the Church to run smaller Scientology operations called Missions. These were franchise operations delivering lower-level Scientology Tech. Generally, they had been left alone by Church management and many had become quite profitable. They were a major feeder line of new people entering Scientology. But all that was changing. Church management, fearing the growing power and resenting the profitability of these franchise operations, had become more and more aggressive and demanding, and it was coming to a head.

The Mission Holders who survived and lived to tell of the hellish nightmare attacks that unfolded have already written about what happened in books of their own. To make a long story short, what happened is the Mission Holders fought valiantly and were persuasive with their arguments for a need to re-examine and change the relationship between the top and the bottom of the Scientology hierarchy. In the end, they didn't win or even make any progress at all.

Eventually, L Ron was made aware of the situation, and he was infuriated with the "mutiny." He released his Kraken, David Miscavige and his army of Finance Police on all Mission Holders worldwide. All were made to turn over the majority of their bank account holdings to the Scientology Finance Police. This was done to drive them effectively out of business. Yeah, that's the polite, short version.

A complete version of what happened at the Mission Holder revolt can be found in a most excellent book titled *A Piece of Blue Sky* written by Jon Atack. Atack joined the church at the age of nineteen in 1974 and was based largely in the Scientology British headquarters at Saint Hill Manor in East Grinstead, Sussex England.

I remember hearing rumors from other Flag staff about a takeover and revolt, with top Mission Holders drawing lines in the sand. Jeff Walker, who was the Senior Case Supervisor at Flag warned the Qualification Division staff that there was the potential for us having an increased flow of people who were being ordered in for correction because they were "squirreling"! Squirreling is a term used by Scientologist to describe anyone using some other "Technology" not authorized by L Ron. It could also mean altering Technology authored by L Ron.

Apparently, some Mission Holders had come up with their own "Technology" to help people overcome negative comments and influence, and they called it "De-Dinging." There was a big problem with this, mainly because L Ron didn't think of it. Anything other than L Ron's "Technology" in his organizations was simply not tolerated in any way.

David Mayo, the Senior Case Supervisor International, was the first person from International Management to show up at the Flag Land Base to quell the Mission Holder uprising. As it turned out, the Qualification Division staff would not get involved in whatever it was that was going on between Top Management and Mission Holders. Nothing was more important than delivering services and making that money, so I didn't hear much more about the situation until I was transferred from Clearwater, Florida to the Gold Base at Gilman Hot Springs, California.

This is how that transfer came about: It was during this time that a previous associate of mine named Mike Eldridge returned to Flag on a special mission. I hadn't seen Mike for more than a year since he'd gone "over the rainbow." Going over the rainbow was a term we used to describe a Sea Org member who mysteriously disappeared to go and work directly for L Ron Hubbard. I was the person that replaced Mike when he went "over the rainbow," and now he was here for me! At first Mike was pretty close-mouthed about his mission to the Flag Land Base. After about a week had passed, he eventually came to see me with the details of his confidential mission.

Mike and I had worked together as Qualification Division staff for a couple of years prior. He told me he was on a mission to find the person that was the most qualified Course Supervisor (like a teacher) and Cramming Officer (quality control person) and he was to bring that person to work with L Ron, to train, correct and establish an ideal International Management structure for his Scientology movement. I remember when Mike explained this to me I was thinking "this is what I get for being too nosey." This was more information than I wanted to know. I tried to end the conversation pleasantly, but he insisted that I sit and let him finish explaining why he was talking to me.

Mike went on to explain that he had selected me to go through the qualification process to determine if I could be a candidate for the job. Mike told me that he had traveled to other International Advanced Level Organizations scouting for candidates and Flag was naturally the last stop. He explained to me that it was an honor for me to be even considered for the position. I just smiled and agreed to be interviewed. I had previously noticed Mike interviewing other staff members, and that took the edge off my concern that he was there to get *me*. I never thought I had a chance at the position, so my attitude was just to submit to the paperwork and questioning with the hope he would eventually go away. I was content with my level of participation and interaction with my job at the Flag Land Base. In fact, everything seemed ideal in my life, the only exception was my fire-hot failing marriage to Sonny.

Mike already had full access to the many personal files every Scientology institution keeps on its members. He arrived as a representative of L Ron himself. This was a bit much for me to take in right away. I mean Mike and I use to drink beers on the weekend, flirt with the women and complain about our wives together. We'd sit around and talk about what we use to do before we got involved in Scientology; drinking, chasing women and getting as high as possible on the rebel drugs of the 60's and 70's baby boomer culture. In our conversations, we would reminisce about taking all the different LSD products and smoking the various types of marijuana. Somehow after all of the Scientology processing we had, those youthful days still gave us bragging rights and a good laugh.

Anyone being sent over the rainbow was thoroughly vetted. Part of the vetting process requires completing a Life History form. The information required for the Life History form included listing the name and address of the individual's family members, disclosure of any connection with military or intelligence organizations, a record of every school attended, a record of all sexual encounters that included the full names of sexual partners, details of the sexual acts performed in the relationship as well as the total number of times the sexual act was performed with each partner. The vetting process included getting hours and hours of security checking. Security checks involved being interrogated by an investigator with the use of an E-Meter machine.

Everything seemed to be moving along with my vetting process until I had to try and do a full disclosure of my sexual exploits. Apparently, I'd had too many sexual exploits, and was accused of not telling the full truth. I ended up getting extra security checking to verify if I was telling the truth or not. In my youth, I was sexually active and may have had up to 20 different partners. When I had to add up all to the times I'd had sexual intercourse, the number was over 100. This was outrageous to Mike and whomever he had to report to. Besides being accused of lying about my sexual history, I was also made to go to the Health Department in Clearwater to get checked for sexually transmitted diseases. I was told to explain to the receptionist at the Health Department that I was indigent. I was checked and of course was found to be disease free.

I remember becoming concerned because I was getting too much unwanted attention from Mike and his mission. The truth was I had no intention or desire to go over the rainbow; I was content with how my life was going and I didn't want any surprises. My concerns were warranted, within a few days of completing my vetting process Mike came to see me again. He told me he was submitting my name to his handlers as the person to go and work with L Ron. He looked at me and smiled and asked me what I thought of that. I asked him if I could just speak to him as a friend; he said yes. I told him I did not want to go over the rainbow, and I had no desire to go back to the Los Angeles area.

Dennis Erlich had earlier pulled me aside when he noticed what Mike was doing with me. He advised me not to go with Mike, and told me I had a right to say no. This was not what Mike wanted to hear, and he began to explain to me what a privilege it was even to have an opportunity to work with L Ron. He went on to say that he was going to pretend like he never heard me say I didn't want to go. He went on to tell me that my life would be ruined if I refused the job. He told me I would be kicked out of the Sea Org and consigned to extinction. I didn't want any of that action, so I agreed to go.

After we had cleared up our little misunderstanding, Mike turned back into the nice friendly guy. He told me my wife would also be fully vetted. If she qualified, she would be allowed to join me at a later date. If she didn't qualify, I would have to divorce her. Mike asked me if I had any questions. I told Mike my primary concern was how I would get my motorcycle from Florida to California.

I was not the only person leaving to go over the rainbow. My other associate; Ray Mithoff was called to go as well. Ray was the most senior Case Supervisor at the Flag Land Base. The technical hierarchy in Scientology began with L Ron Hubbard, next in line was David Mayo and after him came Ray Mithoff. Ray was from El Paso, Texas and was very soft spoken. He and I use to drink beers together sometimes and talk about all the drugs we'd taken before Scientology. He was a nice guy and could be fun to be around. We had worked together for some years training new and old auditors at the Flag Land Base.

Mike informed me that a truck was being rented to transport the possessions of all who were headed over the rainbow. All was in order. I went around to say goodbye to my co-workers, and it made me sad to leave. That evening I was on an airplane headed for Los Angeles.

5

THE CHOSEN ONE
1982

THE FLIGHT FROM CLEARWATER to Los Angeles was uneventful. L Ron's trusted Messengers were caring for me, but this felt strange. For the most part, staff members would rather avoid too much direct contact with L Ron's Messengers.

When I arrived at LAX Airport, a van was waiting at the arrival baggage claim. We drove to the Commodore Messenger Organization located in the Big Blue facility in Los Angeles – the same place I'd left from when I transferred to Flag a few years before. I immediately began to feel uncomfortable being back in Los Angeles. I sure hadn't missed the smell of that thick yellow layer of pollution that covers the sky like clouds in the summer months. Mercifully we spent less than an hour at Big Blue before we continued the journey.

Here is where it got interesting for me. Until that point, I was unaware of any other Sea Organization facilities in California. The van driver joked and told me I would have to be blindfolded for the rest of the trip. I just looked at her; she smiled then laughed and said, "You should see the look on your face!"

There were at least eight other people in the van, and this broke the ice. The driver was a Messenger, and she explained to me that where I was going was a paradise, and I was in for a treat! I asked her if L Ron lived at the place we were going. She replied it was not her place to discuss any personal details of L Ron's location or activities. She told me all of that would be explained to me when I arrived.

I remember casually telling the people on the van about myself and that I was there to work in the new Inspector General Network being formed at the International Base. Some looked at me with wide eyes. A fellow named Gabe laughed and said, "We'll be calling you Sir tomorrow."

We headed east on Highway 10 from Los Angeles towards Riverside and exited onto Pomona Highway 60. We then exited onto Highway 79 headed towards Beaumont, then headed down Gilman Hot Springs Road towards San Jacinto. In 1982, Gilman Hot Springs Road was a poorly lit two-lane highway along the foothills of the San Bernardino Mountains.

It may have been a new moon the night I arrived because the only light I recall seeing was starlight. There were no major cities for miles around. I looked up and saw a night sky I'd never seen before. With the absence of ground light, the sky looked like it was in super-high definition. The stars were both near and far, glistening in the blue-black velvet sky. I was in a high desert area, and for the first time I could see what a desert looked like. There was nothing but small cactus and shrubs to see for miles and miles. No houses, no cars and no people. As we approached our destination, I could see the landscape was sandy, with cactus-type shrubbery scattered about. On our left were the foothills of the San Jacinto Mountains.

In the distance, I could see what looked like the lights of a small town. Can't say I would have ever guessed what I saw next. In this rocky desert area, I saw what looked like a well-lit three-masted sailing ship sitting atop a small hill! As we approached, I could see both sides of the road were lined with a tall black fence. The sign on the side of the Highway identified the area as Gilman Hot Springs, California.

As we approached, the van entered a gated entrance where a security guard waited. The van driver allowed the security guard to inspect visually to see who was in the van. After a brief stop we continued up a road past a row of cottages on a slight incline on the right side of the van where the ship was, on the left-hand side was what looked like a health spa. At the end of the spa was a two-story white building that looked like it may have been a renovated hotel. I later learned this building was known as Del Sol, home of the Watch Dog Committee (WDC), International Finance Police, and the Executive Director International.

As I exited the passenger van, I began to see people that I'd known from Flag, and others I'd known from the Los Angeles area organizations. Mike Eldridge was there to greet me and lead me up a small hill to a row of Villa style offices. Mike informed me that these were the offices of the Religious Technology Center, commonly referred to by its acronym RTC.

Mike took me into the office of a fellow named Steve Marlowe. who was the current head of RTC. I knew Steve and his wife Laura because we had all worked at the Flag Land Base. Steve and Laura had been Messengers at Flag, as had the majority of the other Messengers at the Base. I felt more at ease when I saw Vicki Aznaran sitting in Steve's office. I knew both Vicki and her husband Rick from Flag. Rick and I had worked together as technical staff at Flag; his wife Vicki had been an Executive Messenger. Rick and Ron Miscavige Jr. would often take me to the gun range in Clearwater and teach me how to shoot their guns.

Steve gave me the welcome talk for new staff members. RTC as an organization was a new concept. Steve explained that L Ron Hubbard had turned over all registered trademarks owned by Scientology, Dianetics and all of their affiliate organizations to RTC. It was now the duty of the newly created Religious Technology Center organization to police and enforce the correct usage of all trademarks by Scientology organizations worldwide. I asked what about the copyrights? Steve explained that L Ron maintained all copyrights, and a new corporation called "Author Services" were created to collect L Ron's publishing royalties. There were hundreds of books and tapes authored by L Ron and their use was mandatory for all Scientology and Dianetics organizations.

Steve went on to inform me about the physical dimensions of the property and said it was over 500 acres. All senior management organizations of corporate Scientology, as well as a film production organization called Golden Era Productions occupied the property. The fact that all of Scientology's international management was located here was top secret. To the local community, we pretended we were just a film production company. The place was referred to by insiders as Int Base or Gold Base, or just "the Base."

My next question brought a look of surprise to Steve's face – I asked him where L Ron was. He told me he didn't think he was on the Base today. He pointed out to me where L Ron's house was at the top of a small hill at the base of the San Jacinto Mountains. He told me David Miscavige would brief me later about protocol concerning the proper way to address L Ron, and I was warned not to act shy because he was very much against that. I guess the look on my face made them smirk. Steve said he was joking, and he knew I'd be fine.

I already knew the majority of the executives in RTC because we had worked together at Flag before. I reacquainted myself with Vicki Aznaran, now an RTC executive. She was a tall blonde woman, as rugged and beautiful as a Texas sunset on a cool late fall evening. She was a Texan and had that drawl that always seem to remind me of an Eagles song, any one of them. She had pale powder blue eyes that you could feel when she stared at you. Vicki had a reputation, and the only way I can properly describe it is to use vernacular language here. Vicki was one badass bitch that had a mouth on her so sharp she could cut wood with her words. Anyone who was her equal had a healthy respect for her and the good sense to stay out of her way. Those who were beneath her did what they could to curry her favor.

We smiled at one another and carried on with small talk, but Vicki and I were friends. I knew when we had some private time we would talk, and she would look out for me in any way she could. We had a bond and an innate trust of one another. I had done some simple auditing on her before, at Flag. Usually when I would audit (apply Scientology technology) to a strong woman, it wouldn't be long before they were in tears crying like a little girl, such was the power of the Tech.

No slight on women here because there are plenty of men who react the same way sometimes. In short, it was my job to make her feel better and return her to confidence. Vicki was no crier, and I felt intimidated the first time I tried to do some simple auditing on her. Well, after I saw her cry I guess I looked just as surprised about that as she was for crying. We ended up laughing hard about it together and at that moment we became friends for life. We would go on to create and accomplish many things together.

There was only one other person that I had to report to before my first day at the Gold Base was done, and that was David Miscavige.

I don't remember who it was that took me to David's office, but it was in one of the uppermost Villa's that overlooked Highway 79. This uppermost row of Spanish-style Villas was visually obscured by healthy and well-watered grape vines that hung in front of the Villa doors on tall green trellises that blended well with the environment. When I entered the office, Dave was furiously writing something as he read something else. He looked up with a broad smile and asked that I give him just a minute to complete whatever it was he was doing. It only took a few minutes before he looked up and said he was done. He came over and gave me a strong handshake and welcomed me to the base. I am an open admirer of physically beautiful women and hardly notice beauty in a man. David, while short in stature, was what could be considered to be a handsome man. I think he was in his mid-twenties. He had perfect teeth, blonde hair, and a square jaw line with bright and alert blue eyes. He also had an uncanny deep voice that could make a room reverberate. He was not the whispering type; to the contrary he spoke at a volume slightly louder than average, all the time. He probably had a pretty good singing voice that was never developed. I smiled and firmly shook his hand and told him I was happy to be there.

This was not our first meeting, I'd met him already as well. I'll quickly tell how we met the first time.

Maybe two years earlier, while I was still staff at the Flag Organization in Florida, I was sent on a mission to the Scientology organization in Seattle, Washington to make it produce more income for the Sea Org Reserves fund. I went on a mission with Cathy Rinder and some other woman whom I don't recall right now. Cathy and I were initially briefed and fired on the mission to Seattle by Ron Miscavige Jr., the brother of David Miscavige. At that point in their lives, Ronnie and David could have passed for twins. Only by taking a closer second look you could see that David was the younger brother. Both were short in stature, visually handsome with those bright eyes and deep voices. I knew Ron Miscavige Jr. and his wife from Flag and we were all friends. Ron had a nice gun collection, and he would take me with him to a gun range in Clearwater and let me shoot his guns. Vicki's husband, Rick Aznaran was an ex-marine and gun enthusiast; both of these guys took the time to teach me some basics for the safe and effective handling of firearms.

We had prepared all day and all evening for the mission, being briefed and being security checked with the E-meter to verify our readiness for the task at hand. Finally, Cathy, me and the other woman took the red-eye from Clearwater and flew into LAX early the next morning. We were instructed to report to the Messenger Organization in Los Angeles. I know I was pretty tired from the lack of sleep but as soon as I arrived at the Messenger Organization the first person I see is Ron Miscavige Jr.! I said "Ronnie, how in the hell did you get to LA before we did?" David looked up and smiled and said "You think I'm Ronnie. I get that a lot. I'm his brother David, and he shook my hand. I smiled at him and said "Man you guys look alike for real." I introduced myself and told me I was on my way to Seattle for a mission. He informed me that he was on a mission as well doing "corporate stuff." We wished each other well and went on about our business. My first impression of him was that he seemed like a very dedicated person, and he was courteous. We parted with mutual respect for the work we were doing as Missionaires.

Now I was seeing him for the second time, as he welcomed me to the Gold Base. David said I should take some time to become familiar with the Base and the organizations therein. He said he was tired, but he still had a few things to wrap up then he was going to bed. He asked if I was hungry and told someone to make sure I had something to eat.

As I left his office, I felt a moment of bliss. It felt magical to be there; I knew the big bosses as friends before they were big bosses. They were all happy to see me and gave me a warm reception. It just felt too good to be true. The other big change for me was I was now a big boss in training. In a twinkling of an eye, I was a sort of overnight sensation. I was instantly a big boss over 95% of the staff at the Gold Base. I knew I'd have to get used to that. That euphoria didn't last very long!

For the next few days, I spent time reacquainting myself with familiar friends. I guess it was apparent that I needed a new wardrobe to command that executive snap and pop when I came on the scene. Vicki helped me with shopping and transportation to stores in LA. Some of the clothing stores, I shopped at were on Rodeo Drive in Beverly Hills, CA. I had never done that before. I settled into the Banana Republic fashion line of clothing. This was perfect apparel for the civilian desert camouflage look for where I lived now. It was a cool bohemian style that just projected an Indiana Jones adventure. Vicki was a fan of the Banana Republic too, so there you have it.

There were many follow-up meetings I had with David to help me establish my place in the matrix of the system we were in. In Scientology culture, this is known as doing a Non-Existence Formula. I had to make myself known to my superiors and fellow staff at the Gold Base. What I had to do is go around and visit with staff in each of the organizations at the Base to let them know what my title and position were in relationship to their title and position. This included asking the staff what, from my position, they would need and want from me. I in turn would inform them what I would need and expect from them.

This procedure was part of what L Ron called his Ethics Technology. The simple explanation of what ethics technology is based primarily on western culture and moral principles concerning what is appropriate ethical human behavior. The nonexistence formula is part of a series he called Conditions of Existence. It was his contention that by applying a certain sequence of steps and individual could go from being a virtual unknown at the workplace or a new relationship, anything really, to a state of not only becoming affluent, but also attaining the maximum level of power with whatever came with a new job position, relationship or whatever. This ideology probably extends way past any employee handbook you ever got from the workplace.

When I went to see David Miscavige to do my formula with him, he was very casual about it. He told me the best thing I could do to help L Ron was to give the key managers priority handling to make them more efficient. That included Ron's Messenger Organization (some of whom were also members of the Watch Dog Committee) and executives from what is known as the Executive Strata. Without getting too elaborate, I was supposed to find out what was preventing these people from performing their jobs efficiently and correct it using the technology of Scientology.

This invariably involves doing counseling on the person, as well as finding out what the person didn't understand or was confused about in relationship the duties they were expected to perform. David advised that I start studying the case files of the individuals concerned to see if the person had been mishandled or had the technology incorrectly applied to them.

These were tall orders and hard work but this is what I was trained to do, and I did my work well.

As of yet I still had not seen hide nor hair of L Ron. He was the last and most important person I needed to complete my Non-Existence Formula with.

Dave told me L Ron wasn't at the Gold Base. He told me the house being built for Ron at the Gold Base was not ready to receive him yet. I was also told not to ask questions about where L Ron was or what he was doing unless I wanted to court serious trouble. At the time, this warning made perfect sense to me, and I didn't question it, even in my mind. Dave told me to write my formula in the form of a dispatch and address it to Ron. He said he would make sure Ron would receive my dispatch.

Dave was the carrier and liaison between wherever L Ron was and the Gold Base. He drove a black Chevy Van when he went to pick up the recorded Dictaphone tapes that contained Hubbard's orders.

Life at the Gold Base revolved around the times Dave would drive alone to meet with a man named Pat Broker on some desert back road in southern California or Las Vegas and exchange banker boxes of information from the corporate directors and managers of Scientology with recorded Dictaphone tapes from L. Ron. Pat Broker and his wife Annie were with L. Ron, wherever he was, and Pat was the liaison from that end.

Both David Miscavige and Vicki Aznaran helped me write a proper Non-Existence Formula dispatch to L Ron. Of all of the things I knew how to do easily, writing that dispatch was not one of them. For one thing, I didn't know how to type at all. In fact, I had little to no experience with using a typewriter. During this time, word processing on a computer did not exist for the average consumer.

Dave couldn't touch type, but he had put in a lot of hours using a typewriter. He had a three-finger method of hunting and pecking those keys really fast. He could keep up with a person who knew how to touch type and would often do a better job with the grammar. Back in those days, unless you were using an electric typewriter you had to press the letter keys pretty hard to make an impression that would not only imprint on the first page, there was always that carbon copy page to worry about as well. The typing and retyping were very frustrating for me, and I'd spent nearly a day trying to get it done. Finally, Dave told me what to say and how to say it, and Vicki typed it for me.

With all that I could do, my typing and writing needed work. This was my first real embarrassment. As soon as I was able to I went down to the Qualifications building where my office was located and enrolled on a typing course. Within a month, I was able to touch type and handle a typewriter, but I was still not able to type as fast or as accurate as Dave with his three-finger method.

6

The Real L. Ron Hubbard

I WAS GIVEN ACCESS TO and told to study a new issue type from L Ron that I'd never seen or heard of before, called "LRH advices." Both Steve Marlowe and Vickie Aznaran made sure I understood these letters from L Ron contained direct *orders* to Sea Organization executives across the corporate spectrum that constitutes the Scientology enterprise. I was informed that in the eyes of the law, it was impermissible for L Ron's to be perceived as the managing agent for the corporation.

The reason for this was simple: all Scientology corporations had filed papers to be recognized as non-profit, independent churches. According to their own bylaws, the organizations are supposed to be administered by the corporate board members of said organizations. Nothing could have been further from reality, and these "advices" confirmed L Ron was the absolute unquestioned dictator of the Scientology enterprise he and others created over the years. There were hundreds, maybe even thousands of these advices the contained orders which were being issued to staff that involved the day-to-day operations of Scientology management. Ron had the Sea Organization and his Messenger Organizations to enforce his orders on any level within the Scientology enterprise.

In an attempt to sidestep the issue of control, Ron's orders were referred to as *advices*, and it was perfectly legal for him to give advice. During the application process for 501(c)(3) non-profit status, the U.S. Internal Revenue Service among other things was looking for evidence of L Ron being the *de facto* controlling agent of all Scientology corporations. Additionally, they were looking for evidence of the money Scientology corporations were making inuring to L Ron's personal bank accounts.

In the beginning, I was given paper copies of L Ron's advices as he issued them. Within a month, I had a five-drawer file cabinet full of L Ron's advices concerning every aspect of Scientology. It became impractical for me to try and keep copies of advices that didn't directly or indirectly require action from me. I would shred the copies of advices I and others were done complying with and it was hard to keep up. It was also my responsibility to ensure L Ron's advices were fully complied with by others.

Advices were received on a weekly basis that covered every major operation Church Management. From reading these advices, I began to see an aspect of L Ron that I never knew or even suspected existed.

The many books and published volumes by L Ron are properly edited for consistency, relevance, grammar and so on. After reading L Ron's books and listening to his lectures for so many years, I'd subconsciously created in my mind a personality for him, as a benign, patient masterful teacher. From what he'd written, I also believed he was an intelligent and compassionate leader. To the contrary, these advice letters were straight from L Ron's mouth to a Dictaphone and showed a different side of L Ron that was vile and pernicious.

Within L. Ron's Household Organization, there was a department that did nothing but transcribe and process the Dictaphone recordings from Ron. During all the training courses I'd taken since being in Scientology, I was only familiar with reading or listening to material of Ron's that had been properly produced and carefully edited. These advices were something entirely different. I didn't recognize the personality who authored these advices.

To summarize, the way L Ron spoke about what he thought of some of the staff members at the Gold Base was horrific. He accused executives and janitors alike of being in collusion with the FBI to destroy his Scientology. He would also do his best to denigrate and demean these people that had given most of their lives in servitude to him. It was like watching a horror movie that features a complete narcissistic sociopath with plenty of money ranting and berating others. Even though I was a true believer in L Ron at the time, this is when I began to see more clearly what was really going on.

What was equally shocking was the fact that everyone else at the base acted like this was perfectly acceptable behavior, and they would respond accordingly. There was a whole routine that went into effect the instant Dave Miscavige would return from picking up the tapes Ron had recorded. The tapes would be transcribed and the next thing you know certain staff members were marched down to a manmade lake to jump in fully clothed. I some instances David would have to go around to staff L Ron was particularly upset with and spit in their face. If someone really made L Ron angry, David would spit tobacco juice in the face of a true believer, and dedicated staff member. This is what L Ron would advise Dave to do to some of the staff at the base. Besides being incredibly juvenile, unsanitary and crass, it was completely opposite to what I'd been trained to do.

For more than a decade, I'd been trained to have nothing but the highest respect for my fellow Sea Organization members. There was a code that we would have to read aloud regularly that included the following promises:

1. I promise to exemplify in my conduct the belief that to command is to serve and a person was only as valuable as he can serve others.

2. I promise at all times to set a desirable example in appearance and conduct.

3. I promise to lead effectively, care for and train those under my care...

These are just a sample of the many policies L Ron wrote concerning what proper conduct was for Sea Org members. They were to be highly respected and cared for at all times. This is so not what was happening at the Gold Base. The staff was constantly being removed, demoted or sent to a Sea Org RPF work camp a few miles away at a place called Happy Valley. At the time, Happy Valley was also jokingly referred to as "The Institute for the Criminally Insane" by the staff.

I was really taken aback by all of this. I would have never believed this could happen, however I was seeing it and living it.

L Ron began to create new Technology that basically amounted to deprivation and torture. Ron called this new technology The Running Program.

The Running Program was based on an advice that called for putting up a telephone pole in the ground in a relatively flat area in a field. A large circle extended from the center of the pole. The circle was large enough for a person to be able to jog around; I don't recall the exact circumference of the circle. Some staff had to jog around this large circle in the high desert heat for more than five hours a day every day. In the advice, L Ron said he remembered this technique from some millions of years ago. He said this was a quick and easy way to snap a person out of a funk and get them productive again. He said this idea originated from a time when people didn't have physical bodies; they were just spirits. He described an area in space that had this big maypole in the center of it. Spirits were required to go round and round the pole until they were cured.

There were ex-executives that I'd known and worked with at the Flag Base, who were assigned to do this program by L Ron himself. He was extremely vindictive with these people and wrote that he wanted them to run around that pole long enough until they created a ditch around the pole. The results were tragic for some of these staff, and some were crippled by the experience. I had never known or seen this type of deviant behavior before, and it left me shocked and confused.

I was the outsider in that others around me seemed to understand and accept the torture as if it were preordained. I felt like I was trapped in a horror movie experiencing all the accompanying fear and panic. For reasons unknown, I couldn't stop watching or participating in the confusion. I'd enjoyed horror movies since I was a young child. For me, the speed, intensity and shock of living non-stop drama was somehow perversely hypnotic and mesmerizing. It was a freak show, and I couldn't stop or break the trance.

My dilemma became how many chances could I take before the madness would turn its ugly head to bite and eat me? I watched in abject horror and fascination as staff members I'd personally known for many years were now being labeled as FBI informants or subversives who had been sent in by shadow government agencies to destroy Scientology. I had no knowledge of or belief in shadow government organizations, so I had to make sense of the madness somehow to keep my sanity. The accused were people that had given their entire lives in servitude to L Ron and his Scientology ideology. These tortured souls were just as surprised as anyone else to find out they were a sleeper mole that had been sent in to destroy Scientology! L Ron got this idea from something he'd read about Sirhan Sirhan being brainwashed to carry out the the assassination of Robert Kennedy Jr.

Now these loyal staff were being discarded as criminals after being tortured and disgraced. This happened as they were being excommunicated. I witnessed and participated in the process of "thinning the herd" at all levels of Scientology corporate and management levels during these turbulent times which began in 1982 and continued in 1993. This was only the beginning of what would only get worse.

I found myself playing this game of Russian roulette on a daily basis with fellow staff who in the past were friends of mine. The casualties were too numerous for me to write about here, but I will single out specific examples and persons here soon.

By November of 1982 L Ron's top captain of his International Messenger Organization and myself were exiled to the Scientology Advanced Organization in Denmark, Copenhagen for nearly a month. We were sent to Denmark and told we would have to stay there and live as the staff lived until the Organization was on track and producing income for Sea Org Reserves at an acceptable rate. The person's name that I was exiled with was Marc Yager. To my knowledge, he is still hidden away in the Sea Organization even now.

Marc and I survived this ordeal and made it back home to Golden Era Productions for the Xmas holidays. Strangely enough, The Sea Organization staff celebrated Christmas in the typical secular fashion. There was time off, exchanging gifts, a big decorated pine tree, a traditional dinner that included plenty of turkey, ham, and sides for all. There was also plenty of alcohol on hand, which was supplied by each organization for the staff. In the evening, a band called The Golden Era Musicians performed late into the night for the benefit of the staff. It was usually during these times some staff would get together and have sexual relations with people they were not married to although that was strictly forbidden!

Ultimately, by the end of 1983, there was only a handful of executives remaining that L Ron hadn't accused of being a spy or a subversive. We all had come to dread the times when Pat Broker would make contact and arrange to meet with David. By default, this was the precursor to the next act in L Ron's madhouse play. I can't speak for the others involved, but for me I couldn't help but continue to play L Ron's deadly game of roulette with those who remained. I can best describe it as a macabre game show of high stake wins and losses, favor or exile. As we all played L Ron's deviant game of roulette with each other, there was an unspoken rule never to get emotionally involved. There was a definite unspoken resentment against L Ron's tendency to contradict his set-in-stone policies as he meandered from one sector of Scientology to the next leaving a trail of destruction.

7

THE PURGE
1983

1983, I WAS TWENTY-NINE YEARS OLD. So many staff and executives at the Gold Base, had been or were being removed from their respective corporate and staff positions that it's not feasible for me to try and name them all. Staff who had held executive positions in L Ron's Messenger organizations and Management organizations were excommunicated and gotten rid. After they were gone, they were watched and pursued by Scientology's Office of Special Affairs. Of all the staff who eventually were purged from the Gold Base and branded as FBI dupes or CIA operatives, none was more reviled and harassed by Hubbard than David Mayo. It was a well-known fact by Sea Organization and Scientology members alike that David Mayo had been the next top Scientology technical person after L Ron.

I was ordered by L Ron to take David Mayo in and interrogate him about who his external connections were. I could hardly believe he was sitting across from me totally demoralized, his skin appeared like it had been over exposed to the sun, he looked horrible. I had been told that David Mayo accepted money from Mission Holders while he was out on a Sea Org mission to quell the Mission Holder uprising that happened at the Flag Base a year earlier. In addition to accepting money from the rebellious Mission Holders he also had an extramarital affair with his young assistant during that mission assignment. At that time, David Mayo was married to someone else. During my interrogation of David, he admitted to accepting the money and the extramarital affair with his assistant but there was no evidence whatsoever of any external influence, CIA or FBI connections.

Despite there being absolutely no supporting evidence whatsoever, Hubbard insisted his ex-auditor and confidant David Mayo was under the influence of secret government operatives bent on the destruction of his precious Scientology. Hubbard is the person who ordered Mayo to run around a telephone pole in the desert until he ran a trench around the pole. Hubbard ordered this torture that would eventually cause David to be temporarily crippled from knee and ankle abuse.

L Ron created his own justice system for Scientology. The most severe justice procedure that could be levied against an individual is called a Committee of Evidence.

A Convening Authority, usually the L Ron representative in an organization is authorization to initiate a Committee of Evidence. This person acts at the request of another church executive. The committee is composed of a Chairman, a Secretary, plus two to five other members. Their task is to read and hear evidence for and against the accused church member. They have two weeks to complete the Committee of Evidence. Committee of Evidence policy explicitly bars any representation by legal counsel for the accused.

After reviewing the evidence, the secretary, and members vote on whether they think the accused church member is guilty or not guilty of each of the presented charges. Conviction on a charge is by majority vote. The Committee of Evidence then recommends punishment, which, in principle, must be done in accordance with L. Ron's policies. The results of a Committee of Evidence is issued in a document called the "Findings and Recommendations." All Committee of Evidence members must sign this document whether they agree with it or not. The only means of recourse are: A Review Committee of Evidence, where the committee is only allowed to listen to the recordings and review the documents of the original Committee of Evidence, then issue new Findings and Recommendations; a petition by the accused church member to have the Committee of Evidence cancelled, which is directed to an executive highly-placed in the church hierarchy; or a Board of Review in which the charges are reviewed by newly appointed members. Both the Board of Review and the Review Committee of Evidence have the option of making new recommendations.

Within this internal system, justice is an illusion. The only real hope an individual has of being exonerated from the misery of a Committee of Evidence is to curry the favor of some executive who by position is above those in pursuit of the individual.

More often than not that person would be L Ron himself. He would step in and be the hero and set new policy, on his up days.

In my past experience before coming to the Gold Base, an individual or a small group of two or three individuals could simultaneously receive a Committee of Evidence.

I was put on as chairman of a Committee of Evidence that involved no less than 18 staff at the same time! This went on for months and was a complete waste of time. Hubbard had already decided what crimes and high crimes these individuals had committed against his Scientology organizations. It was the task of the committee to come up with the evidence, which in this case for the most part did not exist.

David Mayo was at the top of the list along with John Nelson, who was the ex-Commanding Officer of Hubbard's Messenger Organization, and sixteen other shocked and surprised staff members. The great majority of the 16 staffers were people that I'd worked with for years at the Flag Land Base, who were totally loyal to L Ron all of their days.

Hubbard was on this kick to find and terminate staff that he accused of being knowingly or unknowingly under the influence of someone or something outside of his control. These external influences could be FBI, CIA or some other subversive organization out to destroy Hubbard's precious Scientology. He really believed this, and many people were made to suffer because of that. Not once was anyone ever found to have any connection to any of these organizations. No matter how many times I or anyone else put a person on the

E-meter and checked, no one was ever confirmed as having such connections. Evidence was created against these innocent and loyal staff to support Hubbard's accusations. By now everyone knew what the consequences of not going along with Hubbard were.

Again, the staff being prosecuted and persecuted acted as if it was all preordained, and they were just going through the motions. Many of them pled guilty as charged and went along with whatever Hubbard said or ordered without resistance. Because I was an executive in the Religious Technology Center it was not necessary for me to get my hands too dirty manufacturing evidence, but I did have to agree to and approve all of the lies being created against these staff as Chairman of the Committee.

This was a point in time where I began to become numb to the confusion and violence leveled against staff members who had given their whole life over to L Ron. Their reward for being loyal was to be mocked and ridiculed for their loyalty by their idol L Ron. To stay in the game meant keeping a poker face on always, even while sleeping. I was at a moral low with a steep drop off coming right around the corner.

David Mayo was accused of being a dupe in collusion with external influences that were hostile to Scientology. That whole Sirhan Sirhan operation must have really influenced L Ron, and he was adamant about ferreting out all dupes and external influences at every level of Scientology. So practically every head of Scientology corporate and management personnel were removed or changed. Briefly, the Executive Director International, Kerry Gleason, was removed. The Commanding Officer of the Messenger

Organization, John Nelson, was removed. The Commanding Officer for Golden Era Production was also removed. Separate from the 18 people that were under Committee of Evidence, the new head of the Religious Technology Center, Steve Marlowe was also removed.

Hubbard's madness seemed to run in very unpredictable cycles. The only thing that seemed to soften his mood was when he'd distract himself by talking about science fiction. While reading Hubbard's unedited advices, in some instances he would be in a vicious rage over a trivial mistake by a staff member and distract himself and write about robots and building computers to replace human management. Then he'd go on about things he claimed happened many millions of years ago. He'd come up with some sort of Buck Rodgers type event from the distant past that explained the present. Sometimes he would amuse himself and temporarily come out of his horrible mood.

Because Hubbard claimed to be the only valid authority on mental health, a Scientologist is not allowed to study related subjects like psychology or psychiatry. In fact, Hubbard had nothing but contempt for psychology and psychiatry and made this well known in his writings and published works.

To that end, it is my opinion that Hubbard created a situation that made it impossible for him to get the help he truly needed. His death was not pretty. All of his money didn't save or help him get treated with the dignity usually reserved for the dying and the dead, but I'm getting ahead of the story.

David Mayo and the majority of the other executive staff at the Gold Base were removed and

The Purge 1983

expelled from the Sea Organization and Scientology. Not all at once; the people were gradually released at different times throughout the year.

It was during this year that I became in part responsible for seeing certain legal cases against various Scientology corporations and organizations were successfully litigated.

8

SCIENTOLOGY ABOVE THE LAW
1983

BY SPRING OF 1983, the principal executives of the Religious Technology Center, CO CMO International and the Executive Director International would meet once a week on Friday at Author Services to review and report on the overall progress and income of the various sectors of Scientology. This is the year that I "matured" and began to act more like an adult. As a novice Scientologist and Sea Organization member, I had always supported the idea of doing something to change the world and make it a better place. Now I was actually working on programs and strategies written with the intention of taking over cities, countries and governments all over the world. Sounds crazy but it was true. Financially, the only entities that could compete with Scientology were countries with their own government and armies.

We were required to wear military uniforms, and we conducted our business and daily affairs like people who are in the military. We were at war with government agencies in the US (IRS) and government agencies abroad (Ministry of the Interior in Hamburg, Germany) just to name a few.

Every aspect of Scientology and its Sea Organization was micro-managed by L Ron directly through his advice letters. There were four senior management organizations created with the primary intent of ensuring L Ron Hubbard's orders to any and all aspects of Scientology were fully complied to. In descending order of importance, these organizations were: Author Services Inc., Religious Technology Center, Commodore's Messenger Org International and the International Executive Strata.

In March of 1983, I became the Deputy Inspector General and a member of the Board of Directors for RTC as Treasurer. There were only two others board members: The President was Vicki and the Secretary was Warren McShane. At the time I was appointed as a member of the Board of Directors of RTC I was made to sign an undated letter of resignation. I never asked for the promotion, it was given to me by Vicki and approved by David Miscavige and Anne Broker. This was standard practice for all Scientology corporate board members. Signing undated resignation letters is another means by which the Scientology corporations are controlled while giving the appearance of corporate autonomy.

During this time, the management organizations and corporations of Scientology were supervised by and received instructions from L Ron through a small group of individuals that were staff of L Ron's new literary organization Author Services Inc.

Author Services Inc. presented itself as the literary agency for L Ron Hubbard. It was actually where top

Scientology managers and Corporate Directors met each week to report on their respective sectors and to receive orders from L Ron. All of Scientology was being directed by L Ron from the boardroom of Author Services Inc.

The whole corporate structure of Scientology was being reconfigured to shield L Ron and other Scientology entities that were being sued or were involved in litigation.

My job title was Deputy Inspector General, External. In name and on paper I was also responsible for activities outside the body of Scientology. This included being responsible for all litigation by or against any Scientology organization, the Scientology intelligence network known as The Office of Special Affairs, the registration and maintenance of the trademarks of Dianetics and Scientology as well as issuing and enforcing licensing agreements to all Scientology corporations. On paper, The Religious Technology Center was the top of the Scientology food chain. L Ron was the top of that food chain, and he was able to exert control through his literary agent Author Services Inc.

There was a standard order of business in these meetings. David Miscavige was always the chairman and host of these meetings. David was also known as Chairman of the Board or COB for short. The order of business at the meetings began with a discussion of the most urgent and pressing issues facing the various corporations. An example would be a fresh lawsuit served on any Scientology entity or any severe threat such as a raid by the police or some other government agency, or the threat of having a Scientology entity being forced to close its doors.

Legal threats took up the lion's share of these meetings because there were many legal battles being fought by Scientology at the time. Right at the top of the list was a case brought by former Scientologist and Sea Organization member Lawrence Wollersheim. There is much that could be said about this case, but the bottom line is a California jury awarded Mr. Wollershiem 30 million dollars in damages against the Church of Scientology California (CSC). Based on the advice from L Ron the corporate mantra in response to the judgment was "not one thin dime for Wollersheim."

There was also another lawsuit referred to as the Kristofferson case in Oregon where the plaintiff, who was an ex-Scientologist, was also about to be awarded a multimillion dollar judgment against Scientology. If successful, these lawsuits could open the door for others to sue for damages with multimillion dollar judgments against Scientology and its assets.

Each of the above legal situations posed their own unique threat to the growth and well-being of Scientology as an institution, but there was an even greater more urgent threat. Through our intelligence network, we learned the Internal Revenue Service in America was considering executing raids on key Scientology corporations. At the time, none of the churches of Scientology had received tax-exempt status.

One principal reason why tax-exempt status had not been granted was the IRS's position that Scientology founder L. Ron Hubbard was actually the managing agent of Scientology in complete disregard of the corporate structure of Scientology. We knew this to be a fact but also knew that it violated IRS rules and so had to be hidden.

There was concern that the IRS would obtain the hundreds of daily, weekly and monthly LRH orders written by Mr. Hubbard and distributed throughout Scientology. These orders were commonly referred to as advices to avoid the appearance that LRH was the managing agent for Scientology. The principal concern expressed at these meetings was that the LRH orders or advices would be used to prove L Ron Hubbard as the managing agent of Scientology.

Because of the already existing fear of an L. Ron advice might fall into the wrong hands, the orders from him were written in a way we could deny it was from him. His name was never on the advices. He was never cited in the advice except in the third person. There was never a signature and salutation in reply was never more than Dear Sir. The routing at the top referred to L Ron merely as *, an asterisk. However, if a person or an agency got enough of these, there would be little doubt that we were in touch with Hubbard via ASI, and he was telling us and every Scientology corporation what to do to make him more money.

David Miscavige specifically stated that ASI was already dealing with the problem, ridding ASI of any documents that would implicate L Ron Hubbard as managing agent of Scientology. He stated that under his directive the LRH orders or advices were being collected and transferred by truck to a recycling plant in Riverside County where the documents were being pulped. This method of destruction was better than shredding. I was also given instructions that I was ultimately responsible for purging the remainder of the Scientology organizations of LRH orders and advices. This was to include the Church of Scientology of California, the Church of Scientology International and the Religious Technology Center. It took weeks to purge all organizations of all the LRH advices.

Several weeks after this first meeting I attended a second meeting at the ASI offices concerning the continued destruction of Scientology corporate documentation.

Although there were four corporations at the top of the Scientology hierarchy, there was just a handful of people responsible to L Ron for executing his orders within the various corporations. There was Norman Starkey from South Africa who represented Author Services. There was Lyman Spurlock of ASI. His official title was Director of Client Affairs, and he was also a trustee on the Board of Directors for RTC. Vicki Aznaran was the Deputy Inspector General and President of the Board of Directors of RTC. There was Marc Yager, Commanding Officer of CMO International, and Guillaume Lesevre, the Frenchman who was the Executive Director of the Executive Strata. And of course, there was me and David Miscavige. Miscavige and Pat Broeker decided to have these meetings with all the above persons to act as a think tank. Each week we met and discussed the most pressing issues facing Scientology, and we would coordinate our individual efforts at these meetings, and a report would be sent to L Ron of progress and recommendations. Every major activity this think tank would engage in had to have the approval of L Ron before initiation.

There were others that came and went according to what situation was being dealt with at the time. Marty Rathbun was always present when legal, and intelligence matters were on the table for any of the Scientology corporations. We were supported by many other staff but at this particular time there really were only a handful of people that were ultimately responsible for the care and well-being of Scientology.

Given the gravity and variety of the legal problems Scientology was facing at the time, we employed a simple strategy as instructed by L Ron. An overall general legal strategy was programmed and executed in all our legal cases. We had a simple one-size-fits-all approach. L Ron wrote:

> *The defense of anything is untenable. The only way to defend anything is to ATTACK, and if you ever forget that, then you will lose every battle you are ever engaged in.* NEVER BE INTERESTED IN CHARGES. *Do yourself much more charging, and you will win.*

L Ron had little regard for the legal system in America or abroad. Instead of using a civil lawsuit for retribution or justice he figured out a better way, that undermines the legal system completely. L Ron wrote this about lawsuits:

> *The purpose of the suit is to harass and discourage rather than to win. The law can be used very easily to harass and will generally be sufficient to cause [the enemy's] professional decease. If possible, of course, ruin him utterly.*

It was the responsibility of a small group of individuals and the best lawyers that money could buy to implement this scorched-earth policy towards our legal endeavors, so we did that.

The Expert Witness

In the early part of 1983, I also became aware of a lawsuit filed by L Ron Hubbard Jr. against his father L Ron Hubbard, the Church of Scientology California, and the Church of Scientology International. The lawsuit was filed in November of 1982 in the Superior Court in Riverside, California. The suit alleged L Ron Hubbard was either dead or incompetent. He was trying to take possession of his father's estate for himself and his siblings.

This lawsuit turned out to be a major game changer for everyone involved in the supervision and management of the Scientology enterprise.

Hubbard's control over anything Scientology or Dianetics was absolute. Anyone who dared challenge him in anyway was immediately intimidated mentally, physically then quickly gotten rid of. L Ron was brutal to anyone who dared question him in any way. He was the god of Scientology, and he demanded reverence. L Ron himself failed to predict, so he didn't realize the ultimate consequence this lawsuit brought by breaking his stranglehold on his Scientology Empire.

Because of the lawsuit filed by L Ron Junior, it became the burden of L Ron and his lawyers to prove he was alive and competent. At the beginning of the lawsuit, L Ron tried to micro-manage the defense of the allegations of the lawsuit against him. He attempted to order or command his way out of the lawsuit based on the strength of his will. This approach didn't pan out, the judge in the case began to lean towards the opinion the case would be over and done with if L Ron simply made an appearance to disprove the allegations expressed in the suit. There was a long list of "advices" from L Ron concerning how to dispose of the case. L Ron didn't want to make a public appearance, but if forced to, he agreed to make a video of himself and submit it to the court under seal to satisfy the argument of whether he was alive and competent or not. This turned out to be a huge problem.

L Ron Senior was being represented by the law firm Lenske, Lenske and Heller. The subject of the lawsuit was on the table for discussion. Steve and Sherman Lenske were present and the discussion became more of an inquiry into the possibility of whether or not a statement by L Ron on video under very controlled circumstances would end L Ron Junior's lawsuit against his father. The question was brought up by one of the attorneys. I don't recall specifically which one of the Lenske brothers brought it up. It could have been Larry Heller I'm not sure. At this particular Think Tank meeting, it was decided to allow the attorney to have direct access to L Ron to discuss the possibility of making a video. He wanted to verify if L Ron was up to the task. The attorneys were high class, well connected and were paid handsomely. Those of us who were not attorneys knew better than to even suggest such a meeting at all.

No one in the Think Tank had seen L Ron for some years, if ever. There were six people who were part of L Ron's personal staff. These were the only people that had regular and routine visual access to him. For a lawyer to have access to and discussion with L Ron was a big deal. No lawyer anywhere in recent history could claim such access to him. I remember being present in the board room at Author Services for the initial meeting when the idea was being considered. Those in attendance were the Lenske brothers, David Miscavige, Norman Starkey, Vicki Aznaran, myself and Marc Yeager.

Maybe two weeks passed before another meeting was held in the board room of Author Services Inc. We discussed flaps and handlings. A flap in Scientology is defined as a sudden or extreme problem or incident that threatens or harms any Scientology organization or its repute. At the end of the meeting, David asked Vicki and me to come to a different office where we met with one of the Lenske brothers who had gone to meet with L Ron. David specifically wanted Vicki and me to hear what the attorney had to say about his conversations with L Ron and the probate case by L Ron junior.

What he said sounded rehearsed, but he was weak on his delivery. He explained to us that because we were devoted to L Ron as our Spiritual Leader our view of Hubbard was one of reverence and respect. He went to say that normal, regular people who didn't have our Scientology training and commitment to the Technology would view Hubbard as strange, esoteric and marching to the beat of his own drum. Simply stated, a regular person might perceive Hubbard as being insane, and therefore he was not ready for prime time. Lenske informed us that another solution was being worked on, and he left the room. While he was talking, Norman Starkey came into the room, He said nothing, nor did he look surprised by what was being said. David explained to Vicki and I that he was glad the attorney had the opportunity to have direct contact with L Ron because that saved him from getting his ass canned! Someone had to explain to L Ron the amount of legal trouble he was currently in, not to mention the Church of Scientology International and Church of Scientology of California.

There was the looming threat of an IRS raid to obtain documentation to prove L Ron was the managing agent of any and all Scientology corporations. These threats were not new news. What was new news to me was that L Ron was delusional and could be considered incompetent! It took a lawyer to confirm what most of us already knew but were too afraid to say: L Ron was certifiably insane to normal, common people, but we had to revere him as the god of his religion or be persecuted. After the attorney had left the room, David explained how it was up to us to get L Ron and our church corporation out of legal trouble. He said no one can save us, but we have the technology to save ourselves.

He mentioned that L Ron had been told that if there was ever any hope of corporate Scientology surviving the legal attacks we were under, he had to agree to give more of an appearance of corporate integrity. The attorney explained to L Ron that on paper he had to be financially and administratively separate from his other church entities or he could be legally enjoined with and liable for any criminal or civil lawsuit brought against any church corporation, because he was their managing agent.

This was not a pleasant experience for the attorney, but it was personally profitable for him; he got paid well to put up with L Ron.

Dave explained that it was up to us as a group to navigate our way out of the legal liability facing L Ron and the Scientology corporations. We became the rulers of the mother church. L Ron agreed to back off and let those who were appointed secure our corporations and endeavors while all the while making more money for him.

Dave confided with Vicki and I and said the actual command line started with L Ron, then Annie Broeker, Pat Broeker, he and Norman, then Vicki and me. He said we had to protect each other, even from L Ron. We had to be careful of the type of information we were sending L Ron to make sure nothing ever required him to do anything. We didn't want or need any more advice from L Ron. Via dispatches, we would assure him we had the situation under control by making sure he got the money he needed to pay for his own lawyers plus anything else he asked for.

With L Ron being advised to take a break from issuing orders to Scientology corporations by his lawyer, he decided it was a good time to finish what would be his final science fiction work the *Mission Earth* series.

David also informed Vicki and me that L Ron was in failing health. The stress of pending court decisions only added to his increasing bad attitude. This was another reason to qualify the information sent to him. We also had to prepare for the worst. David said L Ron's will would probably need to be changed to ensure the survival of all Scientology corporate organizations. He had to make sure all of L Ron's estate inured to corporate Scientology entities, not to any individual or collective of family members of L Ron.

In the event, L Ron died before he could change the will David and Norman Starkey had been practicing writing L Ron's signature. I was given a pen and a stack of paper and encouraged to try and duplicate L Ron's signature. I remember sitting in that board room feeling odd but numb to this unusual request. Here I was trying to duplicate L Ron's signature in case important documents like a will needed to be signed. I went to Dave with what I was able to do, and he laughed at me. He let me check out Normans attempt and asked me what I thought. I told him Norman's was okay. Dave was pretty good at it too. It seemed obvious to me they had practiced trying to duplicate L Ron's signature longer than I had. Dave showed me his attempts to duplicate L Ron's signature. He asked me what I thought of his rendering of L Ron's signature. I looked him in the eye and told him it was better than Norman's, and we both had a good laugh.

At the time, I never considered this to be anything more than a prank. David explained we didn't need to worry about L Ron's will. He said L Ron would sign a new will when the time was right. We would be told what L Ron wanted to be done as usual. I felt a deeper bond with David, Vicki, and Norman and to our common commitment to serving L Ron. I was humbled by Dave and Norman's demonstration of trust in me to show me and reveal to me these things. I started to feel like I'd really made the cut; I was a Boss for sure, and I was playing in the big league as a Boss. Being the Boss meant making hard decisions and becoming numb to the consequences.

David told Vicki and me always to look after and protect Marc Yeager and Guillaume Lesevre. Marc Yeager was the recently appointed Commanding Officer of L Ron's international Messenger Organization; Guillaume Lesevre was the recently appointed Executive Director of corporate

Scientology International. David went on to explain the obvious that it would be in his, Vicki's and my self-interest to make sure these two did their jobs well, because it meant we wouldn't have to bypass and do their jobs for them. He went on to say we would only be successful if we worked together as a team for the team. He instructed us always to keep a close eye on them and not to get too friendly with them, or else they'd get confused and so would we. Being a Boss socially meant being alone or in a limited company most of the time. This was not my style, but I learned to live with it.

9

MISSIONS WITHOUT MERCY

I HAD BEEN DAVID'S AUDITOR for most of 1982. We established that relationship at the behest of Annie Broeker, presumably by order of L Ron. We had gone out and accomplished a mission together that was an instant financial success. This was accomplished by summoning all Scientology and Dianetics Mission Holders doing business on the US west coast to meeting at an expensive hotel located in downtown San Francisco. They were told to make sure they traveled with their main business bank account checkbooks. These were people of means and had made a successful career of getting new people into Scientology and extracting their money for Scientology courses and auditing.

Instead of appreciating the work these Mission Holders were doing and the money they were sending to our reserves, we robbed them on sight, and that's a fact. We even videotaped our gangster activity as proof to show L Ron we did as he instructed. We brought L Ron's lawyer Larry Heller to scare the crap out of the Mission Holders to make them think they were going to jail for criminal negligence of our trademarks! We robbed the Mission Holders using our E-meters instead of guns.

Each Mission Holder was connected to an E-meter, interrogated and intimidated with yelling and threats. Then they were ordered to take out their checkbooks and write checks that emptied their bank accounts. We robbed these people using our own police force. We called our police force the International Finance Police, and they acted with authority and efficiency over the Mission Holders bank accounts. There was little to no resistance. The Mission Holders acted like this was all predestined, and they had no will to change anything that was happening to them. In a strange way, it seemed like the Mission Holders had expected they'd be robbed. When the taking was done, they quietly and without resistance accepted the fact they had been robbed. On their way out the door; when they were allowed to leave, a representative from the International Finance Police informed the Mission Holders that their organizations could be searched for hidden bank accounts at a later date, and a few were excommunicated from the Church (declared Suppressive Persons) on the spot as an example for the rest.

All of this was new to me, and I followed the safe route and did as I was told. L Ron directed our activities via Annie and Pat Broeker. When we got back to the Gold Base, a video was quickly edited to show in detail what we had done to take all of the money we could find from the West Coast Mission Holders. L Ron was pleased with the level of carnage we were able to accomplish in the Bay Area after the money we were able to bring home was counted and verified.

Right around this time I was tested again. L Ron was made aware of the fact that his oldest daughter Diana had requested to leave the Sea Org to pursue a career outside of Scientology. The problem with this was that she was taking his only granddaughter with her. L Ron wanted to keep his granddaughter within the confines of Scientology. He had devised a personal program for her called the Princess Program. The grandchild's name was Roanne, and her father is Jon. Besides being L Ron's son-in-law, Jon was his personal audiophile person. Jon was very much a committed Sea Org member.

L Ron didn't seem to mind the fact that his daughter was leaving the Sea Org, but he preferred she turn over custody of her child to her husband Jon, whom she was divorcing. Diana refused this request. Dave Miscavige was told to handle Diana and get her to relinquish custody of her child, but she refused. Both Vicki and Marc Yeager attempted to get Diana to relinquish custody of her child, and they had also failed to accomplish the task. This was something that bothered L Ron, and he ordered through Annie Broeker that another attempt be made to get Diana to turn over custody.

David told Vicki to send me on a mission to the Flag Land Base to confront Diana and persuade her to turn over custody of her only child to a husband she was divorcing. Vicki briefed me on the situation, and the previous attempts to persuade her. Diana was described as being totally unreasonable and uncooperative. Because of my training, it was expected of me to go and do what the others had failed to do. This confused me because it seemed like I was just being sent on a suicide mission. I was already told that if I failed to accomplish the task, there was a very high probability that I would be sent to the Rehabilitation Project Force. Of course, there was no mention of what would happen if I accomplished the mission.

I read previous information collected about the situation in my briefing. I was interrogated to make sure I did not have any other intention concerning getting the project done. Finally, I was given a package of legal documents that I was to have Diana sign to relinquished custody of her only child.

The following day I left California and flew to Florida to the Flag Land Base. When I arrived in Florida, I was met by L Ron's Messengers and set up with the room to meet Diana. I had no real expectations for what I was there to accomplish.

Diana lived at the Fort Harrison hotel at the very top in a penthouse that was on the 11th floor. For some years I ran an internship located on the balcony of a ballroom located on the 10th floor. Only a few times I had seen Diana coming and going. I always thought she was beautiful. She had long red hair and full lips that she kept nice and red. She also had a bit of a British accent, and I always thought she was a nice person.

Anyway, Diana was summoned to the room. I was there as she approached I stood up shook her hand and smiled. She smiled at me and shook my hand, we began to chat. I told her who I was, and I told her I had worked at Flag for years before. She mentioned that she had seen me working on the balcony, training

Scientology auditors. Then we discussed briefly the internship and the people that I had trained at Flag. I told her I had always admired her but never had the courage actually to talk to her, and I told her I thought she was beautiful. It seems like we made small talk for as long as we could, but it was time to get down to business. I briefly explained to her why I was there. She replied that she completely understood, and she asked me to give her the papers and she would just sign. All of the papers had a big X to mark where her signature was required. She seemed totally familiar with the process, and she signed and dated where her signature was required. As she signed the papers, tears began to roll down her cheeks. She brushed the tears from her cheeks with the back of her hands then wiped her eyes with her fingers. Diana rapidly regained her composure. Now her expression was perfectly stoic as she passed me the signed documents. For some reason, I experienced pain in my chest area as I took the papers from her, and I was unable to speak for a second or two. She looked at me and said "It's okay, at least this is done now." The moment passed, and she asked me if there was anything else. I told her no. She stood, I stood, we shook hands, and she left. I don't think I ever saw her again. The whole incident took less than an hour.

There were one or two Messengers standing by the door in case we needed anything. After Diana had left, I asked one of the messengers to bring me a phone. Before leaving Gold, I'd been given a phone number to call when I finished the meeting with Diana. This number connected to Vicki's office at Golden Era. I told her that I had completed the mission and all the documents were signed, and I requested to come home. Vicki was shocked that I was calling her to tell her the documents were actually signed. She asked me if I was sure the papers were correctly signed, which meant all the places where there was an X. When she asked me the question, I thought about Diana's attitude about what had happened, and I was stoic too. As politely as I could, I answered with a simple yes. I didn't offer any further explanation. The line went silent, and she asked me to hold the line. The next voice I heard was David Miscavige, and he sounded like he might have been slightly out of breath. He asked, "Are you 100% sure you have all the signatures you need on all the documents you were given?" I was stoic with him as well, and he got the same simple yes answer. He didn't threaten me directly, but he said, "you better be fucking sure because if you fuck this up…" Whatever he was saying didn't matter because I gave him a one-word answer again. I simply said okay.

I was on a plane on my way back to Golden Era from Florida within a couple of hours after that phone conversation. When I arrived at LAX, I was met by a Scientology courier who brought me from the airport directly to the Gold Base. When I arrived at the Base, I was directed to go straight to David's office where he and Vicki were waiting. I walked in, handed Vicki the papers, smiled and sat down.

David grabbed the papers and carefully went through them, and then he looked at me with the craziest look. He said "Motherfucker, how did you get her to sign, these papers?"

I put on my best Clint Eastwood stoic face, and I said "I just did the mission."

Dave understood what I was doing, he just smiled and said "Jesse you're a bad motherfucker. Good job." He stood up and shook my hand and hugged me, and we had a good laugh. He said "Jesse, that was very well done. That was excellent. Seriously, thank you."

I just smiled, and we changed the subject. I wanted to know what was going on at the Base since I left. "Don't worry," he said, "You'll find out all about it later. Make sure you get some fluids to deal with the dehydration from flying."

Maybe a week or so later I received a dispatch from L Ron personally thanking me for handling his daughter to turn over custody. I was also gifted with a gold necklace and a black Members Only jacket. I also received either $500 or $700 as well. This incident was a game changer as far as my recognition among my peers. I had personally done something that pleased L Ron, and he recognized me. Not to mention the fact that no one else had been able to accomplish the task.

Something I should mention here about life at the Gold Base. In 1979, all television sets were removed from the personal living quarters of every Sea Org member by order of L Ron. No explanation was given, and none was really needed. We never had time to sit around to watch TV. We all ate our meals together every day at the same times, and this gave us a feeling of family. Every staff member at the Gold Base would sit down to eat at the same times each day for breakfasts, lunch, and dinner. Looking back on it I think this one civilized ritual was honored as sacred. Business was never discussed during the meals. We all ate together as a family in the Lodge hall that was known as the Massacre Canyon Inn.

The Expert Witness

For stress relief, I joined a Racquet Ball club in the nearby town of Hemet, CA. David and I would play racquetball a couple times a week. Our games were intense, and we would explode two or three balls against the wall from hitting them so hard. We'd laugh watching the little blue ball fall apart all over the court. I felt the power and confidence of a leader. Dave and I were friends and would often hang out and talk. He was always interested in how I'd lived my life before Scientology. I'd talk to him about the drugs I'd taken and the women I'd had sex with, just stupid things men talk to each other about in conversations. We'd talk about music, sports and pop culture.

We were neighbors and lived in an area of the Base known as the Villas. We also were into buying high-end audio gear for personal use. I remember buying my first commercial CD player for some outrageous price. I'm the one who introduced David to what would be known as Heavy Metal music. I'd play my Jimi Hendrix albums as loud as my bi-amped Magneplaner speaker system could stand. I'd also play my collection of Led Zeppelin, Johnny Winter, John McLaughlin and Frank Zappa albums. I also enjoyed my fusion jazz with the Return to Forever band at the top of my favorite list. I had fallen in love with the Return to Forever band many years before I ever knew what Scientology was. I can remember how odd David would look at me when I played him some of my music. Sometimes he'd just shake his head and say okay. Dave was slightly younger than me, so that qualified him to be like a younger brother to me. It was part of my duty to keep him well and functioning. It was my job to ensure he stayed healthy and performed his job. During these times, Dave and I took orders from the same bosses, first L Ron, then Annie then Pat. For me, Dave and Vicki were the Bosses who were between me and the Broekers.

By early fall of 1983, L Ron slowed his rampage of orders and executions of staff at the Gold Base, things began to calm down. With L Ron gone, the panic level decreased. Staff members could go to work and get a job done without the degradation and distraction of L Ron and his Messengers. I was also considered to be an Executive Messenger of L Ron although I'd never served him in that capacity. I took a few Messenger courses, for the life of me I have no memory of exactly what those courses were.

Things were changing in my personal life as well. When I arrived at the Gold Base in 82, I was married to a woman named Sonny. By 1983, Sonny and I were divorced, and I had a new love interest named Molly. That's not her actual name, but it's close enough. I'd see Molly around during Renovations Day which was every Saturday. For the executives, on Renovation Day we would usually catch up on paperwork while the rest of the crew worked on the buildings and grounds. Sometimes Dave would watch sporting events on TV with others who were interested in team sports, I never have been interested in TV team sports.

A few times I'd go and pick up my old friend Bill, whom I had known at Flag. Bill was a top executive as well. He was a Watch Dog Committee (WDC) member supervising Golden Era Productions, the organization producing Scientology films and other materials. Sometimes during renovations day Bill and I would head off to town for a 12 pack of beer, and drive around the town of Idlewild, in the mountains above the Base. Sometimes we'd get our other good buddy, Spike, involved, and we could really get some trouble going.

Molly was a Messenger at the Messenger Organization on the Gold Base. Her job was to make others comply with L Ron's orders into Golden Era Productions, and the cinematography organization. During a Saturday Renovation Day, I was walking around the ship with David and Marc Yager and we spotted Molly sandpapering old varnish off one of the masts of the ship.

I don't know how she managed to do it, but that had to be the sexiest thing I'd seen, and I wasn't the only one. Molly resembled a young version of the actress Gina Davis. She had a mass of dark curly hair and powder blue eyes. She was wearing Daisy Duke Style shorts. Both Marc and David were blushing as they watched her sanding. She was totally oblivious to us.

When we passed her, I remarked that I wouldn't mind dating someone like her. Dave said, "You can date her, all you have to do is get divorced first." He went on to say, "I think Molly is a nice girl, and she is gorgeous." That sealed the deal for me and within a year Molly and I were married. That happened in the spring of 1983.

During this time I was also the personal auditor/counselor for David's wife, Shelly. When I met Shelly, she was a mess. She had a reputation for being vicious and screaming stridently at her fellow staff. Not only was Shelley herself a Messenger, but she was the wife of the most powerful man on the Base, David Miscavige. Shelley had to be maybe 20 or 21 years old at the time, and she had little if any life experience outside of Scientology. Like the other Messengers, she didn't have formal education and was illiterate. I doubt she even went to high school, and she could barely read. I ended up spending a lot of time with Shelley, auditing her or just talking to her. She was trying to get her life on track so that she could really be a part of the group that we were in.

I remember after one session I talked to David about his technical training. He told me he had trained at St. Hill Manor in England up to the level of Provisional Class IV Auditor. I asked him how he liked auditing others. He laughed and told me he wasn't very good at it. He told me a story about a person that he had audited/counseled at Saint Hill, a young female, and how he had gotten into an argument with her and ended up slugging her. That was the end of his technical training.

According to David Miscavige's auditing file he never graduated elementary school. He only made it to the 7th grade. After that, his only education was in L Ron's policy and technology. Admittedly, he was horrible at the technology part.

10

Rise of the Independents

It seemed like I was just busy all the time in 1983, but no one predicted the horrible storm that was just on the horizon. David Mayo, John Nelson, and other high level declared Scientologists were getting together and forming the Independent Scientology Movement. There were also several Mission Holders who had been abused by the International Finance Police joining the movement as well.

This was when I learned how we would play hardball with these former members we had humiliated and kicked out. Somehow this was an unpredicted surprise to us. When these people left, we made sure they left with nothing of Scientology origin with them. Not one dispatch, or any photo of anything left the Gold Base when these people were excommunicated. We weren't concerned about these people in the least. Arrogance had blinded me and the others to an obvious truth. Once we were no longer able to control these ex-Scientologists, over time they wouldn't fear us as much as they used to and would eventually go into rebellion. We were only used to dealing with people who were submissive to our control. Here was a new situation whereby these ex-members were calling into question our authority, a mortal sin in Scientology.

The Office of Special Affairs was directed to get spies in place where these ex-members were gathering and planning to create their own Scientology Organizations. The other problem was what these excommunicated people were saying to other Scientologists, who were still in good standing. It seemed like the entirety of Scientology public were upset with the New Management, and in particular, with David Miscavige and RTC. People who had been Scientologists for decades were publicly resigning their memberships. The independent movement was rapidly gaining traction, and there was nothing we could do. We were totally unprepared for and surprised by how strong the resistance was and how rapidly it was spreading.

Because we were inexperienced in handling anything but willing members, there were mistakes made in trying to handle the situation.

L Ron became aware of the situation and advised RTC, as owner of the trademarks, to issue a document to Scientology public titled "The Story of a Squirrel." The document was a compilation of all of the "advices" we had to date from L Ron that really demonstrated how vicious he could be towards another human being. The document was written to say awful things about David Mayo, and it went on and on. This was another example of L Ron thinking he had the power to will away the rising Independent Scientology movement. The document was issued under Steve Marlowe's name, so L Ron didn't get blamed for the disaster the issued caused. Even more people publicly resigned and gave as their reason for leaving the issue, "The Story of a Squirrel." The public hadn't been exposed to that side of L Ron, and no one believed he even knew of the document's existence. This totally backfired on RTC because the document seemed to confirm a rumor going around that L Ron may be either dead or incompetent and was not informed about what was happening in the Church.

L Ron got back on the kick of looking for external influences affecting Scientology, so paranoia came back to haunt us. As it turned out, L Ron was not far from the truth about relating to an external influence hostile to Scientology.

During the rise of the Independent movement, a long term devoted Scientologist named John Zegel also resigned from the Church of Scientology and he was being very vocal about it. The problem with this was that John Zegel was the step-father of Marc Yager. Marc Yager was the Commanding Officer of L Ron's Messengers internationally. John was married to Marc's mother, Vivian Zegel. In Scientology dogma, if a person has a connection to a source that is hostile to Scientology they are labeled as being a Potential Trouble Source (PTS) for Scientology. When this happens, the person with the connection is denied services until they handle or disconnect from the source that is hostile to Scientology.

Had L Ron known that his own executive Messenger was connected to a source hostile to Scientology, Marc would have quickly become a distant memory. David, Vicki and I discussed the situation and Dave asked us to handle John and Vivian Zegel. We agreed to not inform L Ron because none of us wanted to replace Marc or find a replacement for him. This was our secret to keep, but Vicki and I went to Los Angeles for a couple of weeks to deal with John.

To make a long story short, John was no longer under our influence, and he basically told us to go to hell! He showed none of the usual respect or obedience demanded of Scientologist for management. To the contrary, he was loud and hostile. I got loud with him once, even grabbed him. He looked at me like I was crazy, flipped me off, got up and left with his wife. He simply didn't go along with our routine, so it didn't work. John was also making tapes that were being passed around that only served to disaffect Scientology public with the new management. This was my first direct contact with the rising Independent Scientology Movement, and it was clear these people were going to create their own Independent Scientology churches and use the trademarks RTC owned to make money and take our public from us.

Vicki and I quickly set up offices in Los Angeles at Big Blue, and we began to recruit personnel to work on the Squirrel Project. A squirrel was anyone using or attempting to use our trademarks without authorization. The unit was set up to get people to infiltrate the Independent movements, starting with Mayo, so that we could wage war with the Independents. We only knew one way to deal with non-compliance, and that was to apply scorched-earth policy to the situation.

Later in the fall and early winter, I made a trip to Mexico City. The Think Tank group decided as part of establishing ourselves as the new Managers of Scientology, we would tour our larger facilities abroad. Marc Yeager, Guillaume Lesevre and myself traveled to Mexico City. We arrived early that in the day and we checked the facility where the event was scheduled to take place, everything seemed in order. I had never been to Mexico, and I was told not to drink the water. Since our event wasn't until the next day, Guillaume suggested that we take a cab to see the Teotihuacan Pyramids, just north of Mexico City.

As we walked down the main road called "Street of the Dead" towards the pyramids, little children ran up to us with what looked like ancient Mayan arrow tips for pesos. I was just in awe of what I was seeing. Being a mile high in altitude, I felt an energy I'd never experienced before or since. I climbed the long row of stairs to the top of the Sun Pyramid. One side of the pyramid had a black stain that ran all the way to the bottom of the structure. I learned this stain was from the blood from all of the human sacrifices that were performed by ancient Inca priests. It was a perfectly clear day, and I could see for a mile from the top of that pyramid.

After a few hours, our visit ended, and we headed back to Mexico City to find a nice restaurant. The food was great, and I slept well that night. The next day we were the speakers for the event. They had laid tables with nice tablecloths and such. On the table were glasses of fresh cold water covered with plastic. I unconsciously grabbed a glass and started to drink the water as I reviewed my speech and waited for my turn to speak. Guillaume saw what I was doing and shook his head and said, "I told you it's not a good idea to drink the water," but it was too late.

My stomach began to swirl like a washing machine, and I began to sweat. The next thing you know, it was my turn to speak. I gave my speech as fast as I could. When I finished, I headed straight for the bathroom, and I was in there for a while. I sure didn't mind heading home the next day.

So, the year 1983 came to an end and I still had not seen L Ron. I'd seen plenty of dispatch communication but hadn't physically seen him yet. It's strange but even now it seemed like he was right there because everything we did was for him all the time. I traveled to Europe a few times during 1983, but by winter I was home. This turned out to be a perfect time for me to focus my attention on Molly. On Christmas Eve, there is a big party for all the staff at the Gold Base and the party is called the Bosun's Party, a tradition left over from when the Sea Org was actually on ships. Here the staff dance and drink like nobody is watching if only for a day. It was during this party that I summoned the courage to ask Molly to dance. We spent the evening talking and holding hands. After that party, I quickly went into town and bought Molly Christmas gifts. She had no other gifts from anyone, and neither did I for that matter.

Within the next day or so we went on our first date to the movies and kissed the whole time practically. I asked Molly to marry me, and she said yes. I was so happy and looking forward to 1984.

But the Independent Scientology movement had not gone away, and it was about to get worse for us.

On December 9th, an ex-Scientologist named Robin Scott, along with Ron Lowery and Morag

Bellmaine, had executed a plan to steal the most precious confidential technology Scientology owned. All three individuals posed as Sea Organization Missionaries and pretended to be on a Scientology Mission to our Advanced Organization in Copenhagen, Denmark. These three individuals planned and executed the theft of several New Era Dianetics for Operating Thetans (NOTS) course packs. This was the highest level of Scientology technology offered at that time and could only be obtained in authorized Scientology organizations. They planned to make this material available to anyone who could afford it. For Scientology, these materials were invaluable. These guys executed their plan like an episode of Mission Impossible. They were able to pass as actual Sea Org members on mission which made the staff submissive to them. They were able to slip in, get the materials and make a clean getaway back to the United Kingdom.

When we found out what had happened, shock waves went through Author Services and the Religious Technology Center. The independents had raised the stakes, and now it was our time to turn up the volume. L Ron wanted everyone involved put in jail. He also wanted everyone who was currently using his trademarks and copyrights without his authorization also to be criminally prosecuted and put in jail, and that is exactly what we did.

11

THE WAR BEGINS
1984

THE YEAR 1984 BEGAN WITH Vicki and me attending frequent meetings at Author Services with David Miscavige and the others. We were scrambling to figure out a legal strategy to contain the expanding Independent Movement and to recover the theft of the confidential materials that were stolen in Denmark. At this point, David Mayo and anyone else who decided to use Scientology technology outside of the Church were in violation of our trademark rights and became a target for Scientology's Fair Game Doctrine.

The Fair Game Doctrine is a matter of corporate policy authored by L Ron for Scientology. The doctrine is an instruction from L Ron for how to treat someone whom he had determined was a Suppressive Person (SP). A Suppressive Person was defined as anyone who was labeled an enemy of Scientology by L Ron or someone operating on his behalf. The Fair Game Doctrine stated anyone who is determined to be a Suppressive Person may be deprived of property or injured by any means by any Scientologist without discipline of the Scientologist. The person may be tricked, sued, lied to or destroyed. This policy permitted any Scientology staff or public person to attack, with the intent to harm or destroy, ex-members, or persons not even associated with Scientology who were deemed to be an "enemy," like a psychiatrist or people employed by government agencies (FBI, CIA, or IRS.)

L Ron was infuriated with Mayo and wanted his new group destroyed using any and all means possible. We began to create a separate intelligence unit within RTC that was tasked specifically with incarcerating Robin Scott and the others. A staff member by the name of Jacqueline Kavennar was put in charge of getting the offenders jailed, and she proceeded to do just that. The first person that was jailed was Robin Scott. Immediately following the original theft, an authorized corporate representative of the Scientology Advanced Organization in Denmark filed a theft report with the Danish police. The Danish police issued an arrest warrant against Robin Scott, Ron Lowery, and Morag Bellmaine. The complaint stayed active on file until we were able to lure Robin Scott back to Copenhagen. Our strategy was to appeal to Robin's greed and offer him a payday for a copy of the materials he had taken from the Denmark Advanced Organization. The only condition being is the deal had to be done in Copenhagen.

A Scientologist, who was still loyal to authorized Scientology named Peter Glass, was used to lure Robin back to Denmark. Peter used a suitable guise

The War Begins

that he was a successful musician working in Denmark making good money, and he wanted to receive Scientology upper-level services without going into an authorized Scientology organization. Peter put on that he was disaffected with Scientology's new management and didn't want to go back to a Scientology Organization to receive services. He invited Robin to join him at a resort under the pretext he was on holiday. He informed Robin they would discuss the details and exchange money and so forth once Robin arrived.

The whole operation to get Robin Scott jailed was carefully planned to take place on March 13 of 1984. The reason this was significant is; March 13 was L Ron's birthday. We wanted to give him the birthday gift of Robin Scott being in jail. On March 13, when Robin boarded a plane from Scotland headed to Denmark, Copenhagen he thought he was meeting Peter Glass at a resort in Copenhagen. As he exited the plane, a policeman stopped him and verified his identity. We had Office of Special Affairs agents on the scene taking photographs and video of the arrest. I was told Robin went pale and was visibly shaking as he was being interviewed by the police. It was a flawless operation from beginning to end.

Robin was taken to a holding area in the airport where he was questioned. His luggage was searched, and the stolen documents were found. He admitted to the investigator that he was, in fact, the person that had gone into the Scientology Organization in Denmark and used deception to possess our protected materials illegally. He was then escorted to the local jail where he would spend the next month incarcerated for his crimes. We happily reported to L

Ron that we had put Robin away on his birthday, and he was happy for a change. He even complimented us for a job well done, and we all took a collective sigh of relief!

Even though, Robin would eventually get off with minor infractions for his criminal act, putting him in jail set a precedent. L Ron wanted anyone who would illegally use his trademarked and copyrighted materials put in jail or worse.

We knew the financial damage caused to our organization as a result of the theft was beyond anything the Danish authorities would understand or recognize. We knew that copies of the stolen materials would be made and sold abroad, specifically to David Mayo and his group along with others. The spies we had carefully placed within Mayo's group informed us of the plans to distribute the stolen materials. John Nelson worked for David Mayo at his Advanced Ability Center in Santa Barbara, California. Through our sources, we knew that John had made several phone calls to Ron Lowery in East Grinstead to arrange to meet and secure the stolen materials for Mayo's group and we needed to act quickly to get John put in jail just like Robin.

Because of his history in the Scientology movement David Mayo was the natural Technical successor of L Ron Hubbard in the minds of Scientology staff and public alike. Now by default, he was the leader of the Independent Movement. People who had defected from authorized Scientology looked to him for leadership and technical guidance. It was only natural that he receive a copy of the stolen confidential materials as soon as possible. After all, he was the new Scientology technical leader of the

Independent Movement. Most people who identified with being an Independent Scientologist had a healthy respect for him.

Vicki and I began to feel overwhelmed by the momentum of the Scientology Independent movement. We had Scientology breakaway centers springing up in Germany, Spain, Italy, United Kingdom and all over the United States. We were scrambling every day just to keep track of the breakaway groups. These new groups were feeding on the same people who had been Scientologists in good standing before they resigned. As far as we were concerned, Scientology was hemorrhaging money and parishioners over to our enemies, and we needed that to stop.

Vicki and I created another intelligence-based unit within RTC. Their first order of business was to propose a program to infiltrate and disrupt the activities of anyone who was using our trademarks (The Technology) without authorization. They came up with a detailed plan and called it the Squirrel Busters Project. We started with two staff for the new intelligence unit. The staff were Gary Klinger, who was the head of the unit, and Jeff Shriver, who held the position of Case Officer. Both had prior experience in intelligence operations and working with private investigators to do Fair Game on whoever was targeted. Both of these staff had worked before under the Guardian, who was Jane Kember operating under the authority of L. Ron's wife, Mary Sue Hubbard.

Their first primary target was to locate and place loyal Scientologists who could be trusted and were willing to spy and report back to us. Bob Mithoff, the brother of Ray Mithoff (Who replaced David Mayo as the new authorized Senior C/S International) and his wife Sammy, had previously resigned from Scientology. They were handled and brought back into line. Now we hired and paid them in cash to infiltrate David Mayo's new group. They were instructed to report back on their findings on a daily basis. We also used two former staff members, Bill Yaude and Nancy Many who had worked for the previous Guardians Office when it was managed by Mary Sue Hubbard, and they worked for free. None of the informants were allowed to know about the others. Each informant was cautioned that we had multiple sources working the case, and if they slipped up we would know very quickly.

Bob Mithoff began to provide financial and membership information to RTC from Mayo's new group, as well as other fledgling, Independent centers being created by Mission Holders who had resigned from authorized Scientology. The fact of the matter is, Mayo had drawn a good amount of people who use to pay for services at our Scientology Churches.

There was a combination of scandals that occurred that really soured paying Scientology public members and caused some people to resign from authorized Scientology Organizations. Each of these scandals was tied to and created by L Ron himself. The first scandal was the continual price increase month after month for Scientology services. The price for Scientology services automatically increased at the end of each month. Scientology paying public were being gouged for money all the time to continue receiving services from authorized Scientology organizations. The truth is there was no reason whatsoever to increase prices month after month. This was greed and destructive policy issued by L Ron and enforced by RTC and International Management.

The other scandal was how new management humiliated and excommunicated large numbers of faithful staff who were known and admired by Scientology staff and public alike for no obvious reasons. This included destroying a major income source (The Mission Network) who had faithfully paid their required tithes to Scientology. Hell, they were even willing to pay more. Instead, they were treated like enemies and gotten rid of because that's what L Ron wanted. However, the staff and public were prevented from knowing the actions taken by the new management were a direct result of orders received from L Ron. So L Ron continued to get a pass.

Along with the extreme disaffection against the new management, there was a wave of members writing resignation letters. Along with these letters, the people resigning were also asking for a refund of money they had paid into Scientology for services they no longer wanted. Some of these people even threatened to sue Scientology if we didn't refund their money. At first Scientology management tried to persuade members not to resign. There is a policy within the church that states if a person requests a refund for monies paid into Scientology for services yet to be delivered and they refuse to change their minds they are to be given a full refund. The only condition being they were no longer eligible for Scientology services. Some refunds were paid, and we later found out some of the people that received refunds ended up at David Mayo's Center buying Scientology services from him.

David Mayo and his associates had founded a new center in the Santa Barbara, CA area and began to deliver Scientology advance counseling and training services. Mayo called his new place the Advanced Ability Center, AAC for short. Ex-Mission Holders were also creating Scientology service centers all around California. The trend eventually spread even further from Omaha, to Nebraska to Elmira New York. These new centers were charging a greatly reduced rate for the same services being delivered by authorized Scientology Service organizations, and they were keeping all of the money for themselves. Wonder where they learned that from?

As the weeks passed, Bob Mithoff continued to report the bad news. The fact of the matter is Mayo had drawn a good number of people who were ex-Scientologists to his new organization. Our agents had access to the financial records, and we knew the organization was making $20,000 to $30,000 gross income every week. This was better than most Scientology mid-level organizations. Within four months of its inception, AAC had a standard newsletter it mailed to its adherents. We were hard-pressed to keep pace with the rapid expansion of these independent centers springing up all over America and Europe.

Vicki and I were confronted by David Miscavige after he had read the latest reports from Bob Mithoff. He wanted to know what our legal strategy was to put an end to Mayo and the other rising Independent centers. We were already preparing our intelligence capabilities. The first option we suggested was to bring a copyright suit against the AAC.

Copyrights were the business of Author Services. David Miscavige called in the ASI LRH Personal Secretary, Patricia Brice, to get a briefing on the status of current Church copyright filings. He was sorely disappointed when he found out that no one in the entirety of Scientology was responsible for copyright filings since the Guardian's Office had been reorganized by him. As a matter of fact, the Guardian's Office itself had been remiss in properly filing for copyright and trademark protection in America and abroad. The fact is, many works had fallen into the public domain because the materials had not been registered with the United States copyright office for so many years. David Miscavige discovered that the Guardians Office had failed to register copyrights for thousands of pages of Scientology material written by L Ron.

At that same meeting, David Miscavige specifically ordered Pat Brice to begin the process of mass copyright registration filings for all of L Ron Hubbard's library. This order was given despite the fact that David was already aware that many of the materials in question were already in the public domain. This is the reason most Scientology copyright filings have a date starting in 1983 forward.

It was decided not to pursue any copyright actions in court, however pursuing a trade secrets case seemed to be a viable option. It was decided at the meeting that the Vicki and I would search for a good trademark litigation attorney to advise us on our best course of action.

In the meantime, we began to ramp up our Fair Game activities. Bob Mithoff stole a copy of the AAC's mailing list and provided it to RTC. With the stolen mailing list, RTC operative Gary Klinger designed a newsletter, similar in appearance to the one already being mailed out to the people on the list that contained disparaging information concerning AAC. This list was also used by RTC to contact members of the AAC paying public for the purpose of harassment and intimidation. That list was used to enact "Fair Game" on people who were on the list.

We learned through Mithoff that several other ex-Scientologists had copied and were planning to use Scientology policies and technical bulletins for prophet. A former Mission Holder, Frank Gerbode, had an ongoing project to copy and store on computer all Scientology policies and technical bulletins with the intent to sell them to Mayo or trade them for Scientology confidential upper-level materials. Through Mithoff, we learned that Mayo and Gerbode had come to an agreement, and Mayo's new group was, in fact, more computerized than most Scientology facilities. We wanted to know where and to who all of the money was going.

As a result of our ramped up Fair Game tactics, Mayo and the AAC were successful in getting a Temporary Restraining Order against RTC and CSI because of the constant harassment by people sent in to disrupt their activities. The specific incident which resulted in the TRO occurred when Gary Klinger posed as a Jewish Rabbi and went to a barbecue garden party held at the AAC one weekend No one recognized him at first, and he wreaked havoc at the party. Of course, the police were called but Gary and others managed to disappear before they could arrive. Mayo figured out who was at the bottom of his trouble, and that's why we ended up with a Temporary Restraining Order against us.

There was another insurrection happening that directly exposed the activities of David Miscavige, L Ron Hubbard, and Author Services Inc. This insurrection was being spearheaded by none other than John Zegel, the stepfather of Mark Yager, Commanding Officer of L Ron's International Messenger Organization. John Zegel had commiserated with ex-staff members that were part of the large group of Scientology executives who were excommunicated and kicked out of the church. At least four people from that group had been personal aides for L Ron and did everything for him including feeding, bathing him and caring for him during times when he was sick. Some of these people had cared for L Ron for many years and knew many things about him the general public did not know. John Zegel zeroed in on these people and debriefed them thoroughly about L Ron Hubbard and his personal business.

John Zegel started a taped lecture series exposing intimate details he had learned about L Ron Hubbard, his wife Mary Sue Hubbard, and the takeover of the Guardian's Office by David Miscavige. He also divulged detailed information that exposed exactly how the Religious Technology Center was incorporated and why. These taped lectures also included the details of how Author Services was incorporated, who it was staffed by and the exact amount of money they were extracting from Scientology organizations for L Ron's bank accounts on a weekly basis. The amount was in excess to a million dollars per week! I had failed to handle John Zegel, and David Miscavige told me not to worry about it because John Zegel would now receive special handling. David had a special staff member as part of his entourage that did nothing but handle lawsuits and intelligence activities in the exact same manner as the previous Guardian's Office under Mary Sue Hubbard. Vicki and I were rank amateurs compared to the work these people were capable of.

That person was known as Special Project L, and his name was Mark Rathbun but everyone called him Marty. When things got real bad and real ugly with our legal and intelligence endeavors, Special Project L would get involved. Marty was the interface with our hired guns like ex-police officers, ex-agents of various agencies and such. Over the years, Marty had developed a very good working relationship with certain individuals in the Los Angeles and Riverside County police departments. He primarily worked with people that had previously been employed in law enforcement. The primary value these hired guns had were their current connections with those still hired in the system. Marty was like a secret weapon that functioned as a Terminator at the behest of David Miscavige exclusively. Any and everything associated with John Zegel was turned over to Marty to take care off. I was never asked to deal with John Zegel again.

We learned through our carefully placed spies within Mayo's group that David did, in fact, possess a copy of the stolen confidential material. We learned that John Nelson was also involved with the distribution of our stolen confidential materials as well. As if to add insult to injury, David Miscavige's mother-in-law, Flo Barnett, had resigned from Scientology. We learned from Bob Mithoff that Flo also possessed a copy of our confidential upper-level materials. Now David Miscavige also had a proven connection to an external influence hostile to Scientology just like Marc Yager. Technically, he was a Potential Trouble Source. David was extremely upset over the situation. If L Ron had known of this at the time, there would be no David Miscavige to talk about. His career would have been over because when L Ron got on to anyone or anything he thought was an external influence he wouldn't stop until all connections to the external influence were removed and completely gotten rid of.

The situation posed a direct threat to David, and he went into action. He told Vicki and me not to get involved with the situation with his mother-in-law Flo Barnett. He said she would be handled by Special Project L.

We agreed to go on an all-out offense against the rising Independent Movement. Over several days, we had meetings at Author Services concerning the information that we were learning from our spies.

In addition to our legal activities, we decided to start a new public relations push by having International Management Briefings for the remaining and faithful members of Scientology to reassure them that we were winning the war against people who thought they could infringe on our rights as trademark and copyright owners. These events would feature key speakers that were the new Scientology Management leaders. Usually Vicki or I would speak on behalf of RTC, Marc Yeager and Guillaume would speak on behalf of International Management. David Miscavige became the host of these events.

We coordinated our legal activities with many of the attorneys who were already involved in legal cases and represented various Scientology corporations. The lead attorney of them all was Earl Cooley. Earl was a trial attorney out of Boston with an impressive record of winning. Earl was the cream of the crop when it came to lawyers. He was described as being brilliant among his peers, and he was a force of nature in a courtroom. He had recently been hired to help dig L Ron out of his legal problems. The most pressing issue for L Ron was the looming threat of an indictment by the IRS against him. He really wanted to move into his home at the Gold Base, but he was afraid to go there because he knew he could be cornered which was his biggest fear. L Ron was putting a lot of pressure on his new management team to secure his freedom, and we were doing all we could to that end.

The attorneys were all made aware of the intelligence information we were gathering using our spies. We asked them for legal advice for the best way to utilize the information we were getting. It was recommended that we explore the possibility of bringing a R.I.C.O. (Racketeer Influenced and Corrupt Organizations Act) action against the individuals involved with making copies of and selling the confidential materials that were stolen in Denmark.

David ordered Vicki and me to hire an attorney that had a proven record for successfully litigating trademark and copyright cases. We ended up hiring attorney Joseph Yanny as our lead counsel for RTC.

The War Begins

We began to work night and day battling the Independent Movement. A copy of the materials that were stolen in Copenhagen showed up at David Mayo's new center. In an effort to hide the fact that Mayo had a copy of the stolen NOTs materials, he decided to re-write the documentation to make it look like he recreated the materials from memory. David Mayo did a horrible job trying to disguise the original material as coming from his memory. The documents he reproduced were nearly identical to the materials stolen in Denmark. It's almost like he didn't really bother to try and disguise the materials very well. I can only guess he never thought he would get caught. He was so wrong about that. Since the theft, we had done nothing but assemble evidence to prove the RICO action we planned against Mayo and his Advanced Ability Center's.

Mithoff also stole a copy of the NOTs materials that David Mayo had rewritten, and he provided it to RTC. In order to successfully sue David Mayo and the others for RICO, we had to prove the connection between what Robin Scott had stolen and David Mayo and his operation in America.

Robin Scott cooperated with authorities while he was incarcerated. The original materials that were taken from the Scientology organization in Denmark were returned. However, we knew that copies were made, and the monopoly that Scientology enjoyed with having and delivering the service exclusively was lost forever. While Robin was incarcerated, we sent Office of Special Affairs agents to him to cut a deal. Besides getting all the materials back and accounted for, we had also prepared a special affidavit for Robin to sign, and in exchange we would drop all charges against him. The affidavit in essence stated that there was a large international conspiracy that Robin was a part of. The other conspirators included David Mayo, who had now moved to Santa Barbara and ex-mission holder Bent Corydon, who lived in Riverside California and a variety of other ex-mission holders located in Europe. At that time, Robin refused to sign the affidavit implicating the other individuals, but we knew time was on our side.

When Robin finally did go to trial in Denmark, we were unable to prove the monetary losses based on the theft of the confidential materials. The only charge that really stuck was entering the premises with the intent of taking the documents, and Robin pled guilty to that. The usual sentence for such an offense is ordinarily four months. However, the judge suspended the remaining three months and told Robin he was free to go.

Once Robin returned home to Scotland he was kept under close watch by Scientology private investigators we hired in the United Kingdom. Robin's two accomplices Ron Lowery and Morag Bellmaine were in fear and had gone underground. They had also been contacted by OSA staff and told they were going to jail. In the end, they willingly agreed to cease and desist using and profiting from Scientology technology. Of course, we did everything we could to get them put in jail.

There was another person that started illegally using Scientology materials named Sylvie Herman, who was a former staff member of the Scientology Organization in Munich Germany. It was arranged by OSA staff to collect false information about Sylvia involving criminal activities of embezzling while she was on staff at the Munich organization. False information was drawn up in affidavits of staff still loyal to authorized Scientology organizations. Sylvie ended up being arrested by German authorities and went to jail while an investigation was being conducted.

There was another person in Spain named John Caban was also illegally using Scientology materials in Madrid, Spain. Ex-law enforcement officials in Europe were hired to pose as police officers to harass John and his wife. They were in the process of setting up their own Independent Center but changed their minds.

Word was starting to get around to those trying to establish new alternative Scientology organizations that RTC was prosecuting and putting in jail individuals who thought they could illegally possess and use Scientology technology. As with so many other things, we would take one step forward only to take two or three steps back. The German police eventually discovered the affidavits against Sylvia were false. Within days, the Church of Scientology in Munich and a Scientology Mission in Germany was raided by the German police. The raid was a result of the German police doing their own investigation and finding the original affidavits submitted in support of Scientology's claim that Silvia embezzled and stole money from Scientology organizations.

The private investigators that had been hired to pose as police officers in Spain were also discovered and arrested. We gleefully reported to L Ron about the others being put in jail but never mentioned at what cost. However, none of this deterred or stopped us. We had unlimited income at our disposal and plenty of people willing to fall on the sword for L Ron.

We were just getting started.

12

THE WAR GETS VICIOUS

JOHN NELSON, WHO HAD BEEN the Commanding Officer for L Ron's Messenger Organization before he left the Church, was now involved with helping David Mayo establish his new center. We also learned through our spies that John was planning a business trip to Europe, which included picking up a copy of the stolen confidential materials. John was targeted to be put in jail.

We hired private investigators to track his movements to discover exactly what he was involved in. John was trying to set up businesses outside of the subject of Scientology, and we learned that he would soon be making a trip to Taiwan. An operation was put together to have John put in jail while he was in Taiwan.

A person working on behalf of the Office of Special Affairs (Rick) and a private investigator flew to Taiwan on the same flight as John Nelson. They were able to secure a hotel room at the same hotel he had gotten for himself in Taiwan. When John left his hotel room for a meal or business meeting, Rick and the private investigator illegally entered his room and placed bugging devices in his room to be able to monitor what he was doing. The next day Rick and the private investigator invaded John's room again and placed a quantity of the drug heroin in John Nelson's hotel room. The idea was to report John as drug dealer to the Taiwan police after they set him up.

After they had placed the heroin in the room and had arranged for the police to raid the hotel room when John returned, the private investigator called back to the United States to talk to his handler who was Special Project L (Marty Rathbun). The private investigator in Taiwan informed Marty of the fact that if a person was caught with the illegal drug heroin in Taiwan meant an immediate death sentence. The private investigator told Marty he wanted no part of getting someone killed that he did not know. At that point, the operation was called off. I don't think John ever knew that he nearly lost his life during that trip.

Until that point, the Fair Game activities we were doing against former members hadn't risen to a level of actually getting someone killed, that I was aware of. This was the beginning of a turning point for me. Never in my wildest imagination did I think I would be involved in a murder scheme. The whole prospect of what could have happened made a difference. I felt sick on the inside and felt like I wanted to vomit.

Later, I remember having a conversation with Vicki about what happened with our operation on John and why it went south like that. Neither one of us knew about the death penalty for heroin before the operation. She had been involved in dismantling the previous Guardians Office, and it was known that

Guardian's Office staff members would do breaking and entering, theft and manufacturing evidence, but I had never heard of *murder* before. I asked her if we would actually kill someone; She replied that she wouldn't kill anyone, but she couldn't speak for others.

I think both Vicki and I were in shock about the prospect of ending John Nelson's life over some bullshit. John and I had joined the Sea Org in 1976, and we did our basic Scientology training together side-by-side. This is someone I had personally known, and I knew he was not a government agent or spy or an evil person. He was just a person trying to make a living after the devastation of losing his religion and career. I thought what we were doing was disgusting, and I told Vicki that I would never have any part of anyone being murdered. She agreed.

Shortly after this incident occurred, I spent more time at the Gold Base. One day someone – I don't recall who – brought me the auditing file of Shelly Miscavige, Dave Miscavige's wife, and told me she needed a counseling session. When I examined the content of her file, I saw that there was a report written which stated that Shelley's mother had recently committed suicide. The report stated that Shelley was quite distraught over the death of her mother, and she needed to go in for a counseling session immediately. I prepared a place for counseling and Shelly was brought to me. It was so sad to see her like that. She looked like she had been crying hard for a while. Her eyes were bloodshot red. She had a blank expression on her face, and she sort of mumbled her words. Before I attempted to do any Scientology counseling on her, I decided to talk to her to try and understand what happened. Through her tears, Shelly told me her mother had committed suicide. She said her mother took a rifle and shot herself three times in the chest.

I couldn't believe what I was hearing. I asked her if she was sure that she shot herself three times in the chest. Shelly said that's what she was told. I point-blank asked Shelly "How in the fuck can someone shoot themselves three times in the chest with a rifle?" She just looked at me, then looked at the ground and replied, "I don't know." There was nothing I could do or say to help her feel better and we both knew it. I didn't force any Scientology processing on her, and she appreciated that. I just sat with her for a while and said nothing. After a while, she said she felt better and thanked me for sitting with her. She told me her stepfather was a black person who had been living with her mother. She said David never did like the stepfather, but Shelly did. She told me the man had taken good care of her mom through the years. We both stood up, and I gave her a hug, and she really needed that. I let her cry until she stopped then we waited again. She had put on her game face before she left.

When I left, I went to David Miscavige's office to inform him of his wife's condition. After he had thanked me for taking care of Shelly, he said, "That bitch got what she deserved," referring to Shelly's mother. I was speechless and after an awkward silence, left the room.

I knew why David hated Flo. At one point before her "suicide" Flo Barnett had become a member of David Mayo's Advanced Abilities Center (AAC).

Undercover operatives were sent into the AAC by RTC. We ran operations which included renting the office above Mayo's AAC to for the purpose of placing electronic transmitting devices to hear what was being said at all times. Private investigator Gene Ingram was hired to pose as an investigative reporter and Mayo was duped into believing he was participating in a TV program to promote his new group. That was a diversion to make sure he was not on the premises as our spies copied his business and personal finance information on his copy machine. Through Bob Mithoff, it was learned that David Mayo planned to travel abroad to Europe. When he did travel, we caused him a lot of problems with customs and immigrations. Through investigator Gene Ingram, it was arranged to have Mayo stopped at customs as a suspected drug dealer, which did happen. He was detained for hours based on false information provided to European customs officials through official channels. Gene Ingram received his instructions on these matters from Gary Klinger, an executive in RTC.

Ingram's fee was paid by the Church of Scientology International through the office of John Peterson, who was retained as in-house counsel by the Church of Scientology California. As a note, John Peterson was not fully aware of why his office paid private investigator expenses to Bob Mithoff. He said the less he knew, the better.

RTC lawyer Joe Yanny recommended a RICO complaint be drawn up, as we now had sufficient evidence to prove David Mayo had formed agreements with other Scientology dissidents to illegally exchange Scientology materials for commercial purposes.

In the case of the RICO suit filed by RTC and CSI against the AAC, another type of Scientology "ethics" was applied. L Ron Hubbard believed certain words and catch phrases used together in writing could have a psychological effect on the reader. The words and phrases are part of a confidential course in Scientology called "R6 End Words" or "R6EW." Hubbard ordered his "magic words" to be sewn into each and every legal motion and complaint submitted to any court. By adding these words, Hubbard believed any judge would subconsciously become antagonistic to anyone trying to engage Scientology in a lawsuit. So we are lacing our legal briefs with magic spells against our enemies, and this was a not a joke.

In 1952, Hubbard wrote he had discovered something so powerful with Dianetics that he had to protect us all from his own invention. He wrote a journal called "Black Dianetics." Here is how it starts: "_Death, insanity, aberration, or merely a slavish obedience can be efficiently effected by the use of Black Dianetics. Further, adequate laws do not exist at this time to bar the use of these techniques. The law provides that only the individual so wronged can make a complaint or swear out a warrant for offenders using these techniques._" This journal was required reading for those of us whose job description was to protect Scientology. L Ron wrote that Black Dianetics could be used to drive a person insane, and I began to learn how this was done.

As mentioned earlier Scientology counseling involves asking someone questions while they are hooked up to an E-meter machine. Everything a person says during a counseling session is written down in a short form so that it can be referred to later. Every thought, confession or fear the person may have expressed in counseling is written down. In Black Dianetics, a person's counseling folders are carefully and meticulously gone through to isolate the most embarrassing actions, thoughts or fears the person has disclosed in counseling. These items are then used against the individual in such a way as to create the greatest amount of embarrassment and distress possible. An example would be creating a flyer with the person's face on it and listing either real or imagined despicable acts supposedly committed by the person and papering the person's neighborhood with this information. Or the information could be used to infuriate the person's family or extended family members. Any information that could possibly be used to cause a person to lose their job was also looked for. The intent is to get inside the person's head and make them feel insane while working to destroy the person's life.

L Ron had methods for driving a person insane that extended beyond the use of Black Dianetics. Through the use of ex-police or, ex-sheriffs...etc. almost anyone can be bought. In the example of a judge that may be antagonistic towards Scientology and its ways, that judge would become a target. All available public, school and business records on that judge would be scrubbed to find connections to family, old friends and old lovers especially. The idea is to dig up as much dirt on an individual as possible no matter how long it takes. Once a sufficient amount of potential blackmail information is accumulated it is used to persuade the target judge to recuse him or herself from being involved in any Scientology litigation in exchange for silence and peace.

This same method would be applied to journalist and editors as well. In most cases, the method proved to be very effective. Most ex-law enforcement employees have friends that are still active in law enforcement. These friends can be persuaded to do a favor for money. An example of a favor would be obtaining the police criminal records on any individual that are not available to the public at large. A favor could also be to provide private phone records or bank records of a targeted individual. When business is done with cash practically, anything is possible. Scientology has established these types of back-lines for decades, and they pay handsomely.

This is how we were able to stay one or two steps ahead of the IRS criminal investigation because we had informants that were able to get information only known by IRS employees.

13

MISCAVIGE CAUGHT IN THE CROSSFIRE
1984

BECAUSE OF OUR OVERRIDING scorched-earth policy, even when we had minor setbacks in a legal case we continued to press forward. The game we played using civil litigation against our enemies was not necessarily to win the case. Our overall objective in our legal cases was always to wear an enemy down to make them vulnerable so they could more easily be manipulated or destroyed.

Soon we began to see cracks in the Independent Movement. Besides L Ron himself, our primary concern became the amount of people that were leaving Scientology.

At the end of 1983 L Ron had issued an amnesty for staff and public who had not been excommunicated. There was hardly any response from ex-staff and public at all. We began to encourage Scientologists who were no longer active to accept the amnesty.

In Scientology, amnesty is used broadly to forgive individuals who had strayed from authorized Scientology. All the person had to do was to confess, in writing, to any and all wrongdoing they had participated in, and ask for forgiveness. Once an amnesty petition was verified as being complete and accepted, the person would be back in good graces and eligible to continue with Scientology services.

I think it may have been Earl Cooley who suggested at the time that we look into hiring a public relations firm to help us improve our image. We ended up hiring a very prestigious public relations firm known as Hill and Knowlton to advise us on how to improve our public image effectively.

Scientology had a reputation for being really tough on its enemies and critics. While this was effective, it wasn't always appropriate. At this point, public relations became as much a concern as anything else. Staff were hired and placed in positions to handle public relations for various Scientology corporations. I believe this may be when a staff member named Mike Rinder began to manage Scientology's Public Relations.

As part of our efforts to improve new management's image, RTC authorized an international Board of Review to look into possible injustices that may have been occurred to ex-staff and ex-public members in an effort to recover these individuals as well.

During our public events, we kept Scientology public informed of our legal success with shutting down divergent organizations using our copyright and trademark technology. We also unveiled plans to expand Scientology further into society and encouraged our members to focus on and participate in these activities with us. We held these events in Germany, Italy, The United Kingdom, Australia and all over the United States. The tide of public opinion was beginning to turn in our favor despite any mistakes we were making. Earle Cooley and the other lawyers that were on the team were truly the best that money could buy, and we were able to accomplish our legal goals, for the most part.

We continued to have weekly meetings throughout the year concerning the strategies and programs we were all working on. Summaries of our activities were put together and forwarded to L Ron, who was busy preparing himself to move to the Gold Base. David informed all of the new management members that he had been told by Pat Broeker that L Ron was ready to move into his new home. We were told that L Ron was coming to the Base and when he did arrive we were not to stare.

At this point, L Ron primarily concerned himself with the activities of the cinematography organization (Golden Era Productions) and its shoot crew members. L Ron had authorized new scripts to be written to update his technical training films that had been produced years earlier. I don't think anyone in that shoot crew was really looking forward to L Ron actually being at that Base – many had experienced that awful temper of his. Be that as it may, L Ron was busy berating the staff as they tried to comply with his cinematic dreams. L Ron also had musical aspirations he wanted to achieve for the new science fiction series he was just finishing up called *Mission Earth*.

All of this activity had happened in a relatively short amount of time. It seemed like we were always

The Expert Witness

so busy to the point where there was really no time to think about or process all that was going on. My life was a series of meetings, traveling the country and abroad, and hiring lawyers to file and register our trademarks in every country Scientology was in. We were in the business of rebuilding Scientology organizations to make them bigger and more productive. There was no time for me to have a personal life. My thoughts turned to Molly. I had asked her to marry me, and she said yes. It was now April, and we still weren't married.

I'm not exactly sure, but Dave brought up the fact that I wasn't married yet. I remember him asking me what happened? He wanted to know if I was I still getting married. I told him how busy things had been and there was no time to get married. He said there will always be a lot going on and I should take time to get married.

On that note, some of the more senior Messengers got together with Molly and put her in a beautiful wedding dress. The great hall where we all ate every day was prepared for the wedding, and Molly and I got married. I'm not sure how it was for Molly, but for me it was sort of surreal coming from doing the work that I did, to being married to this beautiful and sweet woman. It took me some getting used to.

We went to Idlewild California and rented a cabin for our honeymoon. I remember it was still cold, and there was snow on the mountain. On our wedding night, I lit the fireplace in our cabin. I had never used a fireplace in my life. I didn't know that I had to open the flue and to say the least, smoke was everywhere including our clothes. We had a great time just the same despite the fact that Molly slipped and twisted her ankle somehow and her foot had to be wrapped, and she now had to walk with a crutch. To say the least, people were laughing at us wondering what we had done. That was certainly the happiest thing that I accomplished in 1984.

Molly and I didn't really know each other well. We hadn't spent a lot of time together, but still we made an honest effort to get to know one another and find a reason to love each other. Molly was pretty straightforward, and she was no mental lightweight. She'd been to college and held a degree of some sort; I don't remember what. She was also an actress and had trained with some notable actors when she lived in Europe as a child. Molly had not received a lot of Scientology counseling or training and did not share the knowledge or information I had on the subject. As a matter of fact, we never talked about the work we did much at all.

Even with all its strangeness, somewhere somehow, we found common ground, and I found myself deeply in love with her. Molly was not an executive; she held a rather low position and was considered a worker. She wasn't materialistic, and she didn't have much in the way of possessions. I changed all of that for her when I gave her a credit card to use at her discretion.

During my travels to Europe, I would often go shopping for Molly and buy her clothes and shoes that were not common in the United States. I even went as far as to buy her a long black rabbit fur coat and jewelry. Molly was envied by her peers, and I enjoyed providing her with nice things.

I think I may have hung around for maybe a month after we got married, but soon I was back at my routine of being gone most of the time. Vicki and I returned to the LA area and began to broaden our attack of our enemies.

L Ron became very interested when he learned we had hired a public relations firm. Suddenly he had a lot to say about how Scientology should be represented to the public. The subject of public relations would very quickly lead to a conversation concerning marketing. L Ron loved talking about marketing and had written many policies based on the subject of marketing. L Ron was entertained by all of this, which meant he was generally in a better mood.

L Ron became interested in Scientology celebrities and began to give advice concerning getting them active in promoting Scientology. We created a project within RTC called the Celebrity Project which in effect began with going through their auditing files to make sure they were happy with their services. Once we knew we had fully converted the celebrity we could direct them to use their connections to promote Scientology to influential Hollywood movers and shakers. This all began innocently enough with offering Scientology celebrities counseling under the direction of the Religious Technology Center. This service became highly valued by Scientology celebrities. Receiving "100% standard technology as L Ron intended it" was the best reward a Scientologist could receive. RTC was there to ensure the technology was available and correctly applied to our celebrities. RTC eventually collected every major celebrities' counseling/auditing files. The files were meticulously gone through to discover the person's hot buttons.

Their counseling files were monitored to ensure the celebrity was always satisfied with their Scientology services. Once a celebrity had been properly processed; they were also used to encourage other celebrities to join Scientology. The RTC tech program was very popular, and the new management had begun to turn the tide of public opinion with Scientology staff and public alike.

L Ron was very pleased with the progress we were making with Scientology celebs. He had plans to use the celebs to be in science fiction movies he had written scripts for. There were also music scores L Ron wanted written to accompany the new science fiction book series he was in the process of writing. L Ron was very excited about the prospect of having Hollywood talent at his disposal to help him create films at the same level being done in Hollywood. He again made it known he was ready to move to the Gold Base. He wanted an All Clear from legal so that he could once again be among his adoring staff.

Through dispatches, L Ron let his new management team know he was pleased with the progress we were making getting churches and missions properly licensed under our new trademark agreements. He was also happy with the results we had been able to achieve so far with defending the trademarks and copyrights. In an advice, he said he wanted pictures taken of the top executives starting with International Management Executive Director, Capt. Guillaume Lesevre and his top lieutenants. Next, the Commanding Officer of Ron's International Messenger Organization, Mark Yeager and his executive cabinet known as the Watchdog Committee. Pictures were also taken of the RTC and

Author Services staff. There was a photography studio that was part of the cinematic studio located at the Gold Base. The person that was the head of the photography department was a person named Ted. Of all of the other people associated with Golden Era Productions staff, Ted was one of the few with a college education. Ted and his department staff took these pictures and put them in nice binders and sent them off to L Ron via Dave Miscavige and Pat Broeker.

I didn't think much of that activity at the time because I was preoccupied. As a result of L Ron making plans to come to the Gold Base, sometimes he would come under cover of secrecy to the house he planned to occupy eventually.

It was during this time that L Ron noticed the scent of rose perfume permeated nearly every article in his universe. It had long been the policy that no one at the base was allowed to use any form of perfume. That included scented deodorant products and scented makeup products. This went on to extend to laundry detergent, laundry soap, hand soap, hair conditioner and so on. Everything, according to L. Ron, had the dreaded rose perfume scent.

There was a Messenger named Janadair, who was assigned to make sure L Ron's new house was perfectly cleaned by the staff known as the Household Unit. Janadair and I joined the Sea Org in the same year, 1976. David Miscavige also joined the Sea Organization in 1976. Janadair was also responsible for making sure L Ron's laundry was done properly. L Ron would not wear any shirt unless it was put through the laundry to wash out sizing (starch) which contained the dreaded rose perfume.

Janadair would go shopping to buy new shirts for L Ron. She would turn the shirts over to the Household Unit, who would wash them in large buckets of water using specially made scent-free soap products. The shirts were always washed and rinsed by hand. At the end of such vigorous washing of brand-new shirts, some of the shirts would begin to fall apart, so there was a special sewing unit that would sew the new shirts back together and prepare the shirts to be delivered to L Ron. More often than not, L Ron refused to wear the shirts because he said the rose perfume had not been properly removed.

At this point, staff began to get in ethics trouble for causing L Ron distress with failure to eliminate the scent of rose perfume properly. This plague began to spread to International Management level because Mark Yeager, who was the Commanding Officer of all of Ron's Messengers, had failed to bypass and directly to handle the situation of the horrible rose perfume.

It was only a matter of time before I saw David standing in my office letting me know that I was now the person responsible for smelling every article of clothing, every dispatch, every bankers box, and attest to the fact these items were free of the dreaded rose perfume. When Dave came into the office, he had a smirk on his face, and he said well Jesse you know shit rolls downhill, and I'm tired of taking the shit all the time. He then told me that it had been my job all along to check packages and anything else that were being sent to L Ron because I was the executive over a unit within Church of Scientology International called Authority Verifications and Corrections Unit (AVC). In short, this unit was the final authority of verifying the correctness of any and all issue types published in Scientology. This included policies authored by L Ron himself to keep things somewhat consistent. If L Ron wanted to issue an order or policy that contradicted a previous order or policy, it was AVC's job to point out the discrepancy and cancel the previous order with notice along with any new instructions.

The truth is, Dave had always done that job, and I had never been responsible for doing it before now. He told me if I fucked this up I would probably end up going to the RPF or something, so don't fuck it up. At that, all of the traffic that was about to go to L Ron was brought to my office, and there was a lot of it.

At the time, I was a heavy-duty smoker. I smoked Camel non-filter coffin-nail cigarettes. I didn't have much of a sense of smell left, and I didn't think L Ron did either because he smoked Kool non-filter coffin-nail cigarettes. I remember just sitting there looking at all the boxes wondering what exactly I would do. I began to think how silly this all was. It occurred to me that my entire career and everything that I had worked for could be callously dismissed because of some fucking rose perfume scent that I couldn't smell anyway. I smoked one of those camel nonfilter cigarettes right then and there and decided I wouldn't panic nor would I pretend.

I was more curious about what exactly was being sent to L Ron. I opened up a few of the boxes and saw the usual management reports being sent to him by us. There were articles of clothing in the boxes and other odd items that seemed harmless to me. A dispatch had been prepared for me to sign attesting to the fact that I had personally inspected the articles that were being sent to L Ron, and they were free of the deadly rose perfume smell. I finished the cigarette, signed the dispatch and called to inform Dave I'd finished inspecting the traffic being sent to L Ron, and it was ready to go.

Dave was the person that would drive these boxes to Pat Broeker, who would then take them to L Ron. I knew it would probably take 2 to 3 days before I would hear back from L Ron concerning the rose perfume smell. Sure enough, on the third day Dave received a call to come and pick up traffic from L Ron via Pat Broeker. When Dave got back, he called me to his office. When I went to his office, he was smiling he looked at me and said you lucky fucker. L Ron had written a dispatch saying that dreaded rose perfume was still faintly present, but it was much more tolerable than it was before. L Ron had discovered that the rose perfume smell was coming from the very ink pens used to sign signatures by staff.

What a relief. But I still began to wonder exactly how long everything that we had worked for in the last few years to reestablish Scientology in society would last once L Ron came back on the scene.

During this time, L Ron, Pat Broeker, and Annie Broeker began to come to the Base more often to inspect the progress of the home being completed for L Ron. No one was ever allowed to be present when he would inspect his new living quarters. To the contrary, we were told to carry on as if he was not even there.

One day, Dave came to inform Vicki and me that Pat Broeker had told him L Ron would be on the property, and if we saw him we were not to stare at him. We were also told that if he asked a question to answer the question only and not to diverge, because that could set him off.

I remember Vicki and me sitting in the office thinking "Oh my God, what now?" After a short while, I was told to go across the street and stand in the parking lot of Massacre Canyon Inn. This is where we all would eat every day. I was instructed to stand on a planter, and told a car would be driving around me, and I was not to look at the people inside the car. I did as I was told, but on that second circling around I looked, and there he was looking like a version of Col. Sanders. He had leaned over from the other side of the car and he was kind of bracing himself with his hands as he looked at me. Then he smiled and leaned back. I could hardly see through the windows due to the heavy tint.

I didn't know what to think, but I was concerned if I was now going to get in trouble for not following orders. I returned to my office, and Vicki asked me what the hell had happened? I told her I went down to the parking lot across the street and did exactly as I was told. I didn't mention that I had looked and saw a glimpse of Hubbard, or that he had seen me in that tiny moment in time when we made eye contact, or that he had smiled. But I did know what that smile meant.

I received gifts from L Ron for finally having his daughter turn over custody of her only child to her ex-husband. In general, I guess he was happy with the counseling I had done on others at his behest. Once, for my birthday, I was given a Ruger Mini 14 assault rifle, which I was told was from L Ron. I guess the biggest acknowledgment that I had somehow stayed off his bad side was the fact that I was still there.

Towards the end of 1984 we received a tip from a Los Angeles police officer advising us there was a pending IRS raid about to happen in Los Angeles. We again went into the mode of destroying the recent advices received from L Ron, which would yet again prove he was still the managing agent for all of Scientology.

We also found out that David Miscavige himself was one of the targets of the IRS CID investigation. David was very concerned about this, because he knew or thought he knew what happened to people of his stature who go to jail. In all honesty, he was freaked out about being sexually harassed even if he went to jail for a short amount of time. It was at this time that Dave began to make plans to leave the country if he had to. I know Canada was one of the countries he would more than likely flee to.

With the information we were getting from our lawyers concerning what the IRS was capable of doing to Scientology, we knew that the chances of Hubbard getting off without incident were next to nil. Dave spoke to Vicki and I, and in confidence remarked that the only way to stop the criminal investigation against L Ron and Scientology was for L Ron to die.

Meanwhile, L Ron was in no way sympathetic towards Miscavige being incarcerated, and he didn't believe an IRS raid was imminent. As a matter of fact, L Ron had another take on why he was being told the IRS was yet again investigating him.

L Ron began to suspect that he was being kept away from Scientology by Miscavige deliberately. He felt his grasp on Scientology was weakening, and he became extremely suspicious of Dave.

I received a phone call from Pat Broeker, and he explained that L Ron wanted me to do a Security Check on David Miscavige to find his crimes. L Ron wanted to know what David Miscavige's motives were for passing along legal advice that suggested he couldn't operate with impunity within his Scientology organizations. David was very upset by this turn of events, and I saw him cry like a little girl. Dave swore to me he was only following L Ron's own orders to get an "All Clear" so that he could travel freely again without fear of subpoenas or worse.

Dave thought it was outrageous that he was being asked questions that questioned his loyalty to L Ron, and he began to suspect that he had come to the end of the road as far as being a part of the new management team. Dave informed me during the interrogation that he was not going down alone. He began to tell me about times he and Pat Broeker had taken money that was being sent to L Ron from suitcases prepared for him and gambled away part of the money. As a matter of fact, it seemed like they both had a problem with gambling and the problem was they were gambling with L Ron's money.

Dave also mentioned being involved with hookers in Las Vegas, all at L Ron's expense. Dave became very critical of Pat and said he had a long history of alcohol abuse and recklessly spending L Ron's money. Dave also mentioned that there was unethical activity going on with L Ron's personal physician Dr. Gene Denk. According to David, he had become aware that L Ron was taking prescription drugs as given to him by Dr. Denk. I got the impression that L Ron was busy taking prescription drugs and was unaware that his doctor was also involved in gambling with L Ron's money in Las Vegas casinos.

After the interrogation was over I dutifully wrote up the required report with the details of what had come up in the interrogation and addressed it to L Ron. I knew, even as I wrote the report, that this was something L Ron would never see. I knew this because I had been a part of those who would censor information going to L Ron. I remember thinking at the time that L Ron would never see the report, but I wondered what he would be told, and how the situation would be handled. It would be years before I would find out what actually happened.

During the year 1984, Vicki and I had established contact and communication with Annie Broeker and Pat Broeker independent of David Miscavige. Vicki helped me draft the report, and she even commented that while this was not something L Ron would ever see, she was curious how Pat and Annie would deal with the information.

Maybe a week or so later we received information via Annie that L Ron was very upset that he could not immediately move into the home being prepared for him at the Gold Base. As a matter of fact, we were told L Ron was so upset that he was disconnecting from his new management and the Gold Base. This information was only given to a handful of people.

We ended the year 1984 unable to secure an All-Clear for L Ron, and he was having a complete meltdown over it. To say the least, Christmas festivities that year were somber compared to the year before. We all resolved just to keep doing the best job we could to make it possible for L Ron to move to the Gold Base at some point in the near future. I remember Author Services, Religious Technology Center and Church of Scientology International staff members purchased very expensive gifts for L Ron for Christmas. But we never heard back from him about his gifts.

This picture was taken in the fall of 1983 at the beginning of my karate training while in RTC. Facing the picture: on my right is a young Micheal Laws, Mike worked in the Intelligence department. The lady behind me on the right side is Alison. She was the lady responsible for getting money from Scientology public for RTC technical services and she was very successful. To the right of Alison is Darnell Bloomberg. She was from Australia with Aborigine DNA. I don't think a more beautiful woman was born before her. I was crazy about her. Directly behind me is the Queen Bee Vicki. Strong, intelligent and compassionate (with men). I learned a lot from her. The person next to me with the head cut out is a fella named Tim. He was Alison's brother. Behind me and to my left is Alan Cartwright. He was my Legal Secretary and he would co-ordinate all legal matters within RTC. To the left of Alan is Gary Klinger. Gary was my Intelligence Officer and he was the senior case officer and executive of the Intelligence department during my time in RTC. As you can see, we all have white belts. We stayed at it until we got our black belts: first degree

Here is a picture of me and Alison having fun at an office party. Given our circumstances of being in a cult we still managed to have fun every now and again.

Here is a wedding picture of me just before the ceremony. To my right is a young David Miscavige. To my left is a young Marc Yeager. Behind me on the right side is a partial picture of Gary Connelly, Behind me on the left side is Greg Ryerson. The person you can't see at all behind Yeager is Paul Shroer, notorious for organizing and an all around good guy.

Left to right - Jason Bennick, Andre Taboyoyan, Jesse Prince, John McGinley, Hans Henrick Peterson, Gary Conley, Mark Fisher, Julie Caetano, Roanne Horwich, Lisa Allen, Carol Bourke, Jennifer Reitman, Fleur Thomas, Jackie True-Parman, and Michelle Yager. This picture is from the wedding of my good friend Mark Fisher back in the mid 80s. The people in this picture represent part of an overall family that I lived, worked and ate with every day at the Gold Base for some years. Roanne is the only child in this picture because she was the only child allowed at the Gold Base facility. I had an additional duty of always keeping an eye on her for L Ron and I did that while I was there. We have talked since she left Scientology. I've explained to her exactly what my role had been in her life. We are friends and she gave me her permission for me to tell the story as I have. I apologized to her for my actions that directly affected her as an ignorant cult member and she forgave me. She knows that daze is over.

This picture is me giving on of the first briefings on a new Association being formed outside of incorporated Scientology. This association was set up specifically to be able to divert funds to an off shore account in case of a raid or any other intervention by the United States Department of Justice or the Internal Revenue Service. The association was named "The International Association of Scientologist."

This is me getting married to my Molly. I hope I don't embarrass her with this but we are still friends forever

Here is a picture of Nori, Paul and myself doing a demonstration at our Black Belt award ceremony in Chinatown, Los Angeles

Here is a picture of how I looked when L. Ron saw me in 1985.

14

Traveling Man
1985

We began 1985 in the same manner we had begun earlier years. We produced a New Year's Event at the Flag Land Base, and the event was broadcast via closed-circuit television to all our organizations internationally. We followed the narrative that had now become a routine: to brief staff and public alike on Scientology expansion news and the success we were having getting L Ron Hubbard's technology applied. Part of our shtick always included anecdotal stories of how ineffective our enemies were.

We had a new look, too! Dave had hired tailors from the Los Angeles garment district to make special Sea Org uniforms for the executives. We had plenty of civilian suits as part of our wardrobe which we began to wear all the time. We had been advised by our handlers at the PR firm Hill and Knowlton to improve our image and that definitely included new custom wardrobes for all involved.

We continued to have our weekly meetings to discuss international affairs just as we had before. The difference was, there was no one demanding reports on our progress. True to his word, L Ron had disappeared as far as we were concerned. David had not heard a word from Pat Broeker, and Vicki and I hadn't heard anything from Annie Broeker. Out of respect, we continued the process of documenting our weekly progress just in case L Ron came around and asked for an update.

In any case, we still had so much work to do to secure an All-Clear for L Ron. We were focused on preparing to file the RICO lawsuit against David Mayo, Robin Scott, John Nelson and the others. We were also involved in lawsuits filed against ex-mission holders based on trademark and trade secrets law. Civil litigation involving trademarks and trade secrets can be very expensive, and that's exactly the position we were putting those being sued by us in. We wanted to ruin them financially.

David was still quite upset over the fact that he had nearly lost his position because he was not able to get an all-clear for L Ron. At some point in these meetings, David declared war on the IRS and the Department of Justice.

On 8 January, 1985 the Church of Scientology Washington DC filed a lawsuit against the Director of the Federal Bureau of Investigation and the Department of Justice. David also vowed to bring civil suits against agents of the Internal Revenue Service. We would apply our scorched-earth policy to the heads of these government agencies. We would investigate them just like we were being investigated, our intention was to make this very personal for the individual agents involved. Just like those before them, we would find their crimes and expose them. David explained that we had no choice but to take these drastic actions, and our backs were being put against the wall.

There was the continuing problem with unauthorized use of the trademarks. Our attorneys briefed the team that as owners of trademarks, according to the law, we had an obligation to take action against anyone who would use our trademarks and profit from them. If someone used them and we knew about it, the clock started to run. If someone could prove, we knew and did nothing to protect our trademarks we could lose our legal rights, under trademark law, for protection. There were plenty of people in Europe who were using the trademarks, and we knew about it. Vicki and I began to plan trips outside of America to secure adequate counsel to represent RTC and the trademarks abroad.

A part of this was meticulously collecting the evidence needed to bring a successful international RICO action for the thefts of the confidential materials. We also wanted to put those directly involved in jail. We needed to explore smart ways to do that, and realized we needed to go and be present at these foreign locations in order to properly assess our options.

From our perspective, the world was always against Scientology, and it was our job to push back. We hardly ever had time to enjoy ourselves, because we were always too busy.

My wife's birthday came in January, and I always made sure she had a good birthday with lots of presents. Molly was not as financially resourceful as I had been, and I didn't allow her to spend our money on me. My own birthday, which is in March, was always uneventful. This year my birthday came, and it was really just another day at the office. Vicki said she was taking me to some restaurant on Hollywood Boulevard as a birthday gift from RTC. We drove down Hollywood Boulevard from the Big Blue complex and headed west towards Grauman's Chinese Theatre. Right near the Chinese Theater there was a huge marquee that towered over the other buildings. As we drove down the street, Vicki pointed to the marquee and said, Jesse look! There was my name in bright lights with a happy birthday crawl going along the bottom. The sign was huge, and Vicki said we were going there, I believe it was the Marquette hotel.

We arrived at the hotel and took an elevator upstairs. A ballroom had been rented, and when I went inside, there were my friends from International Management, and my wife was there as well. David and most of the staff from Author Services also came. There were two long conference tables full of presents that the staff had bought for me. I was completely taken aback. I'd never had that many presents for my birthday, and I just didn't know what to say or do. All of the people that I worked with on a daily basis were at the party, and they were playing music and dancing.

Dave looked at me with that knowing smile because he had been in on the surprise all along. I was pretty quiet as I watched my friends enjoy themselves. When we were done, my staff gathered my presents for me and drove them to my room at the Gold Base. Molly and I spent the rest of the evening together, which was rare in those days. I felt reassured that I was among my true friends and that the work we were doing was worthwhile and important.

About mid-April, Vicki and I, along with RTC staff members Alan Cartwright, Warren McShane, and RTC lead attorney Joe Yanny left Los Angeles headed for Basel, Switzerland. Just as we were passing over Las Vegas, NV there was a loud boom that shook the whole plane. I was already asleep when it happened. As I woke up, I looked out the window and saw fire coming out of one of the engines on the wing of the plane. The pilot announced he was dealing with an engine fire, and he was attempting to put the fire out using a sort of sprinkler that emitted white powder. Well, that didn't work, so he shut the damaged engine down, and that put the fire out, but we were still in trouble. Since we were on an international flight, the plane was full of fuel. The pilot dumped as much fuel as he needed, and we were scheduled for an emergency landing at the Las Vegas airport. Some passengers on the flight were in tears praying openly and loudly calling on the Lord. I think they were Hispanic.

The flight wasn't full, and I had taken an empty row to sleep on the chairs after drinking as much alcohol as I could. This was my way of dealing with long plane rides. I preferred to sleep during most of the flight. After the engine fire, I went and sat with Vicki and the others. Vicki was cool about the whole thing and said something like, fuck it, if it's our time, so be it, what the hell else could we do? Then she made an offhand comment about praying Mexicans. She had also been drinking heavily. As we approached the runway, we could see an awful lot of emergency trucks that lined the runway ready to put out a fire if they needed to when the plane landed. Well, the plane landed without further incident. Some passengers actually got off the plane, fell to their knees and kissed the ground. It didn't take long before the passengers who were on our flight were happily gambling in the airport. But our flying nightmare was far from over.

We were scheduled to take a plane back to Los Angeles in order get another international flight. As we approached Los Angeles, we found out that there was heavy congestion at the airport, and we flew around in circles for over an hour waiting for clearance to land the plane. When we landed, Vicki commented that she wondered if all of this was some sort of sign. She asked me if I thought we should still go I said hell yeah!

We took a red-eye flight out, and we safely arrived at the airport in Basel, Switzerland without further incident. Our first order of business was to check on Religious Technology Center Swiss bank accounts. We rented a car at the airport in Basel and drove to Liechtenstein.

When we arrived at the bank Vicki turned to me and said that I couldn't go into the bank. Only her, Joe and Warren McShane could go in. She explained there were some things that I did not need to know about because I had to stay as clean as possible. I was being prepared to become a witness in the RICO case we were preparing to file. I thought that was a line of bullshit, but I went along with it anyway. Besides, what else was I supposed to do? I was already the Treasurer of the Board of Directors of RTC. These types of inconsistencies are common in Scientology management. The right-hand doesn't need to know what the left hand is doing so even the simplest of information would be given on a need-to-know basis.

We took in some of the fine dining in Liechtenstein and went for a sightseeing walk as well. Liechtenstein boasts economically that it is the richest country in the world. It has the highest gross domestic product per person in the world. The city itself is beautiful with all the Old-World charm of a fairy tale. The sidewalk pavement was formed from granite that was gray in color. There were actually people with brooms made of twigs regularly brushing the streets. Floral arrangements lined the streets of downtown, and the city was immaculately clean and in perfect order.

When our eating and sightseeing were done, we drove to Lucerne, Switzerland, which was the home of William Tell. I remembered the legend of William Tell because it was required reading at the Catholic elementary school I attended in Chicago. In the center of the city was a bronze statue of William Tell armed with his crossbow with his other hand on the shoulders of his young son. The city is surrounded by the Swiss Alps and served as the backdrop for the William Tell statue. The city looked like it was actually built on various different levels in that part of the city was on a fairly flat area, and then there was another part further up the mountain. Then there were homes that extended higher above the second level. This was breathtaking scenery for us all, and we thoroughly enjoyed ourselves in Lucerne.

We ended up getting a hotel and decided to check out the nightlife. We went to a dance club whose name I don't recall, but the doorway which was below street level had a huge green neon spider over the door with lots of red neon spider webbing. It looked like we were going into a giant spider cave. We drank, talked and danced for hours. Joe seemed to be enjoying himself, and that made me happy because I liked Joe, he was a very good person, and he was also a bit of a comedian, let him tell it.

In the morning, we had a wonderful Swiss breakfast with different sausages and egg dishes. The fresh fruit, fresh-baked breads and pastries were a real treat. At some point, we met with a Swiss lawyer that we had hired before we left. Unfortunately, I don't recall who he was or why we had hired him but I'm pretty sure it had something to do with someone who had brazenly decided to use our trademarks without authorization.

Our next stop was Milano, Italy. We decided to drive the Swiss autobahn through the Swiss Alps instead of hiring a plane. Joe insisted he drive so he did. Our rental car was a Citroen that had a top speed of 120 mph. When we got on that autobahn and drove that Citroen as fast as we could, we still had to maintain our position in the right lane. In the left lane were Ferraris, Mercedes-Benzes, Porsches, Bentleys, and even a few Lamborghini Countachs breezed by us as if we were parked. They were going past us so fast that it was hard for me to estimate how fast they were going. Even when we got up to 120 mph, these other cars would pass us and quickly become a speck in front of us and then disappear while we schlepped along in our Citroen through the mountains.

We made a few stops in some of the coastal cities along the way for the purpose of shopping. There were vendors set up like you would see in a flea market. However, the wares being sold were not your average flea market wares. There were vendors that sold Italian gold jewelry, Italian fashion clothes for women, as well as shoes and boots. I purchased some fine gold Italian jewelry for my wife, and Vicki purchased some for herself.

By the time we arrived in Milano, it was getting late, and we were tired. We stopped at the Swiss/Italian border and showed our passports to pass through the gate. Right away, we pulled over to the rest stop to have a cup of espresso coffee. Joe let me know that I was in for a treat. I never really had espresso coffee before, and I wasn't quite sure what to think of the small cup with the brown sludge at the bottom. I drank the top liquid part of the beverage and soon experienced a caffeine high that I would have to drink away to go to sleep.

We grabbed a hotel in Milano, I believe it was the Grand Hotel, which was classic and beautiful. Then we bedded down for the night. In the morning we met with the lawyers we had hired in Italy and discovered we were having a communication problem. We didn't speak any Italian. Joe, our lawyer, didn't speak Italian very well either but he understood more than the rest of us. The Italian attorneys did not speak fluent English. Fortunately, we had Office of Special Affairs staff who were Italian and lived in Milano to help with our translations. This proved to be slightly frustrating because everything was taking longer, and we had other places to go and other things to do. When our meeting was over we went out and shopped for the rest of the day and my wife came out the winner of that deal.

After that, we got rid of the car and took a plane to London to meet with our British lawyers. We arrived in London where I discovered the taxicabs were Bentley and Mercedes-Benz cars. Now we were ready to get down to business. This was the country where Robin Scott, Ron Lawley, Morag Bellmaine, and Steve Bisbee resided. They were at the top of our list to prosecute and incarcerate.

We shared with our British barristers (Attorneys) some of the intelligence information we were able to gather on these people in the US. At some point while sharing the intelligence I remarked to the British barristers that we wanted to create a lot of negative activity for the targeted group of people so that it would appear like they were trying to cover their asses with leaves in a windstorm! Vicki kind of chuckled and went on with her briefing of the barristers, but one of them sat there frozen. He seemed to be trembling, and he turned bright red. I thought he might have been experiencing a medical condition when he suddenly began to laugh uproariously so hard that it infected the entire group. Vicki asked him what was so funny. The barrister apologized for his behavior, and he said he thought the remark about leaves in a windstorm was brilliant. We all had a laugh.

By the end of our meeting which extended over a period of a couple of days we were confident that the RICO action we were putting together had a fairly high chance of being very successful.

On the final day of our meeting, one of our British barristers had a court appointment to attend, and we had a rare opportunity to see how that was done. He went back to a room and pulled out a long black robe, he also had a wig of white hair that he poured liberal amounts of baby powder onto. He put the black robe on and adorned the curly white long haired wig. As he put on the wig, white dust seemed to be everywhere briefly including his face. As if to accent the point, he then added just a bit more baby power to the top of the wig, spun on his heel and exited the room. This seemed so bizarre to me that I didn't think it was real. Vicki agreed with me, but that was the custom of the British court, as we found out.

By this time, we had been gone for nearly 3 weeks and had accomplished what we had intended to accomplish. But we were not ready to go home because we knew we were on a once-in-a-lifetime journey, so we began to figure out what else we could do. We decided to visit Scientology's Saint Hill Manor. We flew from Heathrow to Gatwick Airport in a helicopter then drove to the St. Hill Manor located in East Grinstead Sussex, England. This was the last public home L Ron had before his visa was canceled, and he was told to leave the United Kingdom.

As a result of having his visa canceled L Ron took to the sea and out of necessity the Sea Organization was born in 1967. St. Hill Manor was built in 1792 and was situated on 60 acres of landscaped gardens. The building itself has a rich history of prominent owners. I had heard so much about St. Hill Manor from L Ron himself by listening to many taped lectures of his during my training. Vicki had been to the Manor before, but I hadn't, so I was given a proper tour of the property. This brought back to life the many lectures and idiosyncratic comments made by L Ron during his time at the Manor.

He had lived there with his wife and children. The Scientology Organization had had its share of space in the Manor and the surrounding buildings. Here, students had gathered from around the world to attended advanced classes and learn Scientology technology from L Ron himself. Despite the fact L Ron had been asked to leave the country; the operation continued to be a huge financial success. I considered it an honor to add this piece of history to my travels.

Later on, we met with ex-Guardian's Office staff members who were now Office of Special Affairs members. These staff members were doing the exact same job they had been doing in the Guardian's Office. The only difference was the organization was given a new name to try to separate themselves from their own history of planning and executing illegal activities under Mary Sue Hubbard.

There was a staff member whom I had known for some years named Dick, and he brought us up to speed about the observation and tracking of the people we included in the RICO lawsuit that lived in the United Kingdom. We ended up spending a few days working out new strategies for the purpose of having all the evidence we needed to prosecute these people.

We finished our business in England and were considering making a trip to Spain. We were having problems with a fellow named John Caban, and we needed to prosecute him. We considered other places we would travel to as well. Vicki and I had talked to our executive staff members within RTC and were assured everything had been running fine without any problems. I had personal staff members that helped me get all of the work done. Overseeing the activities of Scientology International and the Watchdog Committee was a staff member named Jim Mooney from Edinburgh, Scotland. He was directly responsible for ensuring the success of Scientology International as was I. Another personal staff member named Hansuli Stahli was the overseer of the RTC Celeb Project and the RTC Tech Unit. Besides having a professional relationship these two staff they were my friends and I was very appreciative of their service and fine work, Vicki agreed was as well.

Well, as usual all good things must come to an end somehow, some way. Vicki received a phone call as we were preparing to leave St. Hill from David Miscavige. He told her we needed to get back to the States as soon as possible. A jury in Portland, Oregon had just awarded a $39 million-dollar judgment against Scientology. The judgment was awarded to a woman named Julie Christofferson Titchbourne.

15

THE PORTLAND CRUSADE

JULIE CHRISTOFFERSON TITCHBOURNE had been a Church member for nine months. The trial had gone on for 10 weeks, and a jury found that Scientology had defrauded her. Her attorney was quoted in the *New York Times* as saying the award, 39 million dollars, was adequate for the punishment that was intended. Julie alleged that church leaders in Scientology told her they could improve her weak eyesight, raise her IQ and teach her more about the mind than any psychologist or psychiatrist. Earl Cooley was quoted in the same article declaring this is a ridiculous decision. Earl went on to say the Constitution is in serious trouble in the state of Oregon, and we will appeal.

Vicki and I caught the next flight from London to Los Angeles. The flight was without incident and before we knew it, we were again in the board room at Author Services Inc.

To say the least, we were all stunned by the news, and we had a coming-together meeting to discuss what our potential involvement would be in this new disaster. David was beside himself and informed Vicki and me that this new threat even trumped pursuing people who were currently violating our trademarks. David said if we allowed this action, then there would be ten more behind it, and soon there would be no Scientology to worry about trademarks. The plan was to create a massive protest in the city of Portland, Oregon and overwhelm the town and its court of law. We were pulling out all the stops.

Thousands of people showed up for the protest, and that number grew daily. Vicki flew to Portland to help organize and execute the plans. I was told that I had to remain in Los Angeles and cover my duties just like before. I was reminded that I couldn't afford to be involved in any questionable activities because of my upcoming role as Expert Witness in the planned RICO case. I stayed at home while my wife and the rest of the staff from Golden Era Productions went to Portland Oregon.

Because of the good work we had invested in our celebrities, ensuring they were all more than content with Scientology services, many took off to Portland to lodge complaints, perform concerts and do all manner of public relations activities. I can't accurately describe the details of how things happened in Portland since I was not there, but I was occasionally given some details of what was happening by Vicki. Scientology staff members had arranged to get permits in Lownsdale Square Park, next to the Multnomah County Courthouse in Portland, for the purpose of holding rallies. Scientology's public relations department, had even convinced ministers of other faiths to join in our cause, as "their church might be next." Ministers from all over the United States were provided with their own mini-stage platforms to preach and pray about the injustice Scientology was suffering.

John Travolta flew in on his private jet and went to a press conference to extol the virtues of Scientology. Actors Karen Black, and Frank Stallone sang, and Scientology music celebs Chick Corea, Edgar Winter, and Nicky Hopkins jammed with lesser-known musicians. Scientology staff members from around the country were being bused in to Portland, and all Scientologists were being urged to head to Portland. Soon there were thousands upon thousands of people there, and we quickly took over the whole town.

True to his word, Earl Cooley drew up a motion for mistrial and turned it in to the court, and a date was set to hear the motion. After a while, all of the members from top management returned to Los Angeles or began to travel back and forth in order to get other duties done. We were assured by Earl Cooley that there would be a mistrial declared no matter how far up the court system he would have to take this. The motion was said to be heard July 16, 1985.

I guess all of those ministers who represented other religions and were praying Scientology would overcome the $39 million judgment had an influence on David. I say this because David did something he'd never done before that contradicted his expressed views about God. We all knew and believed that Scientology was a Godless religion. Minutes before the hearing was to start David had all of us in the board room at Author Services, and he asked us to join hands. He then said he wasn't sure if there was a God in heaven, but he prayed if there was a God in heaven would he please show mercy on Scientology and let us prevail with our motion for a mistrial. I couldn't believe I was seeing and hearing David lead a prayer, and he was serious about it, so we took it seriously even though L Ron said there is no God. L Ron's technology stated God was just an idea falsely put in humanoids' minds during a process known as an implant in Scientology terminology. In this instance, David Miscavige directly contravened L Ron and chose to call on the Lord anyway. Strange, but when the hearing was held the judge was more than ready to declare the mistrial. The judge in the case blamed the mistrial on Julie Kristofferson's attorney, in essence saying he poisoned the jury in his closing arguments by making damaging statements about the beliefs of Scientologists.

This was a huge victory for Scientology and to say the least we were all greatly relieved. Earl Cooley had delivered as promised and he was handsomely rewarded for a job well done. Others who had helped organize the rallies and performed at events were also acknowledged for their help and participation in achieving this victory. We celebrated for days, and the victory became the wind beneath our wings to pursue those who would insist on using Scientology technology without permission or authorization.

16

THE END OF THE INDEPENDENTS

OUR TEAM BEGAN TO ASSEMBLE and verify the physical evidence we had to prove the allegations that would be alleged in the RICO complaint. We needed Robin Scott to sign a document that would definitely establish a nexus between Robin Scott, Morag Bellmaine, Ron Lawley, Steve Bisbee, David Mayo, John Nelson and others regarding the transfer and sale of the stolen confidential materials. In exchange, I believe we planned to offer a deal to Robin to let him out of the suit with the additional promise that he would voluntarily agree to cease and desist delivering any form of Scientology services.

I also had another personal staff member in my office named Kurt Weiland, who was from Austria. Kurt and I spent maybe a couple of days in mission briefing going over the details of the Robin Scott arrest, the legal petitions that were on file in British courts, and the intelligence information we had gathered since the day of the theft.

Soon Kurt and I were on an airplane headed for the United Kingdom. Before leaving, we had gone out and bought new long leather coats because we were informed the weather was already cool in Scotland. We also had several business suits and other appropriate attire in order to achieve that slick and polished professional look which happened to be all the fashion at the time. Once we arrived at the Heathrow airport in London, we took the helicopter to Gatwick Airport where we rented a car. I did not offer to drive the car because the steering wheel is in the exact opposite place to where the steering wheels are on American cars. Kurt was already used to driving these types of automobiles since he was from Europe.

We traveled to Saint Hill Manor in East Grinstead, Sussex to meet with Office of Special Affairs staff who gave Kurt and me the documentation that were needed for Robin Scott to sign. After reading the documentation and attesting to the fact that we understood the documentation, we left Saint Hill and headed for Edinburgh, Scotland.

I believe that happened in October, and there was already snow and ice on the ground. We were headed for Candacraig House, a castle-like retreat in the Scottish Highlands where Robin Scott and his cohorts had been staying, and where they were using the Scientology technology which had been stolen from our Scientology organization in Copenhagen.

The drive up was beautiful. The road we drove on was bordered by a stream with trout swimming in it. As we approached Edinburgh, we noticed a small pub, and we decided to stop there and take an opportunity to organize our thoughts and plan for any eventuality we could foresee in the imaginable future with Robin Scott. After having a pint or two, Kurt and I drove to Candacraig House and knocked on the door using the heavy metal door knocker. It sounded like a sound effect from the Adams family TV show in America.

Soon the door opened, and Robin Scott emerged. We sternly announced who we were and why we were there. We instructed Robin that it was within his best interest to meet with us and discuss the terms of his surrender. Well, Robin was having none of it, and he asked us to leave. He also threatened if we didn't leave he would call the local constable. Those turned out to be the magic words because I in no way could be implicated in any type of illegal or questionable activity in relation to the defendant Robin Scott. We had no choice but to do as he requested and vacate the property. I'm pretty sure we weren't there for more than 10 minutes after driving all that time. To say the least, Kurt and I were pretty deflated by Robin refusing to negotiate with us, although you could hardly call what we were doing a negotiation.

As we were driving back to Saint Hill, I got into a slight argument about what had happened. As we were vigorously arguing, I noticed that there was a car headed straight for us. I shouted to Kurt that he was driving on the wrong side of the road, but it was too late. We had a slow head-on impact with a Mini Cooper. We were driving a midsize car, and as the accident happened I could see that a passenger in the front seat of the Mini Cooper crashed her head into the windshield of the car.

I turned to Kurt, and he said, "We are, we are on the wrong side of the road!" I was just stunned. If I had known this shit would happen, I would've taken my chances driving myself. Fortunate for us, no one in the Mini Cooper was seriously hurt, and, of all things, the people inside the car were Scientologists. They recognized us as being executive Scientologists from America and profusely apologized for the accident. I assured the driver that the accident was entirely the fault of Kurt and myself, and we would ensure they were given a rental car to replace their own car while it was being repaired. The woman who had bumped her head suggested that we catch a taxi and sit down for tea while we waited for each of our cars to be towed.

Kurt called the rental company and ordered two cars. The clerk said there would be no problem and dispatched a car to bring us back to the company to sign out another car. Soon we were headed on our way to Saint. Hill, where we knew we would have to make that dreaded call and report our failure to the team.

In usual Scientology fashion, we were threatened within an inch of our lives and told we had one more opportunity to sort this out before we were recalled and severely dealt with. The Office of Special Affairs Saint Hill staff had gotten hold of Robin Scott and renegotiated a deal for Kurt and me to go up and see him the next day, so we drove up once again to visit with Robin Scott.

It was another long ride from East Grinstead to Edinburgh, with all the accompanying magnificent scenery and landscape. We arrived at the Candacraig House and knocked on the door. This time when Robin Scott opened the door he actually greeted us and extended his hand. He apologized for his previous bad behavior and we in turn did the same. He invited us in to the manor house, which was a classic Scottish castle in every way. Just inside the doorway was Robin's lovely wife, Adrian. It had been arranged for us to spend the night, and we brought our luggage along as we entered the castle. Robin showed Kurt and me to our respective rooms and informed us that we were having a traditional Scottish meal of venison and pudding. Until that point, I had never really eaten deer meat but I decided to make a good effort to try.

My room in the castle had very tall ceiling probably over 12 feet and a bathtub large enough to fit two of me length wise. I refreshed myself by taking a nice hot bath in that swimming pool of a bathtub. As guests normally do, I became curious about what was in the linen closet, so I opened the door for a peek. Like everything else, the closet was enormous. I noticed at the other end of the closet was a narrow stairway that lead down to some other place. All of the notions I had read about or seen in pictures of castles flooded into my mind, and I truly felt like I was in a magical place.

After Kurt and I cleaned up and rested a bit, we joined Robin and Adrian downstairs. Adrian had prepared a meal which included venison, and it was delicious, I have never had better since. After our meal, we all sat down together to discuss the business at hand. I had documents that I needed Robin to sign so that we could effectively prosecute the others who had been involved in the theft of our confidential materials. We candidly discussed the theft incident, and I admitted to Robin that it had been a clever trick dressing up as Sea Organization executives, walking into our organization and walking out with our most guarded secrets. Robin kind of smiled, and he commented that while he may have seemed clever at the moment he was now losing everything including the castle we were in.

Robin convinced himself that since he wasn't going to be delivering any form of Scientology services he certainly had no need for a large castle. I think the Candacraig House was meant to replace the St. Hill Manor and was intended to be used to train European Independent Scientologists in Scientology technology.

Even though, it was obvious that Kurt and I would prevail with Robin this time, it was a bittersweet victory. Robin and his wife were such nice and cordial people that it just felt wrong to discipline them any further. That evening we shared a few drinks and laughed and then retired for the evening.

One might ask how I could sleep at night in a man's house that I was out to destroy. I look back on that now and conclude this was another manifestation of that thing where people do really stupid things for no known reason. We all acted like it was all pre-ordained, so stupid is as stupid does. I slept like a baby that night.

In the morning, Kurt and I got up early. Adrian prepared a nice breakfast for us and when we finished our meal we all stood looked into one another's eyes and said our goodbyes, which were heartfelt. I left the castle with a lump in my throat. Kurt and I made the drive back to Saint Hill without incident and reported our progress over the phone to Vicki. She was happy and excited that we had accomplished our goals. She stated that she knew it would not be easy, but that's why I was sent there to do the heavy lifting. Kurt and I made plans and traveled back to America.

Shortly after returning to America the RICO lawsuit was filed against the David Mayo Advanced Ability Center and the principals of that organization. It was during this time that I began my training as an Expert Witness with Earle Cooley.

It would take some years for me to process and digest my relationship with Earle Cooley and for me to respect him as a mentor, but that's Scientology for you — always driving from behind. Earl and I spent long hours together going over every aspect of the allegations from the lawsuit we had filed. I had been being prepared for this exact moment. I was chosen to represent Scientology in this case because I had none of the baggage that my peers from our team had. Specifically, I had not been involved in alleged criminal activity I also had no history or connection with the previous Guardian's Office and their criminal activities. For the most part, I was well-liked by staff and public alike. Of course, my training and dedication went a long way. As far as we were concerned, this case was going to be a total cakewalk. We were so prepared that we pushed for early court hearings so we could bring the madness to a conclusion.

Because of the intelligence people we had in place at David Mayo and other institutions similar to his Advanced Ability Center, we were the "Eye of Horus" in that we could see and know everything our enemies were engaged in against us. Now it was our turn to bring it home. We knew the day and the time John Nelson had planned to fly to Europe to meet with Ron Lawley to work out a deal to share the stolen Scientology materials. We had a signed statement from Robin Scott, which tied in everyone who had been involved in the theft of our materials. David Mayo had done a horrible job of re-creating the confidential materials that were stolen from our Advanced Organization in Denmark. For the most part he simply just changed the issue number and in some cases the title, but the content of the documents was essentially a mirror image of the Scientology materials which were legally owned by Religious Technology Center.

The lawsuit that we filed was brought in Federal Court, and we ended up with US District Judge Marianna R. Pfaelzer, who presided over our case. The hearings went on for a couple of days and finally my moment had arrived. I was brought to the witness stand by Earl Cooley, and he introduced me to the judge as a Board member of the Religious Technology Center and expert on Scientology confidential materials.

Earl extolled my extensive training to the judge, then we got down to the business of presenting and verifying the evidence we had. I had submitted a declaration to the court whereby I had done the comparison with the David Mayo rewritten version of Scientology confidential materials against the actual true version. Because this was a trade secret we took a short break because the judge herself wanted to compare the two sets of materials. For once we finally did something right and did not object to this we only asked the court to be discreet and not make the information a matter of public record, which she agreed to.

The End of the Independents

One of the attorneys representing Mayo was a fellow named Gary Bright. I don't quite remember who else he had, but attorneys for both sides went to the judge's chambers and sat with her while she reviewed the materials herself. I was surprised by this, actually feeling a little giddy being in the chambers of a powerful female Federal judge, She had a liquor bar, and offered us all drinks, which I accepted. I was nervous, and we all needed to take the edge off. This actually turned into a social event where we were smiling and being extremely civil towards one another.

Like people who believe in and study numerology, times and dates were also significant to us with our legal maneuvering, and we were already casting spells in our legal papers. After the break, the judge was ready to make her decision. She ruled in the Religious Technology Center's favor and issued an injunction against David Mayo's Advanced Ability Center and all those involved to immediately cease and desist using Scientology technology when they were not authorized. That day also happened to be David Mayo's birthday, 23 November 1985.

The Los Angeles times reported that Scientology had won a major court victory over its defectors. Our attorney, Joseph Yanny was quoted as saying "You've just seen history made. It's the first time you've ever seen a decision that religious scriptures constitute trade secrets."

The judge stated in her decision that a nexus had been very clearly established between the program David Mayo was offering and the one offered by the church of Scientology and the stolen materials by Robin Scott. She went on to say that the church material that was stolen is substantially identical in content to that being use at the Advanced Ability Center.

This was when David Mayo and his Advanced Ability Center's knew they were over and it was done. We had effectively and forcefully taken out the head of the Independent movement, and we knew we would shut them down wherever they were.

17

The King is Dead
1986

WE WERE ALL SO THRILLED by this new victory that we felt like we were truly the new Turks on the scene. We were tough, and we were not afraid to play tough when we needed. That's how champions roll. Of course, we went out and told the world, and celebrated for days.

We had recently reestablished contact with L Ron and reported that we had finally crushed David Mayo and his cohorts. We assured L Ron that this was only the beginning. We would chase David and those who supported him all the way to the Gates of Hell. We apologized for taking so long, but we reported that the job was now done. L Ron seemed pleased, but he wasn't as happy as we thought he should have been, and we would soon find out why.

We'd had very little communication from Pat and Annie Broeker in recent times, but they were back in touch now and what we were hearing was not good news. Annie Broeker informed Vicki that L Ron had

The Expert Witness

had a mini stroke and was not doing well. Someone needed to go where L Ron was to attempt to apply Scientology Technology to him to make him feel better. That person was Ray Mithoff, who, as Senior Case Supervisor International, was the current top Technical person in the Church of Scientology International.

A Ford Bronco was purchased by the Church of Scientology International and turned over to Ray to use. He was told by Pat Broeker where to go, which was a ranch located in Creston, California. I watched Ray gather a few things he wanted to take and stayed with him until he actually left the property. I asked him to stay in touch and let me know what was going on. Ray and I had developed a friendship over some years which began at the Flag Land Base in 1979. No one else, and I do mean no one else, was called by L Ron at that time to assist him.

For New Year's Eve, the team went out and spread the good news of defeating David Mayo and the others at our New Year's Event for 1986. When we presented the news of our recent legal victories, at least for me, the news rang hollow. Every one of us at the top felt the apprehension of not knowing if L Ron would be okay or not. I don't remember whether the event was held in Los Angeles or at the Flag Land Base. However, I do remember hastily returning to the Gold Base after the event. During this brief period of time, Ray reported back that L Ron was in rough shape, but he had now stabilized.

1985 came to an end with all of us holding our breath.

Right after the 1986 New Year's telecast event, Ray Mithoff briefly returned to the Gold Base and prepared a package of documents to take with him when he returned to assist L Ron. To my knowledge, these documents were Scientology technical bulletins concerning an end-of-life process. I had learned another Scientology technology referred to as "End of Cycle."

End of Cycle is a process used in Scientology to assist someone who is dying. I had personally been around or involved with Ray Mithoff when he was faced with trying to do something about a person that was in the process of dying. A couple of cases come to mind. There was a Scientology staff member named Diane Morrison, who had been ordered by Ray Mithoff to go through the End of Cycle process. This poor lady had cancer and was not allowed to have standard chemo treatment. She was in constant pain without relief of pain medications. According to L Ron's writings, pharmaceutical drugs had the potential of preventing Scientology technology processes from working effectively with individuals who may have used pharmaceutical drugs. To my knowledge, this concept has no basis in fact or reality. The other person was a personal staff member of Ray Mithoff's office. His name was Ted Cormier. Ted also had cancer and had been told by medical professionals that he had a limited amount of time to live.

Ray was somber as he prepared to head back to the ranch in Creston, California. Again I sat with him and talked until the moment he left. I felt an obligation to comfort him as best I could. Ray told me he was not allowed to discuss the details of what he and L Ron were doing, but he told me that he felt privileged to be there to assist L Ron through this difficult process. He did tell me that L Ron's condition had temporarily improved, and this is why Ray was able to leave temporarily to get some of the things he needed to do what had to be done.

He mentioned that while he was doing Scientology processes on L Ron that he was not verbally responsive. Ray emphatically informed me there was absolutely no one else involved with what he and L Ron were doing. He said no one was allowed to come inside the Bluebird RV motor home where L Ron lay dying but him. He talked to me about how L Ron looked and what his general disposition was. I walked Ray to the Ford Bronco and watched him drive off. Then I went upstairs and talked to Vicki about the things Ray and I had spoken about.

Vicki had been in communication with Annie Broeker, and she expressed to me how deeply all of this was affecting Annie. She was in grief most of the time and seemed pretty helpless. Pat Broeker on the other hand seemed nonexistent. His role, and what he had been doing wasn't yet clear to any of us.

I don't remember why, but I traveled from the Gold Base to Author Services in Los Angeles to meet with David Miscavige. I immediately expressed my concern and anxiety about what was happening with L Ron. Dave said he understood, but he didn't have any more information than I did. He asked me what I had heard from Annie Broeker. He told me he was not in the loop; he had not personally spoken to L Ron, and L Ron had not called for him. The only person outside of Pat and Annie, who are in direct communication with L Ron from our group, was Ray Mithoff. David Miscavige was as bewildered as the rest of us.

Rumors had already spread around the Gold Base that L Ron was sick and possibly near death. This was very upsetting to some staff, and some had to be brought in and counseled. Even though we were making strides towards accomplishing our goal of rebuilding the Church of Scientology, and we had reason to celebrate, the whole base seemed eerily quiet. For some reason no one was raising their voices, for some reason we were whispering to one another, for some reason loud noises became too much to bear.

I'm pretty sure everyone was saying their prayers Scientology-style. Scientologist do a form of praying that is absent from a God. This is referred to as *postulating* or making a postulate. In the Scientology world, *postulate* means visualizing something you want and sending that message out to the universe for reply. There was a lot of that going on by staff at the Gold Base.

For the first two weeks of January 1986, we carried on with our activities just like we had before, except somehow, we had assumed the identity of monks in mourning for our leader.

At that time, L Ron, along with David Miscavige, Norman Starkey and possibly Lyman Spurlock were all being investigated by the IRS Criminal Investigation Division, and they seemed ready to pounce.

On 17 January 1986, L Ron suffered a debilitating stroke. We thought he would die that day. Annie Broeker called Vicki and informed her of L Ron's condition. She was in tears, and this caused Vicki also to weep. Pat Broeker was now fully on the scene and active. He called David Miscavige and told him it was now time to verify and finalize L Ron's will if we still had time. Earl Cooley was summoned and asked to go to the Creston Ranch where L Ron was.

At no time was I summoned to be at L Ron's side at his death. At no time was David Miscavige or the executor of L Ron's estate Norman Starkey summoned to be with L Ron at his death bed. The only people who were in attendance at L Ron's deathbed were Ray Mithoff, Earl Cooley, and Dr. Gene Denk. Pat and Annie Broeker were close by but not directly present. For most of the time after Earl Cooley arrived to help execute L Ron's final will and testament, Vicki was on the phone with Annie Broeker getting the play-by-play.

Within two or three days after L Ron suffered the stroke, we were told that he was in the process of dying and was in the process of willfully shutting down his body. Ray Mithoff was with him doing the End of Cycle process on him. Vicki was informed hourly as to what was happening with L Ron and if he was still alive by Annie Broeker. However, Annie herself was not in the presence of L Ron when this was happening. As incredulous as it seemed Vicki was being informed on an hourly basis whether or not L Ron had died or not.

Finally, on 24 January 1986 L Ron was gone from this world. Upon L Ron's death, David Miscavige was then summoned to the Creston Ranch to meet with Pat and Annie Broeker. Upon his return, David immediately went to Author Services in Los Angeles and called a meeting of the team.

Like so many times before, we sat in the conference room at Author Services, however, this time the lighting was intentionally kept darker than usual. The team was Vicki, Mark Yager, Guillaume Lesevre, Norman Starkey, Lyman Spurlock and myself. We had all been instructed just to sit at the table and wait for David to come. David arrived under the cloak of semi-darkness, and he told us the date and time that L Ron had moved on from this world. At the end of his announcement he gradually raised the lights, and as he did he said he did not expect any big show of grief from anyone because that would mean we did not believe in L Ron's technology concerning the immortality of the human spirit.

Vicki quickly dried her eyes, and everyone else seemed fine with it. For me, it was a relief because we knew that what had happened with L Ron worked out for the best for Scientology as a whole. We had known years earlier that he was incapable of managing Scientology in the way he used to, and we all were relieved to know that we were now truly the new leaders.

We began to plan how we would announce to the world that L Ron had passed. We decided to do international events in the major countries of the world where Scientology had a strong presence. David informed us that he and Pat Broeker would announce L Ron's passing the following Monday at the Palladium theater on Sunset Boulevard in Los Angeles. Mark Yager and I were scheduled to fly to Milano Italy to announce L Ron's passing. Guillaume Lesevre and his aides flew to Paris France and held a similar event to announce L Ron's passing. Our speeches were prepared and written by our speechwriters, and those that had to leave packed up and headed for the airport. We made a tentative plan to meet up again and privately memorialize L Ron's passing at a private home in Los Angeles, formerly owned by famous musician and singer Liberace.

Marc and I finished our work in Italy and returned to the United States to join the party being held at the Liberace mansion in Hollywood. Prior to going to the mansion, we stopped by Author Services to meet David to discuss the public reaction to our message about L Ron. At some point, David pulled me aside and said he needed to speak to me privately. What he then told me put me on the edge for the rest of the evening.

He was not very clear and wasn't able to express himself properly, but he told me something was wrong with Pat Broeker, and he had made an ass of himself at the Palladium. I asked him for details and David told me Pat Broeker had gotten up and started talking about implants and incidents which supposedly happened many millions of years ago, and he was acting like L Ron. David's point was Pat Broeker didn't have the authority or the license to portray himself in that manner to the public. The only person that had ever done that was L Ron himself. David told me he wasn't sure what to do about all of this, but he told me to stay close so that I could help figure this out.

Within a week of L Ron's passing, Vicki and I were summoned to the ranch in Creston, California near San Luis Obispo. For some reason, we drove up in the evening, and it was late evening when we arrived. It was pitch black, there was no moon, and the only light came from the stars above and, of course, the car headlights.

I got out to open the first gate to let the car through and when I got back to the car it seemed like there was a sea of green eyes staring back at me through a misty fog. There were deer everywhere standing in crowds, eating the grass. They weren't spooked or alarmed by our presence, and we cautiously proceeded up the road towards the house.

We arrived at the house and went inside the main cabin, where there was a fireplace burning, and liquor bottles were everywhere. Over in the corner with blood red eyes sat Annie Broeker. When she saw Vicki, she got up and gave her a hug and did the same with me. She commented that she knew she wasn't supposed to cry, but she couldn't help herself and she started crying again.

Soon I left the room so that Vicki and Annie could have some privacy, and I was joined by my old friend Mike, the guy who recruited me for the Gold Base. He walked me over to the bar and asked if I would care for a drink, I said sure, and I think we may have had a beer together. At some point, we walked outside, and Mike began to give me a tour of the property. I had mentioned to him we had seen a sea of deer on our way to the house. He told me that was a common sight. The deer used the property as a sanctuary to escape hunters. Hunting was not allowed on the property, and the deer were allowed to graze freely on the land. We sat on the front porch and talked late into the night. In the end, he took me to the room where I would sleep for the night. He said he would come and get me in the morning.

Morning came bright and early, and someone had gotten up and prepared a nice bacon and egg breakfast with toast. Vicki looked refreshed, and she was with her husband Rick who had also been summoned to provide a security plan for the ranch. True to his word Mike was there very early, and he told me he was taking me on the rounds to feed all the animals. We hopped on a small four-wheel utility vehicle, loaded up with maple oats, and headed up a small hill outlined by a white picket fence.

That little four-wheel vehicle struggled to get up that hill, carrying both Mike and I and the maple oats we had in tow. When we got to the top of that small hill, I saw there were five or six buffalo grazing. Mike had stopped the vehicle by a trough, and we began to empty the bags of maple oats into the troughs. While we were busy filling the troughs, I noticed we were circled by these giant buffalo with eyes the size of a Coke bottle. I could literally feel the animals breathing on my skin, and this was not my idea of comfortable. Mike told me not to make any sudden moves if I wanted to live, and we slowly backed away from the trough. The animals began to eat from the trough as we gathered our empty feed bags and headed back down the hill.

We went and gathered another feed bag of grain with molasses added and drove around until Mike spotted this huge bull with four-foot horns on either side of its head. I believe Mike told me the name of this bull was Bubba, and the feed was for him. Mike went around to the back of the utility vehicle and grabbed a 50-pound bag of grain with molasses, cut it open with his handy utility knife right there on the road, and left it for Bubba to eat at his leisure by himself. Mike told me how Bubba was used to having special treatment around there, and that's the way things were done.

The King is Dead 1986

We then went to a small man-made lake near the horse stables and got into a small boat. Mike started up the small engine and we began taking a nice slow boat tour of the lake. Occasionally our small boat would be attacked by a large black swan who was very territorial, and we were not invited. That swan began to hiss and peck at us. Mike and I made a day of just enjoying ourselves on the property.

Later, Mike invited me to the common room of the cabin. There was a large TV on, but no one was really watching it. I had asked why the TV was on, and I was told that Pat Broeker had been watching TV, and he wanted to record any news stories concerning L Ron's passing. I took a moment to watch the television and wait for them to mention the passing of L Ron. Pat had waited in vain. When the news did come on they talked about the Challenger blowing up. There was a blurb that briefly mentioned L Ron was dead as well. At that, we turned the television off and carried on with our activities which were primarily drinking large amounts of alcohol.

Vicki and I ended up staying for some days on the ranch. L Ron had some fine horses in fresh horse stables that had recently been built on the property. There was even a mock Grand Derby Racetrack on the property complete with bleachers and horse racing paraphernalia. Vicki, Rick and I saddled up three of the horses and rode them around for the afternoon checking out the length and breadth of the property and surrounding areas.

I ended up with a rather large horse and, of course, his name was Prince. Prince was a beautiful chestnut brown horse with a white star on his chest, long black and white legs and white underneath. Prince had a very calm demeanor, and he was easy to ride. I rode him until I was good and sore. At the end of the day, I learned how to take the saddle off, brush, water and feed the horse. I remember talking to that horse quite a bit, but I can't recall any specific conversation I may have had with it. During my time at the property, I remember seeing David come and go with Pat Broker. He seemed to be in a better mood and when it was opportune, I asked him if everything was okay with Pat. Dave replied things seemed okay for now, but we should stay alert.

I think we had stayed at the ranch for one more day before we headed back to Los Angeles. Vicki and Annie decided to bring other staff members to the ranch to help care for the animals, and we discussed a possible use for the ranch. I was informed of a second ranch named Newberry that was nearby, and I was told that would probably be sold.

When we got back to the Gold Base, I immediately sought out Ray Mithoff. I wanted to know the details of what happened when he was with L Ron, and I wasn't taking no for an answer. When Ray saw me he laughed because he knew why I was there. He was prepared to tell me some details. I want to say Ray was prepared to tell me the story not because he was afraid of me or worried about anything I would do or say. Both Ray and I were the top of the technical ladder in the entire Scientology Empire. Over the course of years, Ray and I had worked together and had become friends. When he spoke to me about his experience with L Ron's death, he spoke to me as a friend and he was eager to tell me.

Ray did not tell me anything about the details of doing End of Cycle with L Ron because that was not necessary – it was just a process. He told me that Ron's body was prepared for death, and I had no idea what that meant. He then said Ron chose to be alone when he died, and everyone was asked to leave his presence. Ray said he was allowed to go occasionally inside of the Blue Bird RV where L Ron was to determine if he was dead yet. At the time, this seemed to corroborate the information I had received on the night of his death when Vicki was asking or being told almost on an hourly basis whether or not L Ron was dead.

Ray told me he was relieved when L Ron was finally dead, and Dr. Gene Denk had come in to verify that he was dead. Ray then said it was time to dispose properly of the body. Ray jokingly mentioned that L Ron was a large fella, and it took a few of them to put his big ass in the back of that Ford Bronco. Ray said he and Gene Denk, along with Dan, put L Ron in the back and began to drive the back roads to find a coroner that would properly dispose of L Ron's body.

Ray laughed and said L Ron was bouncing around so much in the back as a result of going over bumpy and uneven roads that he was concerned about bruising and would possibly be jailed for abusing dead L Ron. He mentioned a Hollywood movie called *Weekend at Bernie's* to demonstrate how they were handling L Ron's dead body. This was hilarious to Ray, and I nervously laughed with him as he told the story.

Ray explained L Ron was gone, and it was just a meat body, a big fat old heavy meat body that was a pain in the ass to deal with. All I could do is nervously laugh at what he was saying. Ray described having problems trying to get the coroner to cremate L Ron's body without getting an autopsy first, so he had to drive around with the dead body to find a coroner that was more cooperative.

Earl Cooley was brought out to negotiate with the coroner, and a partial autopsy was allowed to L Ron's body for the purpose of determining that the cause of death was from natural causes as opposed to homicide. Ray said the body was finally cremated, and the ashes were given to Norman and Dave, who said they held a private ceremony and dumped the ashes into the sea. No one from L Ron's family were told about this nor were they present when the ashes were disposed of.

18

WTF L Ron?

IN THE YEARS SINCE L. Ron's death, I've had the opportunity to think about the events that surrounded his demise. And of course, after leaving Scientology, I've had access to a lot of information that is withheld from Scientologists. Here are some of my thoughts about his death, as seen through a very wide rear-view mirror.

As written earlier, in 1983, L Ron's attorney said to me to my face that L Ron could not and should not be made to face the public for fear of losing the Scientology Empire to his son L Ron Junior. At the time I really did not understand what that meant because I was still a member and my mind was still sick from drinking the Kool Aid. The truth is, L Ron Hubbard Junior was 100% correct in his assessment and fear of what was happening to his father under Pat Broeker and David Miscavige.

As I wrote this story, a question began to form in my mind that is still unanswered. My question is how long was it known and by who, that L Ron was mentally disabled and not able to care for himself?

After L Ron was dead, Pat and Annie Broeker came together to run a deception on David Miscavige and the rest of Scientology International management executives. Pat and Annie pretended to be an intact married couple when L Ron died but this was a lie. Both Pat and Annie had other, non-Scientologist lovers they were seeing before L Ron died.

Annie later admitted she and Pat made up the story about being given the rank of Loyal Officer (Based on a character from L Ron's OT 3 nonsense). Annie admitted L Ron told Pat Broeker he didn't want him around the ranch in Creston until he figured out how to get an All Clear for him, so he could live at the Gold Base. Annie said this had gone on for nearly a year where Pat was not allowed to come around the Ranch.

This was at the same time that L Ron asked me to give David Miscavige the security check and he never heard back. I suspect L Ron asked Pat for, but never received, the auditing session report from me about David Miscavige. L Ron knew Pat was covering something up about the investigation of David that he had ordered me to do.

So, Pat Broeker was not around the Gold Base *or* at the ranch in Creston with L Ron for almost all of 1985. L Ron had visited the Gold Base several times in 1984 and he was very anxious to move into his new home that was being prepared for him. L Ron had personally picked out or approved every aspect of the home he planned for himself. He also made sure his granddaughter Roanne Horwich, would also live at the Gold Base.

That there was no All Clear vexed L Ron to no end. Finally, in frustration he disconnected from International Management for nearly all of 1985 in protest, as written about earlier. In retrospect I can honestly say David Miscavige, along with his best friend at the time Marc Yager, were never excited over the prospect of L Ron coming to the Gold Base. I say this because they both were tired of the cycle of replacing people. Both knew from prior experience they wouldn't last long under L Ron. More than likely L Ron would have found some crime to accuse them of and they would be gone just like the many who had come before them. L Ron never tolerated any form of competition and he was paranoid.

Pat Broeker had nearly a year to figure out what to do about the problem he was having with L Ron. When L Ron had the first stroke an opportunity presented itself for Pat.

My good friend Vaughn Young who worked as L Ron's personal Public Relations Representative at Author Services always suspected L Ron was killed. He wrote about the inconsistencies in the Coroner's report that were never challenged by any member of L Ron's family because the details of what happened were hidden from them.

The fact that L Ron had been given so many needle injections of the anti-psychotic medication Vistaril, as revealed in the autopsy report, bewildered Vaughn. L Ron was an avowed enemy of anything to do with psychiatry or psychology and this was no secret to anyone who is or has ever been a Scientologist.

This is what I suspect happened when L Ron got sick and ended up dead:

One clue I noticed right away when I arrived at the Ranch where L Ron died. I wouldn't fully understand the significance of what I saw until much later.

When I first arrived at the Creston ranch I noticed Pat Broeker was his usual drunk self, Annie was drinking heavily and there were liquor bottles all around. At the time the heavy drinking seemed like a one-day event as does happen at times of extreme grief. The problem was the heavy drinking happened every day that I was there, and I stayed for nearly a week. The staff drank heavily every day when the work day was done. The staff looked and acted like this is what they did all of the time. They were out there in the middle of nowhere. There was no other ranch or houses nearby, no local convenience stores down the street, no paved streets and no street lights. They were truly alone out there.

After Vicki and I left the Creston ranch, we sent dedicated quality staff to work at the facility. Within three months of them being there, David Miscavige told me most of the staff that had worked at the ranch in Creston were being reassigned or sent to the Rehabilitation Project Force. I remember asking Dave what happened to these staff. They were perfectly good, qualified people before they went to that ranch. Dave was somewhat puzzled by what had happened with these staff as well but he told me they had all gotten into drinking alcohol everyday even while they were working. Up until then, the notion of drinking while working in the Sea Organization was unknown. Apparently male and female staff alike began to drink heavily after spending as little as two months at the ranch.

WTF L. RON?

Later, I would learn from reading L Ron's autopsy report that Dr. Denk, his physician, reported L Ron had a long-standing history of chronic pancreatitis. Chronic pancreatitis is inflammation of the pancreas that does not heal or improve. It gets worse over time and leads to permanent damage. The two most common causes of pancreatitis are gall stones and chronic heavy drinking.

The person who spent the most time with L Ron in the year of his death was a person named Steve Pfauth, known by his nickname, Sarge. He had worked as a sort of foreman and personal security for L Ron at the Creston Ranch. I never knew Sarge well and he was shy and quiet in mannerism if he didn't know you. Sarge had that same issue with alcohol as everyone else from that ranch. David Miscavige didn't have a very high opinion of Sarge and he had a habit of making him feel uncomfortable by publicly asserting his authority over him.

L Ron's medically documented history of chronic pancreatitis was more than likely due to heavy alcohol consumption. Both Pat and Annie Broeker were heavy drinkers. Sarge was a heavy drinker which means alcohol would have been readily available for L Ron to have his way with. According to Steve, L Ron was taken to a hospital due to a flare-up of his pancreatitis prior to his first stroke. After L Ron went to the hospital, his physician Dr. Gene Denk was called to attend to him after his release back to the Creston Ranch.

More than likely, L Ron drank alcohol on a daily basis as did his caretakers. It was known Pat Broeker was the biggest unspoken-about alcoholic of them all, probably L Ron included. It was an excruciating experience attempting have a rational conversation with Pat after he'd gotten good and wasted on alcohol. He would talk and stare with red drunk eyes, all the while pretending he's not drunk, that he could handle it, that he knew what he was doing. We all know the type, and there's a special name for it: asshole.

Pat was a chronic alcoholic, but he had nearly a whole year to plan and prepare his life for when L Ron was gone. What was his plan?s

In December of 1985, L Ron had his first stroke. There is no record or mention of anyone ever taking him to a hospital after this stroke.

A stroke is a medical condition that occurs when blood flow to the brain stops or is interrupted. The causes of a stroke are either a blood clot blocking the flow of blood to the brain or a vein rupturing in the brain. According to every medical reference I have read, when a person has a stroke it is important to get the person to a hospital for treatment as quickly as possible. Certain drugs that specifically dissolve blood clots are administered as quickly as possible to prevent brain damage. Anyone who is having a stroke should get immediate emergency care.

After L Ron had the first stroke, Pat Broeker showed up in Los Angeles, at ASI and met with David Miscavige. He had Dave get L Ron's lawyers to review all the wills L Ron had signed, to make sure everything was covered. I know these things because I was there at Author Services with Dave Miscavige, being briefed about the scene as it unfolded.

Dave mentioned at this time that he wanted to make sure L Ron's family members did not inherit L Ron's estate. He said they didn't deserve it. He specifically said "Can you imagine that little prick Arthur with all of that money?"

He went on to say *none* of the Hubbard family did anything to deserve L Ron's estate and he was going to make sure everything stayed within corporate Scientology control.

For reasons unknown, L Ron was not taken to a hospital after he had his first stroke. As mentioned before, Ray Mithoff was sent for to give L Ron auditing. While Ray was auditing, L Ron's personal physician, Dr. Denk, along with Pat Broeker, David Miscavige, and other top Scientology executives were in Las Vegas, gambling. I was invited to go and gamble that weekend, but I declined because I don't and never have enjoyed gambling. That same weekend, L Ron had a second stroke. Again, he was not taken to a hospital and his physician was not around to give him the urgent care he needed.

According to the Report on Post Mortem Examination #86-A-015 by the Sheriff-Coroner Karl E. Kirschner, M.D., L Ron's physician, Gene Denk, reported that L Ron had a medical condition known as *dysphasia* eight days before his death. Dysphasia is a condition that occurs as a result of the damage caused to the brain by a stroke. It manifests as a speech disorder in which there is impairment of the power of expression by speech, writing, or signs, or impairment of the power of comprehension of spoken or written language.

There were ten needle marks on L Ron's buttocks as a result of Vistaril injections. This made me wonder. When I've gone to the doctor's office for a shot all evidence of receiving a shot are gone within a matter of a few days at most. The report counts 10 needle marks. I wondered how someone could survive that amount of Vistaril and why would that drug be needed at all. According to information Dr. Denk gave the Coroner, L Ron was given the Vistaril injections to calm his anxiety from having a stroke, but why so much?

I have a theory. Like everyone else at the Creston Ranch, L Ron was a heavy drinker. I suspect after he had the first stroke he suffered damage to his brain and began to demonstrate symptoms of dysphasia and he was no longer able to communicate or think in a coherent manner. I don't think those around him understood him when he tried to communicate after his first stroke.

Here is an example of how dysphasia works: Stroke victim wants a cold glass of water. When he asks his caretaker for a glass of cold water, what comes out of the stroke victim's mouth is "Tell John to bring a hammer!" The same thing happens with a stroke victim's comprehension. Example: Stroke victim is asked by his caretaker if he is hungry or thirsty. What the stroke victim hears is "Please hand me a pencil."

Dr. Denk reported to the Coroner that L Ron suffered from dysphasia for eight days prior to death. I suspect L Ron was also suffering from alcohol withdrawal syndrome. Alcohol withdrawal syndrome is a potentially life-threatening condition that can occur in people who have been drinking heavily for weeks, months, or years and then either stop or significantly reduce their alcohol consumption.

Alcohol withdrawal symptoms can begin as early as two hours after the last drink, persist for weeks, and range from mild anxiety and shakiness to severe complications, such as seizures and delirium tremens (also called DTs).

It seems more probable that L Ron was on the Vistaril because in addition to his untreated stroke condition, he was also suffering from alcohol withdrawal.

I have to tell a short story to make my next point, and I promise to be brief.

I once dated a woman for a few years who suffered from anxiety attacks. When she felt overcome by the anxiety she took a low dose of a drug that was the generic form of Vistaril. When she took her medicine, it changed her. She would become lethargic and withdrawn. She became quiet and acted like nothing really mattered anymore. She would only take the medication when she really needed to. When her anxiety level would get too high, I would gently remind her it was time to hit the reset button. This became a joke we shared between us.

One day, I was feeling pretty stressed out and I decided to try one of my partner's anxiety medication. Within a half an hour I could feel my mind starting to clear out. I had a hard time moving my body. Mentally I felt like I was just a head nod away from being a drooling mess. Any lingering thoughts about whatever were gone. None of my thoughts would linger even when I wanted them to. I remember being out of it for nearly three days after taking that one pill.

When I think about L Ron getting ten fresh shots of Vistaril over a 3-4 day period it seems like he was intentionally kept quiet and still. I can't see how a person could live after having that much Vistaril in their system especially if L Ron hadn't taken or been on the drug before.

In my opinion, L Ron was in no state of mind to sign a will or make any decisions for himself. While L Ron was suffering from all of the above, how could he be lucid enough to sign a document on 20 January 1986 saying he didn't want an autopsy of his body upon his death. I suspect that was the last thing on L Ron's mind.

I've concluded there is no way L Ron knew what he was doing after he had the first stroke. He was kept heavily sedated and was unresponsive most of the time. I don't know what Pat and Annie Broeker were hiding about L Ron's death but I'm certain there was something to hide.

L Ron never once asked to see or talk to David Miscavige prior to his death. L Ron was in the process of getting rid of David Miscavige for being incompetent for not getting him an All Clear to come to the Gold Base.

The fact of the matter is, both Pat and Annie are guilty of elder abuse for the lack of care they gave to L Ron. I also wonder how long they both knew and hid from others the extent of L Ron's deteriorating mental state. L Ron's personal physician, the late Dr. Gene Denk, is also culpable in that L Ron had two strokes weeks apart and not once was he ever taken to a hospital for treatment or rehabilitation. If there is anyone reading this who has ever taken care of someone who is at the end of their life, then you know how difficult this can be. After L Ron had the first stroke it seems his care-takers and his doctor abandoned him when he needed them most.

WTF L. RON?

The memorial event for L Ron was a complete farce and was done for show. L Ron did not decide he had lived long enough and needed to move on. L Ron could have lived if he had gotten treatment after he'd had two strokes. L Ron didn't mind going to the hospital. He'd recently gone to a hospital for treatment of his chronic pancreatitis.

In my opinion, if L Ron were properly taken care of and allowed to live he would have eventually gotten rid of David Miscavige and Pat Broeker and they knew it. Pat was ready to let David Miscavige be sacrificed for not having the All Clear. Miscavige made sure he told me things in the interrogation that implicated Pat Broeker, in effect creating a catch twenty-two situation for Broeker. He had nearly a whole year to plan how he would deal with Miscavige and L Ron.

Miscavige had his own ambitions to take control of all Scientology. Miscavige connived his way to the top anyway he could, and he won that battle with Pat. One big advantage David Miscavige had over Pat Broeker was at that time he was not an alcoholic. Pat Broeker spent too much time in the mental delusion caused by chronic alcoholism and was no match for Miscavige. He eventually disappeared from the scene with bags of money to last a lifetime.

19

Mary Sue Hubbard is Taken Out

A NUMBER OF WEEKS AFTER L Ron Hubbard's death, I was present at a meeting where David Miscavige and a group of 12-17 other Scientology executives coerced Mary Sue Hubbard into relinquishing her legal rights to the Scientology writings of the recently deceased L Ron Hubbard. I participated in the meeting in my capacity as an executive and board member of RTC.

The day before this meeting, David Miscavige told me and a group of other senior Scientology executives that he wanted a group, to go over to Mary Sue Hubbard's home in Los Angeles in order to get her to sign an agreement relinquishing her rights to L Ron's estate. Miscavige said he wanted a group to do this because he wanted, in his words, a "show of force." He added that the group would stay at Mary Sue Hubbard's house until the agreement was signed.

The next day, the meeting did take place. The group that went to her house, including myself, went over with the intent of overwhelming Mary Sue and getting her to sign an agreement. That was something we had discussed and was the purpose and intention of going over there. The meeting lasted about three hours, from about 12:30 to 3:30 in the afternoon. I was personally present at this meeting along with a number of other Scientology officers and officials including David Miscavige, Norman Starkey, Lyman Spurlock, Marty Rathbun, Vicki Aznaran, Marc Yager, Ray Mithoff and Mark Ingber. The legal war machine was also present as well, in the person of Scientology lawyer, Earl Cooley.

At the end of the meeting, Mary Sue Hubbard was forced to sign an agreement in which she transferred her rights to L Ron Hubbard's works to various Scientology entities. Those works included copyrights, trademarks, bank accounts, and other proffered property. In exchange, Mary Sue Hubbard was compensated with a monetary amount I believe it was $100,000. Diana, Suzette, and Arthur Hubbard, the children of L Ron, also received a monetary amount. I believe those amounts to be $50,000 each. All of those amounts, individually and in total, were trivial in relation to the value of the L Ron Hubbard fortune, which I understood was then valued at between $200 and $400 million, possibly more. David Miscavige also personally informed me that he obtained similarly signed agreements from L Ron's other children, from prior to his marriage to Mary Sue.

Based on my personal observations at this meeting, Mary Sue Hubbard did not make the transaction voluntarily. At the time of the meeting, she appeared elderly, in her late 70s and seemed obviously sick. She was overdressed for the occasion in that she was wrapped in clothes in the middle of the summer. She remained seated throughout the whole meeting.

Based on my observations including her appearance, mannerism and some of the things she said, she did not seem altogether coherent. At times, she seemed to rant or speak in non-sequiturs. At the beginning of the meeting, Mary Sue Hubbard was introduced to everyone in the group and told their positions in Scientology.

When David Miscavige asked Mary Sue Hubbard to sign the agreement, things changed. Mary Sue Hubbard stated that she would not sign the agreement proposed by Miscavige because she did not agree with it. She told everyone that she did not trust Miscavige and felt he was destructive to Scientology. She made reference to Miscavige as a deceptive power-hungry person bent on taking over everything. She said she was not going to go along with it.

However, she was confronted by Miscavige and 12-17 others including myself. Most of us were large men who wore the paramilitary uniforms of the Sea Organization. David Miscavige screamed for her to sign the document. He screamed that she would sign the document. Miscavige told her everything that L Ron Hubbard did; he did for the church. We are the church, not you. Therefore, everything is staying right here with us. Miscavige told her that the persons who were there would stay in her house until she signed the agreement.

The combination of Miscavige screaming at her, sometimes very close to her face, and the rest of us browbeating her, was an intimidating and coercive environment, particularly for a frail and the elderly woman. There was an implicit threat that she and her family would be subject to various Scientology sanctions such as counseling, ethics, or interrogation if she did not comply with his demand to sign the document.

Mary Sue was told that the group would stay there no matter how long it took, and it would either be done the easy way or the hard way. During the entire proceeding, she was never left alone; she was always in the presence of Scientology members bent on getting her to sign the legal documents that would strip her of her legal interest in L Ron Hubbard's Scientology works.

Scientology lawyer Earl Cooley was at the meeting, but he did not advise Mary Sue Hubbard of her legal rights. At no time during the process was Mary Sue Hubbard advised of her legal rights, either community property rights or her inheritance rights. She had no personal counsel present at the meeting. The only directions given by the Scientology lawyer was that the agreement would make things better for Scientology, and Mary Sue Hubbard was told where to sign the documents.

I was informed by David Miscavige that although Mary Sue Hubbard and L Ron Hubbard had been separated and had not talked for some time, she was saddened by the death of her husband. Miscavige told me he would use this to his advantage. Also, before the meeting took place, Ray Mithoff told me, in the presence of David Miscavige, that he couldn't wait to tell Mary Sue Hubbard that L Ron had not asked about her before his death. Mithoff seemed anxious for Mary Sue Hubbard to ask him about this and appeared gleeful at the opportunity to tell her no.

Mary Sue Hubbard is Taken Out

At the end of the meeting, Mary Sue did, in fact, ask if L Ron had said anything about or had asked about her before he died. Ray Mithoff then told her that Hubbard had not even mentioned her name. At that point, after the hours of browbeating, the screaming by Miscavige, which was sometimes done very close to her face, the implicit threats, the emotional turmoil, and the general coerciveness of the situation, Mary Sue Hubbard became silent, bowed her head and proceeded to sign anything and everything Miscavige put in front of her. I saw her sign multiple documents, and she didn't pay any attention concerning what the documents said or what they were. She then said words to the effect, you got what you want, now leave.

I don't believe Mary Sue or her family knew that L Ron's estate was worth between 200 and 400 million. I base my opinion on the fact that neither Mary Sue nor any of L Ron's children were on the Board of Directors of any of the umbrella corporations of Scientology, such as Author Services, Inc., RTC, etc.

Under the coercive conditions she was put through, and based on the incomplete information she was given, Mary Sue Hubbard did not knowingly or voluntarily relinquish her claims to the L Ron Hubbard estate. I do not believe that Mary Sue Hubbard would've signed the agreement had she been advised of her own legal rights or had she been provided additional information, particularly regarding the value of the L Ron Hubbard Scientology fortune. This is also my conclusion based on what I witnessed at this meeting.

Mary Sue Hubbard felt very threatened by David Miscavige and the rest of us. Mary Sue was allowed to read the documents, but because of her actions and words that day, I do not believe she understood what she was reading. I regret that I had any part in this and am saddened. It would be years before I would recover my humanity and realize now how destructive and wrong my participation was.

20

POST L. RON, FRAUD ON PARADE

IN THE BEGINNING, I THINK David Miscavige really did try to get along with Pat Broker. As mentioned earlier, the team worked together and broke bread at meals together every day. Pat and Annie were trying to fit in with the routine that was life at the Gold Base.

Initially, David Miscavige and Pat Broeker found common ground, and decided to release new technology L Ron had worked on and prepared prior to his death. These materials were exclusively for Scientologists that had completed all of the earlier required levels in their quest to become superhuman. Pat Broeker had informed David Miscavige and the rest of us that L Ron had completed the research for and developed advanced upper-level techniques that would give us the ability to control Matter, Energy, Space and Time with our minds like super humans. We actually believed that L Ron had given us the keys to developing our minds to control via telepathy matter energy space and time. With our new superpowers, we would control the world.

Even with L Ron dead and gone, hopes were still high that we were in possession of superior technology that gave us an edge to become the rulers of the planet Earth and nearby star systems.

Pat Broeker had sole possession of the secret and precious technology L Ron had created and left for us that would eventually teach us all to fly. Pat decided he would parse out these great universal secrets one level at a time. L Ron had already twice before released technology that he claimed would give Scientologist superhsuman abilities and both times he was unsuccessful in achieving the intended results. As they say, the third time is the charm and L Ron was given another chance to prove himself. L Ron called his technology to create super humans OT (Operating Thetan) Levels and so far we had Levels one through seven.

None of these already-released levels consistently or inconsistently had anyone flying anywhere. Pat Broeker and David Miscavige agreed to release a new level, OT Level 8, and make it available to those who qualified and had dutifully completed the previous levels. Ray Mithoff put together scraps and notes of L Ron that were supposedly the research and development of this new and promising state of mind which L Ron would posthumously gift the citizens of planet Earth once they qualified and paid a hefty price.

The release of the new OT 8 was scheduled to happen on the Scientology cruise ship, the *Freewinds*. I declined the invitation to go to the *Freewinds* with David Miscavige and Ray Mithoff. David was being coy with me in that he wouldn't let me see the information that Ray had compiled and called new OT 8. Since I was still on OT 7, I didn't quite qualify. Of course, the hypocrisy is David was even less prepared than me because he was at a much lower level. That didn't seem to matter. David said it would be a relatively small event in that there were not very many people within Scientology who qualified for the service. He said we would put it out there, and Scientology organizations could begin to collect money for the service.

Dave and Ray took off for the Freewinds Ship to release New OT 8. After a few days they returned. Dave seemed pretty upset when he got back, and I could tell things did not go as planned. Within a few days, I caught up with Ray Mithoff and asked him about the OT 8 release. Ray said the event was a complete disaster, and the new OT 8 materials were not well received. This seemed odd. I had only known of one other OT Level that was generally not well received by Scientology staff and public and that level was OT 3.

L Ron said OT 3 was super-secret and dangerous. He warned, if a person was prematurely exposed to the information contained in OT 3 it would be possible for that person to catch pneumonia and die from sleep deprivation. This is the level that first introduced the subject of "body thetans." Body thetans are supposedly invisible to the human eye yet they have all of the characteristics and personality of a human being except they have nobody to carry on with. Since they don't have their own body, they tend to stick to others that do have a human body.

I know this is beyond the Valley of Bizarre for anyone with good sense to believe, nonetheless Scientologist have paid good money to find this out and they are obliged to believe and respect these concepts.

Ray Mithoff chose not to act like an idiot when I asked to see what was so objectionable about these new super-secret materials they had released to qualified public on the *Freewinds* cruise ship. I discovered that the version of OT 8 they had released had a special super-secret post-mortem message from L Ron concerning certain prophecies from the Book of Revelations in the Christian Bible.

The document that was compiled from notes and research documentation is, in fact, the only document I have ever seen within Scientology that accurately reflects L Ron's state of mind and his intention for Scientology. Without further ado I will read and translate the message from that document now.

The document identifies itself as a student briefing. L Ron begins by informing the reader as follows; by the time you read this I will no longer be occupying the body or have the identity you have known as L Ron Hubbard.

Next, L Ron gets down to business and tells them that the following story has been withheld for reasons which will soon be obvious, but he had to wait until more people were ensnared in the Scientology OT levels.

He goes on to disclose yet again that his identity, L Ron Hubbard was, in fact, the reincarnated Buddha whose actual name is Metteya. However, L Ron must've had some of the Indian god Shiva in him as well to achieve that multi-character effect. While he claimed to be Metteya, he also claims he was busy doing the Antichrist role as explained in the Christian Bible, book of Revelations.

L Ron declares that he assumed these multiple identities in order to fulfill a prophesy. As L Ron documented the wonders and glory of himself, he took a moment to gossip about Jesus Christ of all people. There's no way to make this up so I'll just paraphrase what L Ron had to say.

No doubt you are familiar with the Revelations section of the Bible, L. Ron continued, where various events are predicted, including a brief period of time in which the arch-enemy of Christ, referred to as the Antichrist, will reign, and his opinions will have sway. This antichrist represents the forces of Lucifer, the light bearer or light bringer. Lucifer being a mythical representation of the forces of enlightenment and the Galactic Confederacy. My mission could be said to fulfill the biblical promise represented by this brief Antichrist time.

L Ron goes on to tell us some personal details about Jesus Christ himself. L Ron said Jesus was not the saintly figure he has been made out to be. In addition to being a lover of young boys and men, he was given to uncontrollable bursts of temper and hatred that belied the general message of love, understanding and other typical Space Opera public relations.

I remember sitting in Ray's office reading over this document and wondering why he had allowed this to see the light of day. When this information was given to Scientologists that had been carefully prepared to receive the information, things did not go as expected. I can only go by what Ray told me in that one couple after having read the blasphemy of Jesus demanded a refund of their monies, and they left the Freewinds looking for an exorcist.

Ray reported that OT 8 was not very well received by the public at all, and it would need a total rework.

This is what L Ron left us to work with, and this is how it was being received.

21

POWER PLAY AT THE TOP

IN THE WEEKS THAT FOLLOWED the international Memorial events announcing the passing of L Ron, I watched as Pat and Annie Broeker struggled to find their place in Scientology management. But Pat was beginning to make all the wrong moves.

For one thing, he was a heavy drinker, and more often than not he could be seen drunk staggering around the Upper Villas where RTC offices were located.

Pat had discussions with Vicki, and he had informed her that he intended on updating certain of L Ron's Scientology technology. This is a huge no-no in the Scientology world. Scientology had its own specific technology to help people recover from illness or injury, and this type of technology is commonly referred to as *assist counseling* in Scientology. There is one practice in particular were a practitioner would use his index finger to touch the extremities of one's body such as fingertips and toes in an effort to shift the person's attention from an illness to relieve pain. This was one of the most common and simple forms of counseling practice in Scientology. For some reason, Pat Broeker thought it should be changed. I remember he called me on the telephone in a drunken state trying to explain to me why he needed to change this simple process. He went on and on, I guess the sound of his own voice gave him a thrill.

While he talked to me on the phone about this, I muted the phone and held a meeting with some of my key staff so that we could get our day started. Pat Broeker never noticed, he just talked on and on and on apparently all I was supposed to do was listen to him.

I called David Miscavige about something unrelated, but I did tell him about Pat Broeker's odd behavior. David mentioned that he had also heard Pat comment about things he wanted to be changed as far as Scientology technology and policy was concerned.

I noticed David and Pat were starting to get more catty with one another. Here is an example of how this would play out; Pat would take a stroll through International Management offices, and he would make suggestions or actually give orders to someone. In the Scientology world, this is a huge no-no. The proper way to carry out an executive inspection would also be to have Marc Yager present, who was the actual boss of the Watch Dog Committee members. So when Pat Broeker would do something like this, Marc Yager would be alerted, and would then instruct anyone that had received orders from Pat Broeker to not follow through with those orders until they specifically heard from him. Marc would then alert David Miscavige to the fact that Pat Broeker was not following Scientology policy which was upsetting the rank and file members of International Management.

This is how the split between Pat Broeker and David Miscavige actually began. Seemingly Pat Broeker was unable to follow simple Scientology policy and technology that we had all become so accustomed to. Pat and Annie Broeker still claimed the ranch in Creston, California, as their primary residence so were not present at the Gold Base all the time.

There seemed to be constant tension between Pat and David. Pat had always been the boss of David, and Pat's boss had been L Ron. Annie Broeker had always been acknowledged as the Inspector General of the Religious Technology Center. The other Inspector General within RTC were all *Deputy* Inspector Generals. Corporately, RTC was at the top of the conglomerate known as Scientology. Theoretically, this meant Annie Broeker was the new leader of Scientology. But Pat Broeker had no title or official position within any Scientology corporate structure.

Vicki Aznaran was the first person who brought to my attention there was a new title and position being created within the Sea Organization called Loyal Officer. The only reference to Loyal Officer I had ever read about came from the Scientology upper-level OT 3 course. Briefly, as outlined earlier, Xenu, an evil Galactic Overlord was bent on the enslavement of all humankind and at some point in the way distant past, he got busy hypnotizing and implanting false memories in spirits near and far. Eventually, Xenu was subdued and locked up by a group of an intergalactic police who called themselves the Loyal Officers. According to Scientology secret lore, humankind, still suffers from the debilitating effects of Xenu's depravity. According to L Ron, the only path to relief from the ill effects of Xenu's evil implants is to receive copious amounts of Scientology revelation and technology.

Anyway, according to the documentation solely in the possession of Pat and Annie Broeker, L Ron had awarded the title of Loyal Officers to Pat and Annie Broeker exclusively. Not to be outdone, L Ron also gave himself a promotion from Commodore to Admiral of the Sea Organization.

Vicki had carefully explained all of this to me after Annie Broeker had carefully explained it all to her. Pat Broeker also carefully explained this to David Miscavige. So in March 1986 a Sea Org issue titled "The Sea Org and the Future," was broadly distributed in Scientology world announcing Pat and Annie Broeker as being the new Sea Organization Loyal Officers and of course L Ron the Admiral.

For a short time, this seemed to calm all concern and life began to return to normal. We returned to having our meetings in Los Angeles at Author Services the board room. We continued executing our legal, intelligence and public relations strategies. We returned to doing our weekly reports which summarized all of our activities and we would forward them to Pat and Annie Broeker via David Miscavige. However, our newfound peace wouldn't last.

We soon learned neither Pat nor Annie were anything like what L Ron had been. It's hard to describe why even now. When L Ron was alive, our reports had to be very carefully compiled. Our reporting had to be complete with all questions anticipated and answered. In the past, after forwarding our reports to L Ron, we would all sit on pins and needles wondering how L Ron would receive the information and if there was life for us afterward. This was a very difficult way to live however we had done just that for some years now and were accustomed to that pace.

Neither Pat nor Annie had the capacity to generate the excitement or destruction L Ron had been able to, and we began to realize how we missed that. From my perspective, Pat and Annie were boring, lackluster people. They were not in possession of the fine tailored clothes that we the team were used to wearing. It didn't look like they were even going to try to be that way, so we dumbed down to wearing blue jeans. By comparison, no offense intended, but they dressed like migrant workers.

Soon Pat and Annie faded into the background and were hardly noticed. We, on the other hand were out defending our trademarks and copyrights. We were in the process of ending all legal cases.

The fact of the matter is, we were tired of fighting and had decided to focus our attention promoting the subject of Scientology itself to a new generation of Scientologists and new Scientology celebrities.

22

I Have to Choose

SADLY, IT WASN'T LONG before we again started to have even more political problems among ourselves.

Similar to many other American corporations, the executive leadership and management of Scientology became a boy's club. L Ron was the complete opposite, in that he maintained a healthy number of young, beautiful, underage, impressionable young females in his company. David Miscavige preferred and kept young and older men in his administration. The only two females that held power positions with him were Vicki Aznaran and Annie Broeker, and they did their best to stick together and support one another.

Vicki Aznaran was my boss, yet I found myself on the international stage at our televised events representing and speaking on behalf of the Religious Technology Center. David preferred Vicki to fade into the background as far as being the public face of the Religious Technology Center, and Vicki didn't care.

Vicki and I discussed this, because it was not something we were unaware of, and we were truly friends. No matter what, we would support one another. Vicki said she had no desire to stand on that stage and talk to these people because it made her very nervous, and she was just not comfortable with it. I assured Vicki that I would properly represent the Religious Technology Center to our adoring public, and we both had a good laugh about it.

I ended up doing many public events which Vicki could have done. At least for my part, I can honestly say I never felt the need to compete with Vicki about our leadership responsibilities. I secretly loved her, and that may have had something to do with my judgment. Our friendship transcended Scientology morals and dogma.

On the down-low, Vicki and I adored and served another lord and master, his name was Richard Prior! Richard's comedy had helped us to endure some of the most difficult times we would experience in Scientology, and that was our secret and strength.

Vicki began to come to me more and more to tell me about disagreements between Annie Broeker, Pat Broeker and David Miscavige. Vicki told me that our allegiance was to Annie because she is the person that L Ron had trusted with his life, not David. Pat had started to try and act like L Ron with the Scientology that we had created and fought so hard for. I felt conflicted about this. However, my bottom line was Pat was just an alcoholic, and there was no reasoning with the drunk. I wasn't quite sure what to think of Annie besides the fact I thought she was manipulating Vicki in a bad way.

I Have to Choose

Vicki and I began to have private meetings to discuss how we would move forward, given the situation at hand. Annie began to question the corporate structure and leadership of Scientology. I recalled at some point during the impending IRS criminal investigations Pat and Annie Broeker's names were removed from most if not all Scientology corporate documents. This was done to limit liability for L Ron because Pat and Annie were his personal staff. L Ron had learned through the experience of Mary Sue getting caught and convicted in a court of law that he could not afford to have persons he was intimately involved with also be involved with the corporate structure of Scientology, him included.

Long story short, Pat and Annie were not the directors or trustees of any of the primary umbrella corporations that are Scientology and thus had no legal standing whatsoever to challenge the status quo. The status quo was David Miscavige, Lyman Spurlock, Mark Yager, Vicki Aznaran, myself and a few others who were the legal and documented corporate representatives for the Scientology enterprise.

This came up because Pat Broeke wanted Vicki and me to hire separate lawyers to represent him and Annie so they could corporately take over Scientology. Pat felt like such a fool when he realized just how tenuous his position was, so he went to work acting in his own self-interest for his own future. This would eventually translate into a game of hiding L Ron's unreleased upper-level materials from David Miscavige. Pat and Annie soon discovered the only thing they had to show any connection to Scientology executive management was the document that appointed them as Loyal Officers in the Sea Organization.

The Broeker's created a schism within the Religious Technology Center itself and began to pit Religious Technology staff against staff members in the Church of Scientology International. It seems they were following a pattern that had been established by L Ron himself which was to destroy Scientology management by making Scientology management destroy itself.

David Miscavige began to invite me to Author Services in Los Angeles to try and get information about what Pat and Annie were up to. I told him what I knew and what I suspected. David asked me to stay in place and to refuse illegal orders from Pat and Annie Broeker.

I felt like I had been put in suspended animation. I told Vicki I felt like I was being torn in half. Dave wanted a solid commitment from me as to which side I would take, I told him I'd get back to him. Vicki wanted reassurance that I would follow through with Pat and Annie I told her I'd get back with her as well.

We were already getting into the holiday season, and we were in the midst of a bitter dispute. Dave was staying in LA and no longer came to the Gold Base as often as he used to. My relationship with Mark Yager and the rest of International Church Management had become strained.

Finally, at the end of the year, the team I had known and been a part of would get together for one final time, at the Flag Land Base, where we were putting on an event.

Dave and I had a very difficult discussion about Pat and Annie and their attempt to undermine his

I Have to Choose

authority. He let me know in no uncertain terms that he was giving me one more chance to join his team. This whole thing was so upsetting to me that I began to weep uncontrollably. Finally, David had to take me and walk me around for me to calm down. I had a speech to do that night. After a while, I was able to put on my game face and pretend everything was perfect. Somehow, we got through that event telecast, and we headed for home. I told David I would have an answer for him soon.

When I returned to the Base, I noticed Pat and Annie Broeker no longer had a presence there. As a matter of fact, it was eerily quiet, just as it would be before a tremendous storm. I told Vicki about the ultimatum I was facing with David Miscavige. Vicki told me she was waiting to hear back from Annie so that we would know exactly what we were supposed to do.

We waited for nearly a week, and there was no word. During this time, I took a hard look at my life because I knew things were about to change for me. I came to the decision that I had done the best I could in Scientology and it was as good a time as any to move along.

I remember thinking about the disaster that was OT 8 – incomprehensible nonsense. If OT 8 was any example of the unreleased secret levels L Ron had left behind for us to sell to Scientology staff and public then I needed to start running for my life, but I couldn't make myself move.

I felt like I was stuck in a slow-motion movie with the final scene approaching. I just felt like I had no will or control left, and I was waiting for my own death. I now had an idea of how the many who had fallen before me had felt, in that it all felt so predetermined. And now I was obligated to let the final scene play out.

And with inexorable promptitude, the final scene indeed played itself out.

23

Showdown

THE ATTACK CAME JUST BEFORE DAWN as I lay asleep in bed. There was a rather rough and abrupt knock on the door of my residence. I leaped up from my sleep to see who was at the door. A Gold Security Guard stood outside my door and informed me that my presence was immediately requested in the office of the chairman of the board, David Miscavige.

I quickly put on some clothes and shoes and walked the short distance from where I slept to where David's office was located. As I entered his office, I noticed maybe 12 to14 people fully dressed in Sea Org Class A uniforms. These are the uniforms that look just like the uniforms worn by people enlisted in the United States Navy. I entered the room, and I was instructed to take a seat in front of David Miscavige's desk. Oh yeah, they had gotten the drop on me real good, and I wasn't the only one. I noticed to the left of me sat Vicki Aznaran with tears in her eyes fumbling with a stack of papers.

Dave turned to Vicki and ordered her to sign a letter of resignation from her board and corporate positions within the church of Scientology International and the Religious Technology Center. Vicki complied, and did exactly as she was told without so much as a hiccup.

Then David turned his attention towards me, and something very strange happened. Dave began to yell very loudly at me as he told me I was being removed from my corporate and board positions. He ordered me to sign a fresh letter of resignation from my corporate and board positions as well.

Now a strange thing began to happen. For some reason I gradually began to lose my hearing. I looked at Dave, and I could see that he was obviously yelling very loudly, his body was trembling with either nervousness or rage, I couldn't tell which. He passed me the stack of papers and like Vicki, I signed them without a hiccup and passed them back to him. He took the paperwork and set it to the side, and he continued to yell at me and he told me I was going to the Rehabilitation Project Force along with Vicki right then and there.

For some reason, he ordered me to call him Sir as he slammed his fist down on the desk. I casually stood up, and as I did somehow the room began to change color, everything seemed to be turning red. Everything took on a red hue.

I turned and looked towards David and he screamed at me once again to call him Sir. I just looked directly at him and told him "Go fuck yourself" very matter-of-factly.

At that point, I was assaulted on either side by staff members Marty Rathbun and Greg Wilhere.

They were both similar to me in height and weight. I felt both of them touch my shoulders, and they each grabbed an arm. Instinctively, I remembered my martial arts training and the black belt I had been awarded after successfully competing in a tournament in LA's Chinatown.

This event had made the news and had been a big deal. While David and other staff were taking horseback riding lessons and playing basketball, I'd been learning how to whoop ass! The day I and a few other RTC staff members graduated our training, it was even printed in the *L. A. Times* newspaper, but it made no reference to Scientology or any of us specifically. We never represented ourselves as Scientologist while we were students of karate. The style of martial arts I had studied was Okinawa Goju Ryu.

Years later, Marty would describe to me how it felt when he and Greg touched me that day. There was a certain way I had learned to stand that made it seem like I was stuck to the ground like a tree. I was able to draw strength from the ground and become immobile to my two assailants. I assumed that stance and as Greg and Marty both grabbed me I let them grab me real good and when I flicked them off they both went flying to either side of the room. Marty later described it as some type of Warren Sapp move, and I just flicked them off like flies.

Vicki shrieked and asked me to stop. I slowly and deliberately turned my head and locked my gaze onto David Miscavige. David lifted his hands in the air and told the others in the room not to engage me. That turned out to be the best idea he'd have that morning because I was ready to break bones, any bones, anywhere, of anyone, and that room just kept getting redder and redder.

I calmly walked out of David Miscavige's office without further incident. I calmly headed back to my sleeping quarters. Once inside, I began to unpack my firearms. I had a Ruger mini 14 assault rifle with two banana clips fully loaded with .223 rounds. I also had a stainless steel .45 caliber handgun which I fully loaded and cocked with hollow-point rounds. I put my desert camo military style pants on so that I could carry extra ammunition. I calmly and carefully loaded my guns and myself with as many spare bullets I could carry.

When I got outside the door of my bedroom, I carefully checked to make sure the safeties were off, and the guns were fully ready to engage. I remember the sunlight from the new day was breaking.

I turned and headed towards David Miscavige's office with a gun in each hand. My eyes could see red dripping from everything. David, Norman, and a few others were standing outside of his office when I walked up. Now I had the drop on them.

As I approached I pointed my mini 14 assault rifle at David Miscavige, and I said "Who is Sir now, motherfucker?"

David was speechless, and he held his hands up as if he was about to be robbed. Norman Starkey on the other hand was a little braver, and he shouted to me "You traitor, you can't kill us all!" I turned my attention to Norman and addressed him, I said "Maybe not, motherfucker, but you will certainly be the first to die," and I pointed that 45 at him.

To this day, I don't think Norman cared, and I don't think he was ever totally afraid. For one thing, he was probably already drunk. Norman was a South African cowboy, and he was pretty tough. Dave on the other hand was standing there with his damn hands up and it looked funny. Vicki also began to beg for their lives although she never had anything to worry about from me.

The red mist that seemed to permeate the air began to fade. David pleaded for his life; he asked for a do-over. And he went into this routine. Paraphrased, he said "Jesse, first off, I just want to apologize. I want to apologize for everything that I did in the office. It was wrong." Then he reminded me that we had gone through so much together, and all of us had made huge sacrifices, but he had been forced to do what he was now doing. He asked me to, please put down my guns, and he warned the others not to say a word to me and to give me the respect I deserved.

At that point, it felt like pressure that had built up to far in the red zone was starting to release, and I lowered my guns. David said he would meet with me again very soon down on the clipper ship swimming pool a short distance from my bedroom, but for right now he asked that I go to my room and try to calm myself.

I went back to my room with tears melting down my face. As I entered the room, my wife was sitting straight up in the bed clutching the sheets. She asked me what happened. I told her nothing about how I had just now almost killed my team dead.

After some hours had passed, David and I met on the clipper ship in the middle of the desert. David explained to me that I was more than aware of the whys and wherefores of his actions. It didn't matter what he said because I'd gotten into the complete compliance mode.

In Scientology, there is a theory called "head on a pike." Head on a pike simply means putting the severed head of anyone who is a threat to the status quo, on a pike for all to see and act as a deterrent to anyone who would even think about threatening the status quo. The primary motive for such a drastic action within Scientology was crowd control. Let me be clear no one was beheaded, but we were forcefully removed in the eyes of those who were witnessing events.

In the end, Vicki and myself, along with several other RTC staff, agreed to submit to the Rehabilitation Project Force (Sea Org jail) and we were led away by security to Happy Valley, which we had jokingly called the Scientology Institution for the Criminally Insane.

24

TIME FOR LEAVING

THE FIRST COUPLE OF WEEKS in the Rehabilitation Project Force went by without notice, for me anyway. I was in a daze as I tried to mentally process the events as they occurred.

We began to hear rumors that David Miscavige had decided to cancel all of our Scientology training and counseling certificates. This was completely unacceptable to me and I wrote a note to him informing him of the fact that if I didn't hear within 24 hours the idea of cancelling our certificates was abandoned I would be speaking with journalists from the *LA Times* concerning criminal activities perpetrated by him and others that I was personally aware of. I wrote this in a dispatch to Miscavige and put it inside an auditing file that I knew was being hand-delivered to Ray Mithoff.

In my letter, I gave Miscavige a specific time to relent from the notion of canceling any Scientology certification that I learned during my tenure as a Scientologist. I gave him the Clint Eastwood alternative. I told him he had until high noon to cease and desist any activity that involved publicly berating me to staff at the Gold Base and to cease any notion of canceling any of my certifications.

This ended up being exactly like a scene out of Shawshank redemption. At 12 noon, no one complied with my demands that I could see. I had already planned my walk out with another staff member, "Spike" Bush, he was the best friend I had at the time. We decided we would cease whatever manual labor we were doing, walk out of the Scientology compound known as Happy Valley and head for the nearest town, Hemet, California. There was a staff member who was the security guard for us named Gary Morehead. I believe I told him that come 12 o'clock if I had not heard from Religious Technology Center Executives that I would be forced to take my own course of action, and I was sure David Miscavige would not like it.

Between 11am and noon, I remember constantly asking Gary what the time was. I also informed him of what was going to happen come 12 o'clock. Well, the clock struck 12, and I immediately dropped the shovel that was in my hand and turned to my friend Spike Bush and told him it was time to go. Spike dropped his shovel and said fuck it, together we headed for the gate. From above, I could hear Gary Morehead on his radio alerting security at the Gold Base that Spike and I were making a break for it.

Gary informed me that it would not be a good idea for me to make him come down there to deal with me. I let Gary know that if he tried to interfere with what I was doing I would kill him with my bare hands, and I seriously meant what I said. Gary got the

Time for Leaving

message and did not venture from his perch as he watched me and Spike walk off the property. Before we left, I stopped by the place where Vicki had been isolated from the rest of us because she was very ill with a fever. I had informed Vicki the night before that I would be doing this. Vicki was ill and physically unable to leave with me. I told her I would come back for her.

As we headed towards the main road, I became painfully aware that we were in the hot desert with nothing and no one around to help us. With each step we took, I could feel the moisture leaving my body, and I began to worry. For as far as I could see there was nothing but rocks and dry dirt with the occasional cactus here and there. The sun was hot and blinding as Spike and I tried to make it to the main road which was almost 10 miles away from where we were.

Out of nowhere a pickup truck appeared that was driven by Native American Indians. We were actually physically on their reservatrion, which was called the Soboba Indian Reservsatruion. The truck slowed, and they asked us if we needed a ride. We accepted their offer, and they wanted to know how we came to be walking in the heat of the day in the middle of the desert. We told them that we were being held by Scientology at the property known as Happy Valley. The Native Americans gasped when I mentioned this to them. One of them told me that it was known on the Reservation that Scientology took people to that property and killed them. This was something I didn't know about, and the Native Americans told us that they were taking us to their bingo facility so that we could call the police and report being held captive to try and save ourselves from the Scientologists.

Sadly, Spike and I were too brainwashed to heed their advice, and we asked them to, please just drop us off on the main road. From there we would be able to take care of ourselves. The Native Americans reluctantly acquiesced to our request and dropped us off on Highway 79. We still had several miles to go before we would reach the town of San Jacinto or the town of Hemet.

As we walked down Highway 79 towards San Jacinto, a pickup truck pulled up, with Ray Mithoff, possibly Marty Rathbun and other security personnel from the Gold Base. Ray tried to reason with me and begged me to get into their truck. He told me that he would take me to the best hotel Hemet had to offer, and Spike and I could just stay there until we could figure out or agree how to move forward. This sounded reasonable to me, and we were taken to the Best Western hotel. When we arrived, I told Ray to leave because I wanted to take a nap, and we would be in touch. They had no choice, so they did exactly as they were told.

As soon as they left, Spike and I walked to the nearest Enterprise car rental facility, and I rented a Chrysler Imperial. It was the largest, most gaudy American car on the lot. Spike got in, and I headed straight for Happy Valley. When I approached Happy Valley, the security gate was open, so I went right through. I drove to where Vicki was being held in isolation. I opened the door to where she was, and I said let's go.

Gary Morehead was inside with Vicki, advising her not to leave with me. He told her it would be best if she tried to work things out with David Miscavige and company. Vicki took that as her final clue and she stood up and said "Okay Jesse, let's go." She got into that Chrysler with me and Spike, and we headed for a Mexican restaurant that was nearby, which served Margarita Grandes on the Happy Hour menu.

After eating and drinking as much as we could, we got back into that Imperial and drove to the Gold Base security booth where we displayed the middle "fuck you" finger to security and anyone else that happened to be there. Then we drove to the hotel rooms that had been purchased by Ray Mithoff and took that nap we so desperately needed. This felt very liberating compared to the slave mentality of the RPF, and we were feeling giddy having our freedom and free will again.

While we slept, David Miscavige and the others had some quiet time to figure out what to do with us. David and others worked very hard to convince our spouses not to leave the Sea Organization and instead help him convince us to go to the RPF and do our "jail" time.

Vicki's husband Rick had been called down from the ranch at Creston to help David Miscavige convince his wife to stay on the RPF. Rick didn't do that, he agreed with Vicki that it was time to leave, and they left together.

Spike and I were unsuccessful in convincing our spouses to leave the Sea Org with us, and so a decision had to be made. I remember at the time reflecting on the many things I had given up in my life so that I could participate in Scientology. I had left my brothers and sisters and my dear father behind and hadn't even talked to them on the phone for years. To my father it was like I had died, and he didn't know me anymore. I thought about the love children I had fathered and never financially supported for the sake of Scientology. I came to the decision that I would not lose one more person out of my life for the sake of Scientology. I decided that I would wait for my wife to come to her senses so we could leave. Some years would pass before that would happen.

Spike and I succumbed to Miscavige's demands and went back to the Rehabilitation Project Force out at the Happy Valley compound, for the sake of our wives. I did make it extremely clear to all concerned that no one was to cancel any Scientology certification that I had earned. No one was to talk about me being a horrible person or refer to me as a suppressive otherwise I assured David Miscavige and whoever else would listen if they failed to honor these simple things I asked of them then they could find me somewhere talking to a journalist or FBI agent.

Spike and I ended up being twins on the RPF, which meant we were responsible for each other completing the RPF program and getting ourselves out of there. Part of the RPF program involves doing extensive auditing/counseling programs. It was at this time that I decided to stop brainwashing myself with Scientology technology. I also didn't want to brainwash anyone else using the Scientology technology so instead of auditing/counseling one another Spike, and I played backgammon instead. We would go in a room and put up a notification on the outside of the door that we were in session doing counseling. Instead, we played backgammon for hours upon hours. Sometimes we would just sleep and keep watch for one another. We learned to do anything but audit/counsel one another and I began to feel better. It felt like my humanity was coming back.

Spike and I made up the required reports in our auditing files to make it look like we were doing everything we were asked to do. The truth of the matter is we were doing none of that at all, and they were not able to detect what we were actually doing. Comparatively speaking we spent a very short amount of time on the Rehabilitation Project Force, maybe four months at best before we were eligible for graduation.

During my brief stay at Happy Valley, I ended up having to help save a young girl's life that had been driven insane by Scientology ethics technology and sleep deprivation. The young woman was of Latino descent, and she worked in the department that produced the E meters used in Scientology auditing. They had redesigned the E-meter, and there was this huge push to make as many of them as possible so that they could be sold at exorbitant prices to Scientology public and staff. For some reason, the unit this young woman worked in was running behind schedule, and they were not allowed to sleep until they meet their quotas. This turned out to be a very bad idea and after some days the young woman got on her hands and knees and started barking like a dog. She screamed that she was L Ron Hubbard as she soiled herself.

She was quickly taken to Happy Valley and locked away in a room. Just outside of the room where she was locked was a cactus garden. Some of the cacti were the tall kind, and the others were the flat pancake type with the long 2 inch spikes sticking out of them. The girl acted like she had superhuman strength in her deranged state. She was able to escape from a female who was supposed to be her guard. She escaped and immediately headed for the cactus gardens. With her hands, she grabbed and ripped up one of the large flat pancake type cactus, then she began to jump up and down on that cactus with her bare feet. She made no indication whatsoever that she was able to feel pain. It took at least four of us to subdue her and hold her legs as we pulled the spikes out of her feet and hands. This was a scene straight out of the exorcist where this poor girl had all the symptoms of being possessed. L Ron's physician Gene Denk was called out to treat the young woman.

She was given antibiotics and a sedative to help calm her down. This went on for weeks, and I ended up being the primary person that sat with her day in and day out as she tried to recover her mind. I ended up being the person that sat down on the phone with her to tell her parents who lived in New York that she was having a problem but was being taken care of. Somehow through whatever madness that was happening to this young lady she trusted me and followed my instruction. After weeks of this the young lady was eventually well enough to remember who she was, and she had recovered from her injuries with the cactus. I sat with her as she was more able to talk to her parents and remember who they were. As soon as possible the girl was prepared and sent home to her parents in New York. This was the first time I had had such an intimate experience with a person that had lost their mind as a result of Scientology technology and sleep deprivation.

One day while I was in the RPF I was asked to go to the Gold Base for special briefing.

I had not been around any of the people that I formally recognized as my team for some time. Now, they were all looking at me. I knew these bastards needed something, and I was curious to know what it was. For some reason, David Miscavige could not look me in the eye and constantly averted my gaze. Marty Rathbun was very nervous and constantly asked me if I needed anything or wanted something special. I just looked at them like they were idiots and waited. Finally, everyone left the room with the exception of Earl Cooley

He began to explain to me that I needed to save Scientology despite my current position in the Rehabilitation Project Force. I asked him just to come out and tell me what was going on. Earl told me that he was under investigation by the Federal Bureau of Investigation for judge tampering. Earle reminded me of an incident whereby Marty Rathbun and OSA staff member Lynn Farney had actually gone to a federal judge's private residence (judge Marianna Fauser) in an effort to get her to look at an emergency motion for injunctive relief against David Mayo's Advanced Ability Center. Earl told me the FBI demanded that I show up at their offices in Los Angeles the following day and submit to an interrogation by them.

I was well aware of what Earl was talking about because at the time it happened, Earl Cooley was horrified when he found out what Marty and Lynn Farney had attempted to do. It is highly improper for any party to a lawsuit to attempt to interact with a judge in that way. However, because Scientology has no respect for the law whatsoever, this was not a consideration or concern. Earl told me it was up to me if I wanted to save Scientology's ass. He told me if I did decide to save Scientology's ass he would show me how to do it.

Earl also explained that he understood if I didn't want to save Scientology. He said this was a natural feeling as far as he was concerned given how I was being treated by the people I was now being asked to keep out of jail. Earl told me he would personally have a word with Miscavige if I could find it in my heart to save Scientology's ass and his ass as well. I went ahead and did it, I lied for Scientology, and I saved Dave's and Marty's ass from being investigated and prosecuted for their criminal activity of judge tampering. I only did it because Earl asked me to. I had nothing but respect for Earl Cooley, and I did what I did for him.

Spike and I graduated from the RPF and could be part of Gold Base staff again. It was automatically assumed by the powers that be that I would continue my auditing/counseling/training career since I had done an excellent job with the girl that had been driven insane, but this was so not the case. Even though I had insisted I keep and maintain all of my Scientology certification credentials I never really practiced the subject again with the exception of pretending to do OT 7 just to complete that level. No one was able to detect for years the fact that I was no longer a practicing Scientologist.

L Ron had another policy that was closely followed within Scientology. Simply stated for a leader, it was wise to keep your friends close and your enemies closer. I believe for that reason for some years I was kept very close to David Miscavige and the team that I once belonged to. I had transferred to the music and film department within Golden Era Productions. I soon became the sound editor for Scientology films and videos. I also began to participate as a sound engineer in the international events that I was once a speaker for. So once again I got to travel all over Europe and the United States. During this time. I pretty much kept to myself, no new friends. I spent so much time thinking about my wasted life that I really looked forward to just being dead. I felt like I was such a disappointment to my family, and I had nowhere else to go but where I was.

I remember describing my mental state to my wife, Molly. I told her I felt like a cow out in the pasture chewing grass. Not only was I a cow, I was a smooth brain cow meaning there were no furrows on my brain which meant I had nothing in or on my mind. I felt like I was some type of mindless, low order animal creature. And that feeling was reinforced by daily life on the Gold Base.

I was so confused and depressed that I had forgotten to pray. I had forgotten to ask for help on a spiritual level because I'd convinced myself that my life wasn't worth continuing. I was not able to help anyone, not even myself. I had no friends besides my wife, and I kept to myself for a few years. Then one day, even though I had forgot to pray a miracle happened. My wife came to me and said she finally understood what I'd been trying to tell her about the Sea Org and Scientology, and she wanted to get the hell out of there. My attitude changed so fast; I went from 0 to 100 really quick.

Molly and I carefully planned our escape from the Gold Base and within two weeks we were gone. We escaped to St. Paul Minnesota and began to plan a new life. Well, that didn't last long because we were tracked down and coerced to return to the Gold Base. The sticking point was my wife's sister and father were still active members within Scientology. Molly was informed if she didn't come back and leave properly her father and sister would be forced to disconnect from her, and she would never speak to them again. We went back to leave properly, and it went on for months. Molly became pregnant again. Miscavige, Marty Rathbun, Ray Mithoff and anyone else who thought they could influence me or Molly tried to make us divorce each other. They tried to convince Molly to have another abortion.

This was a living nightmare, but there was a bright spot that I remember. Right around that time the Red Hot Chili Peppers came out with that song, 'Under the Bridge.' I would listen to it on a small alarm clock radio and weep. I marveled at how this group was able to sing about my life under the Scientology Bridge with the trash. I can't tell you how many times I walked out that gate headed for Hemet to find a phone so that I could make that call to the *LA Times*.

Finally, I was able to put more demand on Miscavige than he was able to put on me and he had to let us go. When we left, we had nothing, and we were offered nothing. In the end we both walked out of Scientology's doors forever. That's right we walked out with our heads up, no running.

We decided to go back to Minnesota at the beginning of winter. I owned no winter clothes at all. I did have a black satin jacket that I was given by my wife. I really liked this jacket which was a promotional item from a John Carpenter movie. The back of that black satin jacket had purple and gold letters that said "Prince of Darkness" across the back. I wore that jacket everywhere when I arrived in Minneapolis on the last day of October 1992.

25

Finding My Way Back to Humanity

At this point, I'm not going to write anymore about my ex-wife Molly. I will say that our marriage didn't survive outside of the Scientology structure. However, to this day we are still friends. Molly remarried and had a child of her own. Me, I spent a lot of time doing and thinking.

I preferred to be alone as I worked to sort out from my Scientology conditioning. Maybe that was because I felt like a lunatic. It was very difficult for me to integrate into any corporate job situation. I had no trouble quickly rising to the top of any organization or activity I involved myself in. I had a very difficult time with social skills and ended up making others feel uncomfortable or threatened by my presence.

I was socially flawed in my thinking because I hadn't watched television for nearly 20 years. I hadn't had much interaction with people who were not Scientologist for over fifteen years. For the past sixteen years I had only lived in the structure of the

Sea Organization on, the edge of society. I hardly knew or even cared who the President of the United States was or who the Governor was of the state I lived in. I didn't know or care about what was trending in popular culture.

I experienced a totally unexpected cultural shock when I went out and purchased my first television set, with my perfect credit rating. I thought I was about to have some fun watching TV. I remember plugging that TV in and connecting the antenna. I sat down and tuned the TV to the local news station and watched. After a few minutes, I could hardly tolerate how that TV was making me feel on my insides. It's hard for me to describe adequately how the TV was affecting my emotional and mental state of mind. I know it's silly now, but I felt like the TV was an evil brainwashing machine of the devil! It felt like if I watched it too long I ran the risk of being demonically possessed. I couldn't for life of me figure out why someone would willingly sit in front of a TV, it didn't make sense. I just assumed the problem was with me and I would eventually become desensitized to the things I didn't understand in this new world I found myself in. I just had to keep on living.

As I sat and watched the light images and listened to the sounds, I thought the world I now found myself in was an immoral and violent place to be. I was shocked at the acceptance of open displays of lewd and immoral sexual behavior that seemed to permeate every aspect of the culture. There were sexy clothes, sexy shoes, sexy perfume, sexy cars, sexy men and sexy women, and the flow mindlessly went on and on.

There was a different vibe in the music I was now hearing on the radio of my car compared to the Rock, R&B, Jazz and Soul music that I'd grown up with. There was this new music that was like no other music I was familiar with; it was called Rap music. There were these repeating, idiot simple beats that people were talking over the top of and this was the fashion for emerging new music. There was also another style of music called Hip-Hop which I knew nothing of and didn't care for because I was stuck in my own ways. I think I was only able to watch that TV for 20 minutes before I quickly turned it off. It would be some years before I'd be able to sit down and watch TV without thinking I was really dead and in hell.

I found the majority of television programming to be sexually explicit or sexually redundant for no reason. It was almost as if the society itself was going through the sexual frustration I had lived through as a teenager. It seemed like the new friends that I was hanging out with were successful and had careers but were somehow mentally juvenile with all of this sex silliness. It's hard to explain but it was difficult for me to fit in.

As my mind began to heal, I was able to "see the obvious" and tolerate the consequences. I was able to emancipate myself from the corporate world by learning to earn money selling art for several local art manufacturers. Some days, I would make so much money I would get tired of collecting it. After my divorce, I began to associate with women, some beautiful, some plain and some just butt-ugly. I was lonely for a woman after my divorce and the occasional partner helped temporarily ease my loneliness.

I felt like I could do anything if I put my mind to it. The problem was I didn't trust myself. I knew I needed time to process what happened to me in Scientology. I started my own business selling popular wildlife artwork.

I had begun to do something else that was also making me feel a little bit crazy, a carryover from Scientology. I had begun to study and practice magic again. I also began to cast spells occasionally. These were simple spells for beginners primarily used to attract the attention of angels or devils. These spells didn't require blood sacrifices or any type of self-mutilation.

Before becoming a Scientologist, I could be described as a New Age person interested in alternative ways of thinking and living. I had hoped to learn from and sought after people who identified themselves as Shamans, Transcended Beings, Watchers and Teachers of humanity.

Back in the 60's and 70's, it was considered to be New Age thinking even to consider these concepts amongst the general populace that I was exposed to. I was a child of the 70s. As a teenager in high school, I was radicalized in my thinking by Jimi Hendrix and the Beatles. I had also read all of the Carlos Castaneda books which were about a Native American Shaman's teachings. I had also been raised in the Catholic Church so concepts of life after death, good souls vs. bad souls, and in the beginning as organic to God as humans are.

I found myself reverting to the same issues I had grappled with prior to Scientology. I couldn't believe that I hadn't answered the great majority of the same life questions of who we are, what is the human race and why are we here. I was seriously confused about the whole God thing.

I withdrew from participation in the daily activities of life and focused my attention on making money. I began to sell framed art as a vendor at outdoor festivals being held all around the Midwest area of the United States. I created a perfect display board to showcase 28 titles of popular art pieces. I created panels with individual lighting that could be adjusted for persons interested in the best viewing experience to perceive the art I was selling. During this time, I rarely bothered to shave the hair from my face, but I was always clean.

In the beginning, back in 1976, I had been attracted to Scientology because my recruiter boasted that Scientology wasn't really a religion and was based on actual science and research. I was raised in the Catholic Church and had gone to Catholic school until I graduated elementary and middle school in Chicago. I was tired of religion and had begun to look beyond religion altogether for answers about spiritual matters. I was told the only reason Scientology identified as a religion was for tax purposes. In the last true message L Ron left for his faithful he wrote he'd been living this secret Antichrist life. Even though I'd decided to put religion behind me I was still unwittingly involved with religion through the deception of dead L Ron.

I decided I needed to read the Bible from beginning to end to see what I had missed or needed to know. I'd studied the Bible almost daily in my early Catholic life, but I had never read it cover to cover.

This is what customers would see me doing at my booth as I sold art in shopping mall around Minnesota. Looking back on it I'm amused by just how out of place I must have appeared to others. Just to give you an idea of where I was doing my sales; I covered shopping malls located in North Dakota, Minnesota, Lake Superior area in Wisconsin, and the Upper Peninsula of Michigan.

I always had good manners. I used to marvel at the glow I would see in the eyes of people that would purchase the art I had on display. As I began to interact with society my confidence grew. I began to hang out with groups of customers at the end of the day to share an evening meal.

Force of habit and routine can be a scourge or a blessing. Over the years, I kept going to the same places in the Midwest, and the people came to expect me. Through gentle interactions with people, I began to recover my humanity. I began to feel and experience the joy of life again. I made sure I took slow and deliberate baby steps to walk myself back into the world I now lived in.

Sometimes I wasn't able to bring enough art to satisfy everyone at the art shows I would attend but every piece of art I had was sold. I ended up becoming an employer and hired people to handle mail orders for me. Even though I felt like I was getting better I would act like a depressed person. Sometimes I would stop working for months and wait until I had spent all of the money I made before. Sometimes, I would even wait until I had to borrow money at bad interest rates before I would feel motivated to go out and make as much money as I was willing to collect.

Finding My Way Back to Humanity

Slowly but surely, I began to cheer up. I even began to like some of that crazy Rap and Hip-Hop music. About six years had passed since I finally disconnected from Scientology. The year was 1998.

I began to feel so much better that I began to reach out to old friends and people that I had known in Scientology. One of those people was Stacy Brooks.

26

Stacy Brooks and Bob Minton, Death of Lisa McPherson 1998

STACY BROOKS WAS THE FIRST PERSON I talked to from my past after I left Scientology in 1992. She remembered our friendship from our Scientology daze. She was the only person that I had talked to in six years who actually knew who I had been.

I first met Stacy at the Gold Base in late 1982. At that time, she was actually staff at Author Services Inc. in Los Angeles. ASI was an organization created by L Ron to collect author royalties from all Scientology Organizations. I'd pretty much just arrived at Gold, and my job was to correct and properly train Scientology International Management executives. I knew who Stacy was, but we were not close friends. I was a fast friend with her then-husband, Vaughn Young, but Stacy and I had never really crossed paths in any significant way.

David Miscavige brought Stacy to me in tears and he told me to find out what her "external influences" were. That meant he wanted to know who, outside of Scientology, was influencing Stacy. He believed Stacy was connected to someone outside who was antagonistic to Scientology. I was told to check her for FBI and any other government connections.

This was all the rage at the time, the latest "Tech" from L. Ron. Executives at the Gold Base were being questioned, removed and severely dealt with. Yep, for the first time in my Scientology career I had the privilege of experiencing how L Ron Hubbard discovered and implemented new "Tech" for Scientology. I became a pilot auditor for L Ron to test his new theory of how a person can be unwittingly duped without their knowledge.

All of this was based on a conspiracy theory L Ron had about Sirhan Sirhan and his role in the assassination of US presidential candidate Robert F. Kennedy. According to L Ron, Sirhan, had been influenced by the use of pain, drugs, hypnosis (PDH) and programmed to kill Mr. Kennedy. L Ron suspected the U.S. government was employing these same methods to get at him and destroy Scientology.

Dave explained to me that Stacy was on her way to the Rehabilitation Project Force that very night for being a traitor.

I asked Stacy to close the door and have a seat. She understood what we were about to do and willingly submitted. I asked her to pick up a pair of tin cans, which were connected to the E-meter. As we sat across from each other, I looked at Stacy, and we locked eyes. Looking into each other's eyes is part of the investigation procedure. She was trying very hard to control her sobbing and comply with the process.

As I stared into her eyes, what I saw was a fellow human being in agony and completely defeated. I also understood what it meant to be sent to the RPF as I'd spent nearly two years in there myself. This scene caused me a pain in what little heart I had left, and I just couldn't take her through the process. I told her to put the cans down, and we would just quietly talk. She made eye contact with me again when I said that to her and I detected a smile trying to get out of her face. She put down the cans and let out a muffled laugh and we just started talking.

As Stacy tried to explain her situation to me, I listened, seemingly attentively but in reality, I didn't hear much of what she said at all. In my mind, I'm trying to figure out how I can gracefully get myself out of this situation without throwing Stacy to the wolves.

As I mentioned, I hadn't really known Stacy before, but now I felt like suddenly she's my new best friend in the whole world, and I have to come up with a way to save her ass and mine too. Lucky for us, I had an ace in the hole and other cards that were not showing.

In Scientology world, when it comes to the auditing ritual, the person receiving the auditing must be fully rested and fed. Otherwise any result is suspect and thus unacceptable. As I thought of this, I explained to Stacy how we were going to handle this, and there would be no report of what happened in that room between us.

Stacy fully understood the risk I was taking for her, and she went along with the plan. When she had sufficiently calmed down, I walked her out of my room to David Miscavige and told him I could not perform the action he'd requested of me on Stacy because she was not properly fed and rested. For me to attempt, the action was outside of the rules and body of the procedure. Any person trained in the Scientology dogma knows this.

It was quite a thing to oppose an order from David Miscavige. Most people at the Gold Base would comply with whatever he asked them to do, policy and procedure be damned. David was not used to the word no, when it came to his giving anyone a direct order.

He looked at me like I was crazy for a moment. Then the light of reason came over him, and he thanked me for pointing out to him my reason for not complying with his demands. In retrospect, this was a defining moment for me because, in the eyes of everyone around, I was one of the few people that stood on the conviction of the training I'd received and graduated from. I just said no to him, and he accepted it.

That night Stacy did not go to the RPF; she ended up going some days later but not that night.

When we met again in 1998, both of us now out of Scientology, Stacy was excited. She remembered me as someone who had a good heart and tried to help her when she needed it. She wrote the *following at the time:*

> *I had known Jesse since 1976 in Scientology and was thrilled to see that he was reaching out to re-establish contact. He had been third in command of Scientology, under David Miscavige and Vicki Aznaran, from 1982 until he was busted, along with Vicki and many others (including Vaughn), by DM in 1987. Jesse had always been a kind-hearted person, even when he had every reason*

to advance his own position by becoming one of DM's vicious lieutenants. Jesse never crossed that threshold. He always remained my friend and someone that I and others could trust not to sell us out.

I also knew that Jesse would be David Miscavige's worst nightmare if he decided to come forward to expose what he knows about Scientology. He was not just in the inner circle; Jesse was in the innermost inner sanctum, privy to all of the illegalities, covert operations, destruction of enemies, and degradation of Sea Org staff – all order by Miscavige. He was also a direct witness to the rift between LRH, Pat Broeker and DM which began in 1981 and increased as LRH and Broeker realized with growing alarm that DM was wresting control of Scientology away from them. I was electrified at the possibility that Jesse and I might re-connect. The ramifications of the battle being waged to reform Scientology were staggering.

At the time we reconnected, Stacy was very much involved in the campaign to expose and reform Scientology. She had spoken out against Scientology on CBS 60 Minutes, given interviews, testified in court, and even picketed Scientology orgs and events. She was eager for me to meet a guy named Bob Minton.

Bob lived in Boston, and had never been a Scientologist, but he had become intrigued by the information he'd read on the Internet concerning Scientology. He learned that Scientology had a reputation for having a formidable ability to systematically destroy or eradicate any dissent from past or current adherents. The methods they used, and the lengths they would go to destroy "enemies" lack any concept of mercy or forgiveness.

That this could even be tolerated in America vexed Bob no end, and he vowed to fight Scientology with the great financial resources he'd accumulated as an investment banker. Bob's money didn't fold, and his pockets were hundreds of millions of dollars deep. Bob was in no way shy about how he felt about Scientology's bully behavior.

Bob was particularly incensed by the circumstances of Lisa McPherson's death at the hands of Scientology, and the way they had covered it up. This story has been told in detail elsewhere, but here are the bare bones: Lisa was a Scientologist who had been receiving Scientology auditing at Flag, Scientology's technical center in Clearwater. After a minor traffic accident, she had a psychotic break, throwing off her clothes and walking naked down the street. She was rushed to the hospital, but a group of Scientologists arrived and spirited her back to the Fort Harrison Hotel, There, she was kept in isolation for seventeen days, following a regimen of total isolation, dictated by L. Ron, called the "Introspection Rundown". At the end of that time, she was dead.

The Church of Scientology was indicted on two felony charges, "abuse and/or neglect of a disabled adult" and "practicing medicine without a license." The charges were later dropped after the state's medical examiner changed the cause of death from "undetermined" to an "accident."

Due to the horrific nature of Lisa McPherson's death, Bob decided to create an organization at the scene of Scientology's crime against Lisa in Clearwater, Florida.. It was to be called the Lisa McPherson Trust (LMT), and Stacy was going to be the head of it.

Stacy introduced me to Bob over the phone. He told me he wanted me to come up to his home in Sandown, NH to talk. Stacy made the travel arrangements and off to Boston I went.

She told me I was going to love Bob and that he was my kind of person. She also charged me with keeping an eye on him during my visit because he would tend to get wild and become vulnerable to Scientology entrapment schemes.

I was about to find out how true that was.

27

FACING THE FEAR

DESPITE EVERYTHING THAT eventually happened, I have nothing but eternal gratitude for knowing Bob Minton on a personal level. Wherever he is now (he's dead), I hope he understands that.

My whole journey in the Scientology experience primarily involved extreme and unusual circumstances. I'd spent many years living "extremely" in that system. But nothing in my previous experiences prepared me for the "Bob Minton" experience.

On the third day after I had physically met him; Bob grabbed me by the scruff of my neck and laughingly dragged me through my personal valley of fear of Scientology and made sure I could stand on the other side of it with my back straight.

The Scientology programming runs deeper than deep if you've been involved for a long time. For me, it was sixteen years with them, as a part of them. The intensity and demand of Scientology training often involve much repetition. In other words, you say the same words or repeat the same actions over and over for years until the Scientology way becomes second nature.

The ultimate rule for a Scientologist is first and foremost to protect Scientology from any outside scrutiny or interference, period. The logic being that normal people (called "wogs" by Scientologists) were incapable of understanding Scientology culture. No matter who you were, Scientologist views any outsider as being spiritually inferior to them. Did I mention that I was in there doing that and thinking that for 16 years?

Anyway, there is a physical manifestation that often affects a person after leaving the movement. I can only describe how it felt to me. It was like getting an electric shock from the inside of my body. I have also confirmed this feeling with others who have left the movement as well. I know that sounds crazy, and I'll try to clarify what I mean.

I noticed after leaving the Scientology movement, if I happened to be in close proximity to any Scientology property, I'd get what can only be described as a panic attack. It felt like a physical sensation of dread, apprehension and pain. I'll give you an example of how it felt and what happened.

Sometime in the fall of 1995 or 1996, I was traveling in a car with a friend, and we were headed west to Los Angeles via Interstate 10. My trip had nothing to do with Scientology. I was on totally unrelated business. As we approached the California border from Nevada, I started seeing familiar road signs. Inextricably, I started to feel restless and agitated.

As we progressed down the highway, I saw a sign that was an exit for Hwy 79, Gilman Hot Springs. OMG! I couldn't fuckin' breathe! I broke out in a cold sweat, started hyperventilating. It felt like I was about to have a stroke! I knew exactly where I was located now. I had traveled this road many times for many years.

I knew the Gold Base was nearby. In my panic, I could only wonder how and why in the hell was this even happening! My friend who was driving looked over at me and asked if I was okay. I told him I thought I would be okay once we got down the road 15 to 20 miles away from where we were. He asked me why, and I told him I really couldn't talk right then but asked him to please get on down the road. As the miles between where we were in relation to Gilman Hot Springs increased, my panic started to subside.

I told my friend as best I could about the situation I'd had with Scientology at that location. I could tell by the way he listened and looked at me that he had no idea of what I was talking about. On that he was not alone because I couldn't understand my reaction either.

The answer to this dilemma would come to me years later as I realized something about my Scientology conditioning. After being intensely trained and tested on the Scientology ideology for years, I learned that besides the conditioning effects, my training could produce in me an extreme physical discomfort whenever I found myself in opposition to my Scientology conditioning. Saying it another way, I discovered I had no control over the discomfort I'd experience if I opposed or had bad thoughts about Scientology.

At this time, I'd only been away from Scientology for a few years. This was completely irrational in every way but admittedly very much out of my personal control or will, until I met Bob Minton. Bob *healed* me of that illness in a brutal, no-nonsense way.

After I arrived at Bob's home in Sandown, we spent the first two days just talking. He asked me a hundred questions and wanted to know everything. I asked him a hundred questions as well, and I wanted to know everything. During the second day of our talking, Bob told me he had been picketing Scientology facilities in defiance of its rules and influence.

I told him what happened to me when I got near the Gold Base, and how I felt just going near any of their property. I tried to explain to him how overwhelmed it made me feel and that maybe in time I'd get over it. Bob smiled and informed me that tomorrow he was taking me with him to picket Scientology's facility in the Beacon Hill area of Boston. I felt like I could just shit myself when he told me that, but I just smiled instead, and we took a break.

I called Stacy on the phone and told her of Bob's plans for the coming day, and she told me *not* to do it! She was like, "Please Jesse, don't let him take you out there to picket; Scientology is all over him!"

Bob knew I was talking with Stacy about picketing, and he said to me, "Oh, you think you're going to be a pussy and not go picketing with me tomorrow? Is that it? Oh, you're listening to Stacy, and she's giving you shit? Here give me that phone! Let me show you how to handle Stacy."

He took the phone from me and in a polite voice says, "Hello, is this Stacy? Okay, listen girl, you shut the fuck up about me and Jesse going picketing tomorrow, you understand? I don't want to hear any of your shit about it; we are going, and that's final!"

He then looked at me with the phone near his mouth and said, "You see how I did that? Fuck that, Stacy's not the boss around here, I am, do you understand that?" He then returned to his conversation with Stacy and said, "Anyway, baby, we'll be fine. Stop worrying. Those cocksuckers are going to get a big surprise when I bring Jesse Prince down to that fucking shithole organization!"

I glanced at a small mirror Bob had stuck on a refrigerator in his kitchen where we were talking on the phone with Stacy and noticed my lips were blue from lack of oxygen, I had forgotten to breathe.

The next morning, we drove down to the Boston Organization and began our protest. It was supposed to be a peaceful protest, but Frank Ofman, a Scientology staff member, came out of the Org and proceeded to slap Bob in the face. In response, Bob hit Ofman with his picket sign. Frank fell out on the ground like a professional athlete trying to get a foul call. The police arrived within minutes.

The police did see a video which clearly showed Ofman hitting Bob first. The officers commented that if Bob had responded by kicking or punching back, he would *not* have been arrested. He was only arrested because he used the <u>sign</u> he had in his hands, which was considered a "weapon." Apparently using anything which could possibly be construed as a weapon forces the Boston police to take someone into custody.

The *St. Petersburg Times* later reported on the incident as follows:

> The man considered to be the Church of Scientology's No. 1 enemy was arrested Thursday after a scuffle with church members in Boston. Robert S. Minton, a Boston millionaire who has spent nearly $2-million on anti-Scientology causes, was charged with assault and battery with a dangerous weapon and jailed briefly before posting $25 bail. According to Boston police, the weapon was the stick from a picket sign Minton was holding as he protested against Scientology outside the church's Beacon Street headquarters. Police said Minton used the stick to strike Frank Ofman, a Scientology Public Affairs officer. Minton said Friday that he reacted after Ofman struck him with a fist to his temple and slapped his cheek.

Bob was handcuffed, put in a police car and was taken off to the pokey. Bob told me to call his lawyer, which I did. I was on the phone with his lawyer as I watched a police car take him away. Then I had to call Stacy and let her know what happened. Of course, she flipped out!

Then I had to call Bob's wife and let her know what happened; she didn't say much, but I could tell she didn't like me much!

Later on that evening when Bob got out of jail, and we met up, I wasn't sure what to expect. Bob looked at me silently and very seriously. Then he put on that huge smile of his and gave a big belly laugh and said, "Now that's what the fuck I'm talking about! We gave those bastards some shit today!"

Facing the Fear

When you watch the video of that event, you can see that my phobia was almost instantly healed. As a matter of fact, it's hard to tell I was ever even sick. I was ready to stand, back straight, and face the Scientologists.

As for Bob, the incident only seemed to cement his resolve, because the day after his court hearing on this matter, he purchased a building in Clearwater, Florida, for the Lisa McPherson Trust.

28

Dirty Tricks

In the fall of 1999, along with a few others, I found myself making plans to move to Clearwater, Florida, the last place on earth I wanted to be! I reluctantly decided to go because it felt like the right thing to do. Stacy Brooks was the head of this new organization. As per usual, I was the number two principal of our new organization. We proceeded to scout out a location for what would become the Lisa McPherson Trust.

The Lisa McPherson Trust (LMT) was an organization incorporated in 1999 located in downtown Clearwater, Florida. Ex-Sea Org members along with a few others staffed the LMT.

Back in the day there was no physical location in the United States where people could go to get information about and help with the Scientology problem as it relates to family members who had been "disconnected from." The only other place on earth this service was being provided that I knew of was located in Hamburg, Germany under the leadership of Ursula Caberta.

Our efforts to establish the new Lisa McPherson Trust in Clearwater, was met with immediate dirty tricks from Scientology to attempt to stop us. Stacy tells the story best:

> **Stacy:** *We couldn't find an office building that would lease to us. The Office Manager of the Sun Trust building informed me that the owner had declined to lease to us. Then the realtor for the Nations Bank building told me that he had received an email from the owner of that building saying that the owner had "decided to rethink how he wants to utilize the building." I told the realtor it was obvious Scientology had contacted him. He hemmed and hawed and said he'd have a final answer for us the next day.*
>
> *Next we tried at the Clearwater Tower building. The way that realtor refused us was to tell me the owner had said they would have to get a release from all the other tenants in the building before they could lease to us. The owner of the AmSouth building at first told us there would be no problem leasing to us, but later changed his mind and refused. In a conversation with the realtor for that building, I was able to discover that Scientology had sent him a large package of materials "documenting" the dangerous nature of each of the principals in the Lisa McPherson Trust. He refused to show us the package, but he did mention that the owner wouldn't want to lease to a convicted felon. Stacey told him he was being given false information by Scientology and told him the real story of the assault charge against Bob in Boston and how the charge had been thrown out by the judge.*
>
> *We had an appointment at eleven to look at a building at 33 N. Ft..Harrison. Within five minutes, seven*

Scientologists barged into the room he was showing us and began shouting "This man is a criminal! He was arrested for assault and battery last night! He's violent! Don't do business with these people!" The CPA ordered them out of the building immediately, but they refused to go. We finished our tour and then sat down to talk to him in his conference room. Almost immediately, his secretary called to say that his building was being picketed and that one of his clients had been photographed as they entered the offices.

At this, the CPA instructed his secretary to call the police. During our brief meeting, he got three urgent messages to call Mary Story, the DSA Flag.

"I've asked Mary twice to get Scientology to buy my building," he told us. "They weren't interested. Now that I'm talking to you, suddenly she's frantic to talk to me." He just shook his head in amazement.

Pat Jones arrived with an entourage, demanding to see the owner of the building. He just closed the conference room door and tried to ignore all the frenzy, but soon his secretary announced that the police had arrived outside.

Our meeting effectively disrupted, the CPA went out to see for himself what was happening, while we remained in the conference room. Soon three police officers came in, and one of them said, 'Mr. Minton, I just wanted to shake your hand and welcome you to Clearwater.' The other police officers also shook our hands and expressed how glad they were to have us in Clearwater. They all said they knew what had happened the night before, and asked us to let them know if there was anything they could do for us.

As soon as we left the building we were surrounded by seven Scientologists, apparently public, at least two of whom had been part of the spontaneous grassroots counter-picket in front of the Ft. Harrison the afternoon before. This gang of Scientologists surrounded us as we tried to get to our car and stood behind the car as we tried to back out. They followed us on foot as we drove to the ticket booth, and the woman in the ticket booth called the police to let them know that the Scientologists were harassing us in the parking structure.

We stopped in to see the CPA again on our way back to the hotel. The same set of Scientologists materialized out of the bushes as we crossed the street and surrounded us as we tried to walk up the stairs to our car. There were two men with video cameras, three women with picket signs and two other women whose job seemed to be to chant "Religious bigots go home, religious bigots go home." It was close to dusk and with these people all following us to our car it looked like a scene out of Night of the Living Dead. A policeman happened to be in the parking structure and witnessed all of this. He ordered them to let us get into our car and leave the parking lot.

After my meeting in Tampa, I had to go to Clearwater to set up a Post Office box for the Lisa McPherson Trust. When I came out nine Scientologists - the ones that had stalked us all day the day before, surrounded me on the steps of the Post Office. This time they were actually threatening me. While two of them videotaped me, several others held up picket signs that said 'Religious Bigot go home,' and several of them shouted at me. One of them in particular shouted, 'Go home or else, religious bigot!' I felt very threatened by what was being shouted at me and by the intensity with which I was being stalked. Finally, I managed to get into my car and lock it. As I drove away, I could hear them shouting after me.

I decided to go to Tampa and find Patricia and Peter Greenway. As I walked in Patricia and Peter were both standing up. Patricia was pointing at a man who was ducking into the men's bathroom toward the back of the restaurant. Patricia called out to me, "He was watching for you! He was pacing back and forth looking out the window and talking on his walkie-talkie, and then I heard him say, 'Here she comes.'" After a few minutes, the man came out of the bathroom and headed for the door. Patricia, Peter, and several others from the restaurant followed him out, and then I returned to the phone and began to talk to the Tampa police officer.

I told him my name and asked him if he had ever heard of Lisa McPherson, and he said yes, he knew who she was. I told him I was in Tampa to set up the Lisa McPherson Trust. Then he said, "I can't tell you what I really think of you because this is a recorded line. But I will tell you this: I fully support everything you and Bob Minton are doing. I am behind you a hundred percent." I told him how much I appreciated his saying that, and he said, "We'll do anything we can to help you. Anything."

Clearly, Scientology is going to do everything they can to keep the Lisa McPherson Trust out of Clearwater. But we're moving to Clearwater, and we are going to shine the light of truth on Scientology. There are a lot of people who are very happy that we are coming to town. In Lisa's honor, we can't let the Scientologists frighten us away, and we won't. No matter how much harassment and intimidation they throw at us, we're moving into Clearwater.

After much back and forth, we were able to purchase a building on the same block as one of Scientology's training facilities where I'd worked in 1979. Along with Bob and a handful of others we went about the business of making our location a shelter for distraught family members of those in and lost to Scientology. We also made ourselves available to Scientologists in or out of the movement.

29

THE EXPERT SPEAKS OUT

When I worked for the Church of Scientology, I was used by them as an "expert witness," due to my Scientology training and familiarity with Scientology's processes and procedures. This turned out to be a double-edged sword when I began to use that expertise in court rooms across America against Scientology.

In 1997, in addition to the criminal case being pursued against Scientology for the wrongful death of Lisa McPherson, a civil case against the Church had been launched by Lisa's McPherson's family with Bob Minton financing it. In November 1998, I was retained as an Expert Witness and trial consultant. December 1997, Scientology staff member, Glenn Stilo, brought Lisa McPherson's auditing records to lawyer Ken Dandar in Tampa, FL, by order of the court, for inspection. I was able to study the auditing files in detail, as well as the caretaker logs from the time when she was being held in isolation prior to her death.

The ritual or procedure that Lisa McPherson had forced on her was known in Scientology as the "Introspection Rundown." A "rundown" is a Scientology auditing procedure. Lisa died while receiving the procedure. Images taken by the coroner of her dead body looks as if she had been literally *run down* by a fast-moving vehicle. I was familiar with the Introspection rundown and had seen it applied in Scientology.

In September of 1999, I submitted a lengthy affidavit to the court in the wrongful death civil lawsuit being litigated on behalf of the Lisa McPherson estate. I have included the full affidavit as an Appendix on page 219, but here are a few excerpts from the affidavit concerning Scientology's isolation treatment:

> *26. In 1973, Hubbard announced to the Scientology world that he had solved the problem of how to handle a person in a "psychotic break". Hubbard stated that this was a "technical breakthrough" which possibly ranks with the major discoveries of the twentieth century. He further said his discovery means the last reason to have Psychiatry around is gone. He went on to say the key is what caused the person to introspect before the psychotic break.*
>
> *During my tenure in Scientology, I have observed four instances of people having a psychotic break. In each case the person was sleep deprived; each had been told their job performance was inadequate, and each person was subjected to Scientology ethics.*

> 27. I am familiar with the practice of "Isolation," also known as "baby watch" as practiced by Scientology and I have participated in the "handling "of one Scientologist that was ordered to "Isolation". No one volunteers to go into Isolation.
>
> I have seen with my own eyes how a person is driven to the point of having a "psychotic break" and the subsequent brutality of treatment the person then receives as a result of the handlers following strict Scientology methods.
>
> 28. In the four instances of Isolation I observed, the person was locked in a room with at least two other people guarding the exit door. The people that watch the person in a psychotic break are not allowed to talk to the person at all. They are only allowed to physically restrain the person. The reason there are people guarding the exit door is that the person wants to leave and attempts to leave time after time. By their own policy, the person in a psychotic break is not allowed to leave until the Case Supervisor allows it.

Scientology lawyers told the judge in open court David Miscavige knew nothing about Lisa McPherson death or what was done to her. However, that didn't gibe with what I knew about how RTC operated. I clarified for the court exactly how he knew all about her death in my affidavit:

> 41. RTC receives all reports on situations involving Isolation for guidance from RTC to the Senior Case Supervisor, Sr. C/S. RTC

then reports the matter to Sr. C/S INT, i.e., International, office for further investigation. Senior C/S INT then reports back to the RTC Reports Officer. Ray Mithoff is the Senior C/S INT at CSI, the mother church.

Ray Mithoff, Marty Rathbun, and David Miscavige, as they have done on other occasions within my personal knowledge, meet and discuss various options available to Scientology on how to deal with a public relations flap. No one else has the authority to do so. Lisa McPherson was such a public relations flap to Scientology since she took her clothes off in public and was placed in Isolation.

42. In records I have reviewed provided by FLAG in this case concerning Lisa McPherson; she had previously complained that Scientology was not working for her, and her stats were down. Based on my own experience and Scientology procedures and protocol, these three individuals would have met and discussed on several occasions what to do with Lisa since she was not improving in Isolation.

Many years after the fact, Marty Rathbun, after leaving Scientology, did an interview for the St. Petersburg Times newspaper and confirmed what I has surmised. He reported that David Miscavige not only had full knowledge of the Introspection Rundown ritual being performed on Lisa McPherson that eventually killed her, he actually supervised the operation.

I also noted that:

34. It is obvious from these files that Lisa McPherson complained that auditing and Scientology were not working for her in 1995 and that she wanted to leave and return to Texas. Her "stats" were down, i.e., her production and income at AMC Publishing.

As a result, she was placed in Ethics at her work where the records revealed that she was constantly doing "amends" and writing "O/W's", overts and withholds, which resulted in less time to obtain adequate sleep which further, in my own observations, leads to psychotic breaks. L. Ron Hubbard confirms this in his own writings, "Introspection Rundown Additional Steps."s

35. FLAG at the Ft. Harrison Hotel is "the mecca of technical perfection" according to Scientology. I can attest that it is a high crime in Scientology to alter or ignore the tech. It is also a high crime to lose or omit vital information from any PC folder, including "caretaker logs." The Lisa McPherson "caretaker logs" are missing substantial day-to-day portions, in particular, the last three and one-half days of her Isolation.

This is no accident. Records of this magnitude are not lost. Based on my experience, these missing records were intentionally destroyed to conceal material matters damaging to Scientology. Hubbard explicitly writes in CS SERIES 97 and CS SERIES 98 "omissions from folders and complete loss of folders is a very serious matter...." If proven, expulsion from Scientology is mandatory.

Marty later confirmed what I had pointed out. He had in fact ordered the last three days of Lisa's caretaker logs destroyed, as well as anything implicating RTC or David Miscavige in her death.

Many years after Lisa's death Marty Rathbun gave an interview with the ST. Petersburg times after he finally fled Scientology. He confirmed certain facts about the death of Lisa McPherson that validated the declaration I'd written ten years earlier. However, Marty still left out certain facts about his involvement in the coverup of the facts like where Lisa died. I assume he left out these facts because they would implicate him in the murder of Lisa McPherson. The one fact he does make clear is Lisa's death was no accident.

When this document was submitted and accepted by the court, the panic that set in the Scientology conglomerate was virtually palatable. I could smell the fear and hate oozing from my Scientology adversaries. David Miscavige, Marty Rathbun, and Mike Rinder must have felt like they were in a shit storm being threatened by multiple lightning strikes around their ass area. This sent the Scientology Legal and Intelligence apparatus into overdrive.

The sheer amount of banker boxes full of false and imaginary information submitted to the court on behalf of David Miscavige and his henchmen, Marty Rathbun, and Mike Rinder in opposition to my declaration was staggering. Oh for sure, reading their opposition to my declaration seemed to confirm that I was the real Lucifer, not L Ron as he professed at the end of his life. The Scientology legal conglomerate fought valiantly and fearlessly against it, but in the end the judge allowed my testimony.

I can only speculate that it must have seemed like I had a crystal ball when I submitted my declaration in 1999, placing Marty, Miscavige and Mithoff at the scene of the crime of Lisa McPherson's murder.

Marty, now a self-proclaimed Scientology Technical expert, failed to demonstrate or apply his knowledge of the writings of L Ron. In his writings after fleeing Scientology, Marty rambles on about how horrible David Miscavige is, never mentioning any of the horror's he was responsible for.

30

THE CAMPAIGN TO DESTROY THE LMT

NOW WE GET TO THE PART where David Miscavige, Marty Rathbun, and Mike Rinder go on an all-out assault to destroy the Lisa McPherson Trust, and succeed.

This all-out assault is an excellent reference that should stand as a model for everything Scientology truly represents when it comes to "Attack Campaigns" against a target. Anyone or anything that impedes Scientology growth can become a target. Handling a target involves the utter destruction by any means necessary of the target. A Scientology critic, journalist, protester, or ex-member are often targeted. A person can become a target if they become a plaintiff in an adverse lawsuit against Scientology or any of its many subforms. Collateral damage is a given for any unfortunate associated with the wrong side.

Originally, Bob had taken his concerns to the highest level of Sea Org members he could, and tried to reason with them. This was in 1998. He had a series of three meetings, totaling 15 hours, with two of the top leaders of Scientology: Mike Rinder, the head of OSA International, and Marty Rathbun, head of the Religious Technology Center (RTC) and second in command of Scientology under its dictator, David Miscavige.

Bob hoped to enter into a dialog about ending Scientology's criminal conduct, including fraud, practicing medicine without a license, child abuse, and human rights violations. Unfortunately, the Scientologists had no interest in discussing their criminal conduct. Their interest was solely to convince Mr. Minton to stop providing funds to Scientology critics.

They told Minton point blank that if he quit giving financial support to critics, Scientology would stop harassing and intimidating him, his friends and family.

At the end of the third meeting, Mr. Minton made it clear that he would not stop his financial support until Scientology ceased destroying people's lives through fraud and criminal abuse. In response, the Scientologists intensified their campaign against him.

It was a couple of months after the above meetings occurred when I came into the fray. So by the time I met Bob he was already pretty "wound up," that is, reaching a hysteria concerning what he had gotten himself into concerning Scientology and how that was affecting his life and the lives of those he was close to. Bob just couldn't reconcile how a predator organization like Scientology could exist without threat by government agencies that were established to protect the public in general.

During our conversations during the first three days when I first met Bob, I asked him the same question I later asked Amy at the Hamburg conference. "Why are you doing this? Why do you fight them when it's clear you are going against something that could kill you? If there was a way Scientology could get it done without getting caught or even suspected, you would be a dead man."

Bob's reply to me was a story about something that happened to him earlier in his life.

As a teenager, Bob grew up in a household with his father, mother, and younger brother in Nashville, Tennessee. The house was anything but a home. Bob told me his father drank heavily and to often, would beat his mother. He would also beat Bob for arguing with his him about beating his mother. He described his home life as a living hell. He said one day his mother just packed up her stuff and fled the house, abandoning Bob and his younger brother to fend for themselves.

Bob described his father as a strict disciplinarian, and he beat Bob as he saw fit. Bob said as he grew older and stronger the day came when his drunken father tried to beat him, and Bob fought back and kept on fighting back. At some point during one of the altercations, his father called the police and asked them to commit Bob to a psychiatric institution for evaluation because he thought Bob was insane.

Because Bob was underage and had very few rights, he was taken away and locked up in a mental institution for testing and evaluation. I don't remember how long Bob told me he was locked up in the mental institution, but no one from his immediate family tried to intervene or come to his aid. Bob said his girlfriend's mother finally came and got Bob out of the institution and agreed to take care of him and supervise him until he was an adult. Bob said he ended up living with his girlfriend's family, getting whatever jobs he could to put himself through college. He said he also helped pay some bills where he lived. He told me that with this new family, he finally felt the family love that he had yearned for.

Bob said for as long as he'd live, he didn't think he would ever forget the feeling of utter hopelessness at being held against his will, while in that institution. When Bob heard about the details of what had happened to Lisa McPherson, he cried like a baby. He cried like a baby just trying to tell me about how it made him feel to think how Lisa must have felt when everyone ignored her cries because she was just "crazy."

He said this was the reason why he kept on going despite the persecution Scientology was putting him through, at the hands of Marty Rathbun and Mike Rinder, for questioning its authority. It was during these initial conversations with Bob that I agreed to help him in the fight as best I could. Bob was fighting from his heart for all the right reasons, so I walked with him.

Here is some idea of the sophistication and depth of execution Scientology will go through to destroy an enemy:

On September 28, 1998, Peter Franks, a British private investigator hired by Scientology, spread the word to many friends of Therese Minton (Bob's wife) in England and to Mr. Minton's former business partner, Jeff Schmidt, that Therese, the Minton's' two daughters, and Mr. Schmidt were going to be followed by private investigators in order to bring pressure on Mr. Minton to stop his activities concerning Scientology.

Mr. Schmidt's office had been picketed and leafleted at this point for several weeks, as had his home while his wife and children were there. Franks threatened to go after Mr. Schmidt's clients, one of which was the Nigerian government. Franks said they would arrange picketing of the Nigerian delegation to the International Monetary Fund (IMF) meeting in Washington, D. C., which was set for October 4-8, the next month.

Franks promised that Mr. Schmidt would be caught in a web of an IRS tax investigation of Mr. Minton and in his own investigation by the Inland Revenue Service, England's equivalent of the IRS. Franks said that unless Mr. Schmidt did something to help Scientology go after Mr. Minton, he would have serious trouble on his hands, since the seven-year statute of limitations had not yet run out on the activities he and Mr. Minton were engaged in together (their partnership ended in 1993.)

Franks also said that all of Therese's neighbors would be visited in Boston, and the "whole ugly scene" would be laid out for all to hear. The children's schools would be targeted for the same campaign, which would include teachers, administrators, and parents, to paint Mr. Minton as a pariah. He let it be known that he expected Therese and Jeff to pressure Mr. Minton into quitting the work he was doing concerning Scientology.

In July, 1999, Scientology operatives broke into Jeff Schmidt's London office and photocopied extensive files. Mr. Schmidt was later told by a Scientology private investigator that if he could not convince Mr. Minton to end his opposition to Scientology, all of the files would be turned over to the Inland Revenue and the Nigerian Media. Mr. Schmidt called Mr. Minton and begged him to stop criticizing Scientology. Mr. Minton tried to convince Mr. Schmidt to go to the authorities and report Scientology's conduct as blackmail, but Mr. Schmidt was frightened of what the Scientologists would do to him and his family, and he refused.

Here is a perfect example of Scientology's utter contempt for the law or law enforcement agencies. This is the right time and place to explain how Scientology is able to corrupt practically any government agent or agency. It's the untraceable money flow through the offices of high priced lawyers who then help launder the cash money paid to the field operatives and their friends. Scientology on its books carries whatever the dollar amount paid to eliminate an "enemy" as attorney fees. The law firm carries the dollar figures on their accounting books as fees paid to a private investigator firms who then dole out the money to active law enforcement employees. The lawyers will admit to whom they paid money to for investigative services, but how that money was used and in what sums quickly become unclear.

The operative theory for Scientology and its high-priced lawyers is to keep as many arms lengths from the eventual victim as possible to limit liability. Simply stated, the scam is set up so that all can claim no one knows anything specific, especially those at the top doling out the money. These are the same people issuing the orders and paying for the service. It's just that simple.

The Campaign to Destroy the LMT

Through the hire of high priced influential lawyers. Scientology project operatives like Marty and Mike Rinder direct these lawyers to find the best ex-cop, ex-FBI or ex-Sheriff or any ex-law enforcement person to work for hire. The more connections the potential hire has with current active agents, the better. This is the preferred method of hire because it's easy to get cash money exchanging hands. These ex-law enforcement agents have "favors" they can buy from current law enforcement friends, such as providing a profile or files of someone. An example would be; a hired ex-law enforcement person pays his connection cash for information and hands the information over to Scientology for evaluation. Driving records, cell phone records, tax information and past criminal records can be procured.

This can also extend to getting law enforcement to look the other way while a crime is being committed such as a break-in. Scientology uses these contacts to procure the latest surveillance equipment and bugging devices. This is how Scientology is able to give a person that "I'm being haunted" feeling. Scientology somehow seems to know everything about the target.

After a certain amount of money has exchanged hands between Scientology and working law enforcement agents, the intended Scientology target also becomes a target for law enforcement itself by association.

The following is a story *St. Petersburg Times* reported of an operation Scientology ran on me:

> *You have to be courageous to publicly criticize the Church of Scientology. The organization recently proved – again – how far it will go to investigate, smear and intimidate critics...*

The Expert-Witness

Again and again in recent years, Scientology has claimed that it has reformed, that it no longer engages in the kind of underhanded or illegal behavior and smear tactics that have earned it a sorry reputation around the globe. Again and again, Scientology has argued that it is a religion and should be treated like any other church.

But again and again, stories surface that set Scientology apart. Not only does it have a penchant for secrecy, it will spend virtually unlimited time and money on pursuing, setting up and bringing down its critics.

That's not like any church we know.

During my trial, Scientology divulged it paid private investigators in excess of $500,000.00 in fees alone to set me up for marijuana possession. A few people were paid very well for that.

Mike Rinder's parting shot, when his "project" for me failed to get the intended results, was to assure the *St. Petersburg Times* reporter he would "get me the next time."

This is why any law enforcement agency that decides to investigate Scientology has the added task of investigating itself first, lest Scientology play cat-and-mouse games for years due to infiltration in the ranks of the investigating agency. This has already happened. When the FBI raided Scientology in 1977, Scientology staff were tipped off by a police officer hours before the raid occurred. At that time, it was too late to try and hide files because all files were paper files. This was before the digital age of the Internet, digital files, or personal computers. With today's technology, an early warning could make a big difference as far as what eventually can be discovered.

The Campaign to Destroy the LMT

I invite any active investigator to revisit as a study the information concerning Bernie McCabe as the prosecutor in the Lisa McPherson criminal case. Someone should ask Marty and Mike specifically how they investigated the investigator using the influence of high priced local law firms. Some of those drunken high priced lawyers were starving for cash. Marty and Mike walked in with those huge Xmas bags of money and were able to get a lot done under the table. This is not my story to tell though. Only Marty, Mike and David Miscavige can tell the factual story.

Here is another example from Stacy Brooks of how Scientology hires professionals to do criminal activities against its perceived enemies for money:

April 26, 2001: Jesse Prince received an anonymous fax at the Lisa McPherson Trust that indicated a man named David Amos might be willing to provide information to Mr. Prince about harassment of Mr. Prince by Scientology operatives. Mr. Prince was able to reach Mr. Amos by telephone. Mr. Amos agreed to meet with Mr. Prince in Memphis, Tennessee. That night, Mr. Prince drove to Memphis, accompanied by Patrick Jost, a former Treasury Department investigator who was working with the Lisa McPherson Trust to document Scientology's criminal conduct. Mr. Jost felt that Mr. Prince should not meet with Mr. Amos alone.

April 27, 2001: Mr. Amos agreed to meet with Mr. Prince alone while Mr. Jost watched them from his car less than twenty feet away. Mr. Amos told Mr. Prince that he had worked as a private investigator for Scientology from the fall of 1998 until the winter of 2000. He said that Scientology attorney Kendrick Moxon had told him that Mr. Prince and Mr. Minton were involved in a child slavery ring and that Scientology was trying to expose them to rescue the children.

Mr. Amos said he felt that Moxon had told him this story in order to motivate him to commit illegal acts to try to catch Mr. Prince. Mr. Amos admitted to Mr. Prince that he had illegally wiretapped the telephone in Mr. Prince's Chicago apartment at the end of 1998. He also admitted that he had passed on information obtained via this illegal wiretap to his Scientology handlers. Mr. Amos also said that he had set up illegal surveillance equipment to monitor Mr. Prince, Ms. Brooks and Mark Bunker in their homes in Clearwater, Florida.

Mr. Amos reluctantly agreed to show Mr. Prince where the surveillance equipment had been set up. However, he later refused to travel to Clearwater because he was afraid of what the Scientologists would do to him if they found out. A report of this meeting was sent to the FBI in Florida.

Over time, Scientology is able to manufacture whatever information it needs to suit its own ends.

31

SWITCHING SIDES

IN JANUARY OF 2002, Bob Minton called me from his home in New Hampshire and told me that he felt suicidal.

By this time, Bob had begun to realize the gravity of his situation. He felt betrayed by the very people he wanted to trust. Bob was in anguish, sobbing uncontrollably and was threatening to end his life with a shotgun blast to the head. His plan was to get into his old pickup truck and drive out into his field behind the barn, located a short distance from the front door of his house, and shoot himself. We were on the phone for hours. For once, Stacy was not with him at his New Hampshire home.

Bob said he hated Stacy for information she had disclosed to Scientology in a recent deposition she'd been ordered to attend. He was also upset with her for the pain he felt Stacy had caused his wife and family. He felt deeply betrayed by Ken Dandar; the lead council in the Lisa McPherson case because he felt Ken had extorted him for his money. He said he hated himself the most for letting things get so out of hand. He told me he had let everyone down because he could not stand up for, or help anyone, anymore. For that reason, he thought he was just a piece of shit who was now about to kill himself.

There was also the fact that the Scientology Legal and Intel machine was about to have Bob locked up in jail for contempt of court, perjury, and other "manufactured" charges.

As mentioned earlier, Bob had very strong feelings about being locked up against his will for any reason. It is my opinion the threat of being locked up was Bob's true Achilles heel, and he had reached a fork in the road.

I'm going to try really and distil the exact reason Bob. was so upset with Stacy in the hopes that the concepts are simply understood. So here is what is happened.

At some point in the fall of 2001, Scientology attorney Kendrick Moxon, was deposing Stacy Brooks. Kendrick asked Stacy about her knowledge of a bank account Bob Minton maintained offshore. From what I remember, the specific account in question was established to maintain the Lisa McPherson Trust financially until the end of the Lisa McPherson civil trial. Bob was trying to take himself out of the picture in the Lisa McPherson case so the case could get to trial. We were all confident with bringing the case to trial.

Scientology had been investigating Bob's financial sources and bank accounts for over a year. Bob had a lot of money, and he had it placed in banks internationally. The main mission of those investigating Bob was to find money he had not paid taxes on in the United States. Somehow, during Stacy's deposition she told Kendrick Moxon about an account Bob had that may have had money in it that he had not claimed or paid any taxes on in the United States.

Bob had transferred money from that account to another account to keep the Trust going until the trial could be completed in the Lisa McPherson case. Bob had taken Stacy Brooks and Patrick Joust with him to Europe and had exposed these accounts to them.

I remember the day it happened. Bob and Stacy came back to the Lisa McPherson trust after the deposition and Bob was furious. I'd never seen him that upset before. He was screaming at Stacy and actually got physical with her. I intervened and asked Bob what happened.

He said Stacy told Scientology information about his accounts that would probably land him in jail soon. Stacy said she didn't mean to; it was a mistake, and the questioning rattled her. Scientology was also trying to get her put in jail for perjury any way they could. They had already bounced off of me.

Bob was never the same after that.

For Bob, this had turned into a life or death situation, so I guess that may have been the reason he called me about his planned suicide.

We had already gone through the "life or death" drill a couple of times before. About a year earlier, Bob and I were walking and driving around his property in New Hampshire. I think the property was at least 200 acres and included what can only be called "The Woods." As we were headed back to the house, we ran into a swarm of wasps, and one had bitten Bob on the neck.

Immediately he started to bleed from the bite and his face began to swell. As we entered the house, I noticed Bob seemed to have trouble catching his breath. He told me he was going into anaphylactic shock as he got some pills from his medicine cabinet and took them. Bob also retrieved a huge syringe with a substance in it, and he showed me how to use it on him. He told me if he stopped breathing to inject the substance into his heart with the syringe. He told me I'd have to make sure I punched through the breastbone to get the medication to his heart. Bob had an allergy to wasps, and one had stung him on the side of his neck.

The way he was bleeding it seemed like he'd been cut with a knife. I told Bob it would be best if I called the ambulance now, but he wouldn't have it. He told me he was just going to lay down and if he fell asleep to sit and watch over him to make sure he was still breathing. Bob told me the medication that he had taken would kick in soon, and he did not want to make a scene with calling 911.

I sat there with him and watched him sleep for about 3 hours with the syringe in my hand most of the time. As he slept, I could see the swelling was going down, and he seemed to relax. When he woke up, he was a little groggy, but he put on that big smile of his and assured me he was okay now and thanked me for watching over him.

Another occasion of a life or death situation with Bob happened at a restaurant in Leipzig, Germany. Bob, myself, Stacy Brooks, Mark Bunker, Patricia Greenway and whoever else was there, had just begun to eat our meals when Bob suddenly looked like he was having a seizure. He turned totally red, and he couldn't breathe. This was a shock to all present, and we all just froze. I jumped out of my chair and grabbed Bob from behind and started doing the Heimlich maneuver on him.

His body was rock hard, as if he'd turned to stone. It may have been the third try, but I felt his body relax and he took a gulp of air. I came around to face him and could see whatever happened to him had passed. I asked him if he'd choked on his food; he said no. I asked what he thought happened? He replied he didn't know. He refused to be taken to see a doctor. He did promise to see his regular doctor after the Leipzig trip was over. We all kept an eye on Bob for the rest of the trip.

Back to the suicide phone call, Bob told me he didn't want to talk to Stacy anymore because he felt she betrayed him when she'd told Scientology what they wanted to hear in her deposition. Bob's rejection devastated Stacy, emotionally she was miserable as well.

I asked her myself why she told Scientology about Bob's accounts. She told me it was a mistake, and she didn't mean to do that. She also told me she was going to do whatever it took to get Bob out of and away from the stress of Scientology. She told me she was going to call Mike Rinder and work out a deal. She said she had to get Bob out of the courtrooms with Scientology, and I agreed. Together Stacy and I were able to get Bob to calm down and consider other options besides death.

Bob, Stacy and I had some long hard talks after the above situation calmed down. It was clear that the Lisa McPherson Trust was over. Both Stacy and I made plans to sell our homes and get the hell out of

Florida. This was before Stacy called to make a "deal".

Stacy ended up leaving Florida and going to New Hampshire with Bob to see what kind of deal could be worked out.

After Stacy and Bob started negotiating with Rinder and Rathbun, they quickly let me know the negotiations were confidential and they could not discuss any details with me, but they would fill me in when they came back to Florida, and so it went.

The Lisa McPherson Trust was closed during this time, and the staff was put on hold. I prepared my house for sale and went about the business of home improvement. I had a family at this time, raising two young kids, so a plan B was on my mind hard.

Meanwhile, Bob and Stacy had discussed the situation, and decided that it was time to settle their differences with Scientology. In March 2002, Bob called Mike Rinder in Los Angeles and told him that he felt overwhelmed by the litigation and wanted to get out of it and settle any outstanding differences. Rinder agreed to call Minton back to discuss it.

Rinder called back and suggested meeting in New York on 28-29 March. Rinder had his lawyers create a confidentiality agreement to prevent Minton from mentioning the discussions on the Internet, as happened last time Minton and Rinder met, in 1998. The confidentiality agreement included a clause requiring the participants to hide the discussions from the court: "without trying to anticipate all the ways in which this agreement could be violated, it is specifically agreed that the discussions will not be posted on the Internet; will not be inquired into in discovery in any litigation; and will not be revealed in any court papers or to any court."

Bob first met with the Church of Scientology in New York at the end of March. The meeting took place in Sandy Rosen's office. Present were Rosen, Mike Rinder, Monique Yingling, and Bob's personal attorney, Steve Jonas. Stacy Brooks was also present. Bob expected that the settlement negotiations would involve him writing out a check to the Church of Scientology, and nothing more. It turned out to be much more.

In addition to the Lisa McPherson case, they talked about a number of other ongoing cases that Bob was funding: Larry Wollershiem, Grady Ward, Gerry Armstrong, two cases in France, a libel case in Germany, two cases in Switzerland, and Keith Henson's activities. The Swiss cases involved Jean-Luc Barbier who was suing the Church of Scientology. Minton gave him $25-30,000 and provided assistance from a French lawyer, Michel Pesenti, who Minton paid $250,000 for legal services. Pesenti represented Minton, Stacy Brooks, and Jesse Prince in three libel suits in France).

Rosen showed Minton a "preview copy" of the lawsuit against Gerry Armstrong, where Minton and Brooks are named as defendants. He was also shown a "preview copy" of the counterclaim in the Lisa McPherson case, adding him as a defendant in the counterclaim. Rosen also mentioned that the Church of Scientology had spent approx. $20,000 on a possible RICO suit, $34,925,000 on the lawsuits in which Bob Minton was involved.

Rinder also wanted to discuss domain names registered to Minton that contained the word

"Scientology," mutual releases (each party agrees not to sue the other after a settlement agreement), and an agreement preventing Minton from funding anti-Scientology litigation. The meeting lasted from 9:00 a.m. until 3:30 or 4:00 p.m.

Rinder said that before they can begin settlement talks, Minton and Brooks must travel to Florida and "set the record straight in the wrongful death case and the breach of contract case" Rinder says that if Minton and Brooks "set the record straight," he thinks that the wrongful death case will be dismissed.

Shortly after that, Bob and Stacy came back to Florida and asked the Lisa McPherson Trust staff to meet them at a hotel in Tampa. At the meeting, Stacy confirmed with the staff that the Trust was over. I think there may have been a final paycheck.

I met privately with Bob and Stacy to discuss the new deal. In a nutshell, Stacy told me Scientology would leave Bob alone if he complied with the following conditions:

1. Close the Lisa McPherson Trust.

2. End funding any and all legal cases against Scientology or its affiliates.

3. Destroy the Lisa McPherson case by retracting testimony.

4. Enter into a permanent agreement to end all disputes with Scientology.

Step one and two were already done by the time they came back to Florida, so the priority was to get rid of the Lisa McPherson case and any other cases Bob was funding.

This turned out to be a long day and a long night. For the rest of the day, we didn't talk about the Lisa

McPherson case. Bob wanted to save that for after dinner.

We had dinner that night, and it seems like we talked about everything but the case until much later. After the LMT Staff members and friends had left it was just Bob, Stacy, and I., It was time for real talk. I asked Bob what was going to happen with the Lisa McPherson case. He said he was not sure what was going to happen. Stacy quickly corrected him and said it had all been worked out. She proceeded to explain to me that Scientology wanted Bob to stop giving financial aid to all legal cases against Scientology.

The Church also wanted ALL cases settled, and Bob and Stacy were to assist Scientology in any way they had to. I looked at Bob and asked him if he had joined Scientology now. He said "Fuck no, we'll see what these fuckers have got and dealt with it as best we can, but I am not going to jail, and I'm not going to have my family harmed anymore."

I told him I understood that, but I was unclear on what it all would mean.

Stacy then told me the rest of the deal. She told me that she and Bob were working with Scientology attorneys to draft new declarations recanting their testimony in the Lisa McPherson case.

The plan included targeting the attorney for the Lisa McPherson case, Ken Dandar, to get him disbarred and to end his right to practice law. This is how Scientology likes to gloat when it thinks it has won hands down. The plan was for Bob and Stacy to say Ken Dandar coerced them and gave them bad advice that amounted to perjury.

Neither Bob nor Stacy were concerned about submitting declarations to the court about perjuring themselves. Scientology owned the right judges by then and assured Bob and his attorney that there was little chance he'd go to jail for perjury. They were just going to blame everything on Ken Dandar. Did I mention that Ken had recently had a double bypass heart surgery? I'm pretty sure to this point I haven't mentioned the personal hell he'd gone through at the hands of Scientology paid investigators either.

These were Stacy's instructions from her Scientology handlers and she had set about the task of getting it done. Stacy told me that she was going to do what she could and use whoever she could to get ALL legal cases settled.

What Stacy wanted to make clear to me is that Bob was done with the Lisa McPherson case and would not support it in any way. She mentioned that I needed to start thinking about recanting my testimony in all of the legal cases that I was involved in.

I didn't react to what she was saying. I just listened. She just kept on talking but again I had tuned her out. I was thinking of the gravity of my situation. I'm here in Florida with a family. I was involved in at least four legal cases against Scientology. I'm thinking, these guys have been convinced to not only back off from Scientology litigation themselves, they were also going to try and attack or destroy anyone Scientology could sic them on, especially me!

I told Stacy that I needed to talk with Mike Rinder or Marty Rathbun before I could give them an answer. Stacy said that would be arranged the following day. We all said our goodnights and I went home.

Switching Sides

I called a friend, Frank Oliver, and laid out the whole scene. He was just as shocked about the situation as anyone could be. I told him I'd requested an audience with Mike and Marty and I needed to be prepared. I asked him for a miniature-recording device that I could easily hide but get a good recording at the same time.

I had also decided I would still support Ken Dandar in the Lisa McPherson case. Both Frank and I consulted with Ken on my plan. Frank gave me the device. I had mentally gone through as many possible scenarios as I could think of. The basic plan was to leave the meeting with a usable recording of the event. The only other problem I could think of was just me. I was a ball of nerves and conflicting emotions.

The next day I met with Bob and Stacy at the Adams Mark Hotel on Clearwater Beach. I was somehow able to keep my composure. Bob and Stacy had decided to move to another hotel on the beach and that was where we were to meet with Rinder and Rathbun.

Before the meeting, both Stacy and Bob got in my face about how I really needed to work with them on my recant declarations; they made it clear that unless I complied I was going to starve along with my family.

I tried to remain calm, so I just looked at them, but then I started seeing red.

I told Bob that he had no idea what he was asking me to do. I asked him if he thought I lied or did he think I was trying to trick him about my Scientology experience? Did he think he had done something for me to the point that he could now bargain with Scientology for my soul? I told him he was breaking my heart and I needed a face to face with Rinder and Rathbun. I wanted to hear it from them. I let him know that I was no respecter of persons and I welcomed an opportunity to light Rinder and Rathbun's asses up. I reminded him of what I'd told him about the last time Miscavige and Rathbun tried to force me to do anything.

Bob told me he "felt threatened" and told me that he didn't want to see me anymore.

Stacy ran off to make a phone call, so I waited, thinking Rathbun and Rinder were on the way. After some time passed, I asked Stacy if they were coming, and she said they were not. It turned out that Bob had called Mike to "warn him about Jesse's threats."

I don't have any memory of ever talking to Bob Minton again. The train was on the track and there was nothing more to say.

32

BENDING TO SCIENTOLOGY

BOB AND STACY HAD A NEW TEAM put together promptly. When Stacy and Bob went into negotiations with Scientology, they also brought Patrick Jost and Arnie Lerma with them.

Remember that part of the deal Bob had with Scientology was to convince Lawrence Wollersheim to settle his case with Scientology. Bob persuaded Arnie Lerma to contact Larry and relay Bob's offer to pay him approximately $200,000 personally, and forgive the $700,000 that Bob had loaned him, if he would dismiss his case

I don't know how many people reading here know or know of Lawrence Wollershiem, but the above Scientology drill proved to be a complete waste of time. Lawrence would have none of it.

Lawrence is the only person I know of in the history of litigation with Scientology that brought his case to court, won the case, got paid for his trouble and *never* signed a confidential agreement with Scientology about anything, period. Lawrence and his team (which I joined in 1998) kicked Scientology's ass in the courts, hands down. Anyone else that I know of has sold a piece of his or her soul for Scientology's money by promising to keep quiet.

Accepting Scientology's money in this way allows Scientology to rewrite history. By trading money for silence how can you warn others? It's a selfish decision to know of *something* that actively hunts and preys on good people just like you and not warn them for money, not to mention the lifetime Scientology tether agreement is always around your neck.

The attorney for the Lawrence Wollersheim case was Dan Leipold. I can only describe Dan as being a righteous man when it came to having respect for and defending the truth. I say that in summary of the character of the man I knew. He has since passed on. The true story of how he was able to legally defeat Scientology and the suffering he and his family endured will never be told because he is dead now. A firsthand account is no longer an option.

Anyway, Stacy Brooks, Mike Rinder, Bob Minton, Marty Rathbun, Arnie Lerma, Patrick Jost and a host of attorneys for all concerned set about the task of settling all of Scientology's legal cases one way or the other. They contacted as many people as they could on Scientology's behalf.

The reason or excuse for this new agreement to work between these unlikely parties I suspect had something to do with saving the cash cow, Bob Minton. Bob had continually given both Stacy Brooks and Arnie Lerma large sums of money so they each had a vested interest in keeping Bob safe.

Bob had given money to many critics of Scientology. Scientology had already made Bob divulge whom he had given money to that was a Scientology critic via deposition testimony. Now Scientology used Bob and his new team to attack what he had supported. This is how Scientology gloats in victory. This is what Scientology makes friends do to each other. I also blame the attorney for the Lisa McPherson estate Ken Dandar for being dishonest with Bob Minton about what he was doing with the money Bob had given him for the case.

Even the judge in the Lisa McPherson case was surprised and taken aback by how drastically the court proceedings had changed. For almost 2 years, Bob, Stacy and I sat in different courtrooms in Clearwater and St. Petersburg Florida as a team exposing Scientology for the last three years. The Scientology team always sat on one side of the room while we occupied the other. Now suddenly Bob Minton and Stacy Brooks are sitting on the same side as Scientology in the courtroom in front of the same judge as before.

Stacy was now assisting Scientology attorney Kendrick Moxon with whatever paperwork or preparation he needed. I remember just looking at her as she smiled and joked with Moxon who was on a mission to get Ken Dandar disbarred from the Florida Bar Association.

Besides the Lisa McPherson case, I was also actively working on the Wollershiem case, the Dennis Erlich case and a case against Digital Light Wave that involved an ex-Scientologist named Brian Haney. I had submitted declarations in each of these cases. With the exception of the Brian Haney case, each of the cases mentioned above had received funding from Bob Minton.

Bob had provided funding for many cases. That meant Bob and his new team went to work to reverse the work done with each person he had financially helped fight Scientology.

It seemed like Scientology would prevail in their sweeping plan to silence all critics under threat of lawsuits forever, but that's not how it turned out. Some people refused to cooperate with Scientology and Bob Minton's new team and that made a difference. Dan Leipold refused to cooperate on the Wollershiem case. He went on to settle with Scientology on Lawrence Wollershiem terms that did not involve Lawrence being quiet about his Scientology experience. Ken Dandar fought for his life for as long as he could. He did not get disbarred in the end, but he did cooperate with Scientology during the final settlement of the Lisa McPherson case and he signed a confidential agreement with Scientology to keep the details of the settlement confidential, among other things.

Brian Haney settled his case with Digital Light Wave for north of $80 million dollars, but he had to sign a confidential agreement not to disclose details of the settlement.

Brian Haney is a good man with deep religious convictions. Brian was also a financial supporter for the Lisa McPherson Trust; I think he may have given north of $100,000.00 to the Trust for support. He was the only person that had the guts to let me know how Bob and his new team planned to deal with me.

Patricia Greenway refused to cooperate with Scientology in any way, and hired her own lawyers to fight them at their own expense. Patricia was always right there fighting back against the Scientology onslaught. She and her husband Peter produced the film "The Prophet".

Bob had a healthy respect for Patricia Greenway and she was a confidant for him. Even after Bob decided to go with Scientology he would still talk with Patricia and she would try to get him away from the group he was with so that maybe he could get another perspective on his situation. Patricia reminded him that he could hire whatever out-of-state lawyers he would need to get out of his current mess. She didn't agree that Bob had run out of options. Stacy hated the fact that Bob would consult with Patricia and she eventually convinced Bob to end his relationship with Patricia.

To add insult to injury, somehow Arnie Lerma had insisted on different news forums that Patricia Greenway is an "OSA plant"! I mean, wasn't it Arnie Lerma that went into settlement negotiations of legal cases on behalf of Scientology? Arnie was also fully aware of my situation, and he also tried to get me to cooperate with Scientology to "help Bob." I told him at the time where he could get off. We have since talked, and he again tried to convince me that Bob and Stacy did the right thing. I could only tolerate his betrayal and ignorance for so long. We've had problems since.

Because I refused to cooperate with Scientology, my punishment was "disconnection" and "fair game" as practiced in Scientology. With the exception of the Wollersheim case, Bob and Scientology made sure that I was not paid for any of the work I'd done in the cases they were able to settle. Even though I stood with Ken Dandar till the end of the Lisa McPherson case, I was not paid a dime for my work. It was the same in the Dennis Erlich case; I never even got a call thanking me for helping. The Scientology plan was to starve my family and me and cause us to lose everything we had. Their plans worked, for the most part.

I spent months going thru the stress of foreclosure on my home in Florida. I also had the problem of reinventing a career to support my family, which became an overnight priority. Because Lawrence Wollershiem refused to cooperate with Scientology, I received a payment for my services in the case, which sustained me while I searched for a new career. I became a successful Mortgage Broker within three months and was able to maintain my financial obligations for a while. Then the "Fair Gaming" got intense.

Scientology relentlessly interfered with my employers, and I found it nearly impossible to maintain continued employment in Florida. Scientology practically owns Clearwater, Florida, where I lived, so I was fighting a losing battle to a slow death there. All too soon, I was facing the stress of foreclosure again. My friend Brian Haney was not allowed to help me, but we worked something out. Instead of losing my house in foreclosure I was able to sell it.

Due to the extreme stress of the situation, my relationship with my girlfriend failed as well. I ended up renting an apartment alone, struggling to survive. I accepted the failure of my relationship with my partner on the basis that there was no way I could continue to walk down the dangerous path I'd chosen when she had a family in tow. I parted with her so that she could have peace and a chance at life detached from my madness. My partner had never been a Scientologist, so it was all Greek to her. She hung in there as best she could given the circumstances. We have no malice between us to this day.

My partner was a woman of deep religious conviction, and she was the Receptionist for the Lisa McPherson Trust. Anyone who knew her just loved her and her spirit. She was extremely organized and was a great asset to the Trust.

Until very recently, I've had one or two conversations that I remember with Stacy Brooks after she went back under Scientology's control. I talked to her in 2003 when I found out her ex-husband Vaughn Young died. When I learned Vaughn died something inside of me just broke. I remember the day I received the call informing me that Vaughn had passed. I had just parked in front of a house where I had an in-home appointment with the homeowner to refinance their Veterans Administration home mortgage.

My phone rang, and to this day I don't remember who it was but they told me Vaughn had just passed. I sat in my car, stunned. Time seemed suspended as I tried to rationalize how I could get out of this appointment and find the nearest bar. I felt like I couldn't make it thru a presentation in my current state. That feeling of deep-down grief refused to be contained so I sat in my car and decided to cry just a little bit so I could get through the interview and meet my obligation to my employer. I sat there and cried real hard like a big boy for a while, then I got the Visine out and put it in my eyes, took a deep breath and went to the door and rang the doorbell of my potential clients.

I put on my happy face and introduced myself and handed the man my card. They welcomed me into their home, and I started my presentation. Somehow that grief monster roared and I was crying like a baby again! My clients, a man, and a woman looked at each other in horror, and then they looked at me with pity. I ended up explaining to them that a dear friend had died, and I was only informed as I pulled up to their home. They were very understanding and made me tea to calm me down.

When my grief had passed, we continued the interview, and I ended up getting the deal. At the end of my interview with my potential clients, we all laughed about the idea that if I cried at all of my appointments I'd be a rich man! That couple was very understanding and showed me some love that I'll never forget. I could have been fired from my job for my conduct if my employer only knew.

After that appointment, I returned to the home office of my employer and let them know that I'd be taking a few days off to grieve the loss of a friend, and they allowed it.

When I got home that day I called Stacy and let her know, I'd heard about Vaughn passing, and my heart was totally broken. I don't know why I called her. At the time, I was under the full attack of Scientology's fair game practice seemingly from all sides. I talked to her and cried, she talked to me and cried and said we really should talk. I told her I was not ready to have any dialog with her; I just called because Vaughn was dead. Can't say I remember how, but we ended our conversation and years would pass before we would talk again.

Vaughn Young and I traveled on what I consider to be an epic journey together through Scientology, and we were always friends for different reasons. I have to move this story along, so I'm not going to get into all of the idiosyncrasies of the relationship Vaughn, and I had together as freedom fighters right here, right now. I've missed him every day since he left us. Once Vaughn finally left Scientology, he never submitted to them again in any way for the rest of his life.

However, I will take the time to say this. When Vaughn was first diagnosed with cancer, he was informed the damage was irreversible. The cancer had metastasized to his bones and his days were numbered. Of course, being an ex-Scientologist, he had no medical insurance policy to see him through any form of treatment. He also had no money to pay for treatment that could extend his life and let him accomplish finishing his work for others in the future. I remember the phone call with Vaughn when he got the news. He was devastated and had no idea what to do.

He and I discussed possible solutions when I remembered that Vaughn was a veteran of the US military! As a veteran, he was eligible for free medical care for the rest of his life. I made him go to the Veterans Administration for medical care, and they took him right in and started immediate treatment on him. Vaughn was able to live longer because of the treatment he was able to receive. He spent the rest of his life creating a blog about prostate cancer survival as well as his work against Scientology. The work he was able to accomplish in his life indeed lives on.

Vaughn Young gave up the ghost on June 15, 2003, about one year after Bob Minton and Stacy Brooks descent into madness with Scientology. Even though Vaughn had his personal suffering, he was a rock for me through these maddening times.

He was the only person that never turned his back on me in any way as we fought for the truth without compromise as best we knew how.

33

Reawakening

When Vaughn passed, I felt truly alone in the struggle. I simply began to disassociate myself from the subject of Scientology and just tried to live, while years passed.

I only re-awakened when I attended the 2008 conference in Hamburg, which I described at the beginning of this book. It was there that I realized that I was no longer alone in my struggle with Scientology. With recent defections, there were more ex-Scientologists than ever speaking out, doing interviews, writing books. And there was a whole on-line army that had our backs – Anonymous.

On the second day of the conference, the group who represented themselves as Anonymous expressed a concern. Some were disturbed by what they had read on Marty's new blog. He had apparently written articles about his separation from the Sea Org that caused some to question his sanity. Marty wrote about the oppression he was under from his former boss David Miscavige for trying to preserve the precious Scientology Tech. In his writings Marty, was making comparisons of his life with that of Gandhi and Martin Luther King.

Both Anonymous and Marty were involved in activism against David Miscavige and his brand of Scientology. Marty wanted to remove Miscavige from his position as the leader of the Scientology movement, so he could take over and rule with the precious Technology. Anonymous wanted Scientology investigated and prosecuted for criminal activities. Like me, Anonymous wanted no part of endorsing any form of Scientology.

I could sympathize with my Anon friends over Marty's odd behavior. I explained to those present as best I could that he needed more time to decompress from his Sea Org experience. I advised and predicted he'd eventually come to himself.

My new dilemma was the realization that I had not been specific enough with what I'd asked for when I prayed. I'd asked and prayed for Marty Rathbun to leave the Sea Org, but I didn't bargain that he'd get out and start "auditing" people. I guess I just never considered the prospect of Marty leaving only to turn to auditing! Is there no mercy!

It sure could be worse, that's for sure, and I'm laughing as I write this. I ended up having to defend both Marty and Mike Rinder (who had also left Scientology) at the conference and pleaded for patience on the behalf of my two former enemies.

When I arrived home from the conference, I started to research Scientology on the Internet to see if there was anything that I knew on the subject that had not already been said. In the sea of information available through a Google search, it seemed any researcher could find everything they ever wanted to know about Scientology easily.

My other dilemma was how I could show Marty, his bring-along lost cub Mike Rinder and anyone else that auditing is not helpful for people who have decided to leave Scientology. To do so, only adds insult to injury in my opinion. Scientology had already deceived, lied to and probably robbed the person.

I thought my experience was unique among my peers. I'd been there for L Ron during the last four years of his life. L Ron did not live in the same place where I lived at Golden Era Production nor was he there all the time. He was there some of the time, and that's what I can write and talk about. To date, no one had written anything about the end of L Ron's life, and this became a valid subject for me to write about.

I'd be justified in calling what I realized during my reflection and research as cathartic. I began to understand something in my experience that I'd chalk up as insignificant. I thought this insignificant circumstance could be the cornerstone for how I could explain to others why I no longer practice Scientology as a faith. The word faith begins to explain the paradox with L Ron's bridge to enlightenment. L Ron marketed Dianetics and Scientology as a new science. But Science is a systematic enterprise that builds and organizes knowledge in the form of testable explanations and predictions about the universe. With Scientology, this is the fork in the road because Scientology leans towards indoctrinated beliefs as opposed to facts.

My personal chosen path, when I left, was to leave the movement without any promise of payment from me to the Sea Org for anything past, present or future. I willingly and happily renounced any opportunity afforded me by my Sea Org handlers to continue my journey up their ladders or across any of their bridges.

On the day I left Scientology; I left the subject with them. I had no use for or any desire to practice Scientology at all. That condition didn't begin there; it developed over time during the last four years of my service to L Ron Hubbard. I now consider my history with Scientology prior to direct contact with the source of Scientology, L Ron Hubbard as the honeymoon phase. I can best describe what followed as an awaking from a very categorized and organized confusion.

Admittedly, I have not always been the sharpest knife in the drawer when it comes to common sense. I realized it was what I'd experienced during those last four years of L. Ron's life that finally woke me up from my Scientology delusion.

Scientology makes perfect sense until the very end. When is the end? The end comes when Scientology has extracted all that it can from you, with your consent. The minute a Scientologist or Sea Org member ceases to be useful or no longer obeys; their end with the subject comes swiftly.

34

THE SCIENTOLOGY TRAP

ON MARCH 29TH, 2010 POPULAR CNN news host Anderson Cooper produced a show about Scientology titled "Scientology: A History of Violence." The show is now archived on YouTube and is still available for viewing.

As a consequence of airing the show, Anderson Cooper was personally attacked by Scientology's Office of Special Affairs Dept. Paid Scientology agents disseminated information about his lifestyle and "crimes." Anderson learned a lesson about reporting on Scientology that he'd probably only read about and hardly believed.

As I sat and watched the Anderson Cooper series, I thought one of the most poignant segments involved the ex-spouses of Marty Rathbun and Mike Rinder. These fine ladies were doing their best to debunk the concept of forced disconnection as practiced in Scientology. But anyone who has ever spent at least 6 months in Scientology knows the fact that very early in all Scientology doctrine, the fledgling

Scientology adept is prepared and taught how to reject and disconnect from individuals, family, friends or even institutions deemed "undesirable" or "low-toned".

In 2010, old friends began calling me about a new article written by Lawrence Wright in *The New Yorker Magazine* about Hollywood writer and director Paul Haggis. This is a long-ass article but well worth the read:

I had to stand up when I read the very last paragraph of the article:

> *I once asked Haggis about the future of his relationship with Scientology. "These people have long memories," he told me. "My bet is that, within two years, you're going to read something about me in a scandal that looks like it has nothing to do with the church." He thought for a moment, and then said, "I was in a cult for thirty-four years. Everyone else could see it. I don't know why I couldn't."*

You see, even to smart people Scientology superficially makes perfect sense until the very end. Butter knife or dagger, it makes no difference.

Well, being in the butter knife category I knew I had my reasons for never again permitting myself to be subjected to any further Scientology treatment or training in any way. I thought that as a common person, if I could come out of the delusion that is Scientology, anyone could if given the right information.

When I first began to work at the highest echelons of management, I found out the people at the top of L Ron's corporate organizations did not practice the Scientology I learned and became certified in, at all.

The Scientology Trap

All this talk of helping mankind and freeing souls was just nonsense, and the real focus was building money and power. Many years later I surmised that it was known by those who were caring for him that L Ron suffered from dementia. Pat and Annie decided to keep L Ron out of the public eye until the day he died.

New Scientology adepts are instructed on how to negotiate with friends and family who are deemed a potential threat, by telling lies. Of course, they don't just outright tell you to lie. No one needs to be taught how to lie we already know how that goes. For most people, in general, there are moral implications associated with the act of lying itself. Scientology doctrine trains the adept not to *lie*, but how to tell an "acceptable truth," thus sidestepping any moral hazard associated with the act of lying.

As all new Scientology adepts progress up the ladder to spiritual enlightenment, they become more sensitive to family, friends or people, in general that may become antagonistic by questioning the authority of Scientology. Scientology doctrine trains the adept to lie systematically over time to the potential threat. The logic being to tell continuous lies to the potential threatening person for the greater good of keeping the peace for now.

Masking the truth and telling lies (acceptable truths) is institutionalized in Scientology and starts at the very beginning of the indoctrination. The primary emphasis is to "protect" Scientology against any type of scrutiny what so ever in part by lying about or masking the actual truth. The Sea Org members take the concept of lying to a higher level and no longer need the crutch of telling acceptable truths. Sea Org members, in general, will outrageously lie to anyone with a straight face and conviction in their eyes. This is part of the training and Technology that is Scientology.

The practice of institutionalized lying and deception is not a concept lonely to Scientology. Our United States military, along with any other military on the earth we live on trains' new adept soldiers very early on how to lie and deceive in case of capture. They also learn how to deceive and attack targeted enemies. The adept soldier learns how to communicate effectively with his enemy while giving his enemy the least amount of information possible thru deception or outright lies. As an adept soldier moves up the ladder of privileged information and activity, they become more proficient through training in the practices of deception. This is the same model used to train adherents of the Dianetics and Scientology doctrine and rituals.

Government militaries around the world practice deception as a means to protect the nation or to undermine and/or conquer another or other nations and entities labeled as enemies of the state.

Again, I apologize for the long preamble. The point I am trying to establish is this: any Sea Org member who has left the movement readily admits to lying in the misguided effort to protect Scientology from scrutiny and/or to protect their place in the movement itself.

As an example, in a 2009 CNN interview, Scientology spokesperson Tommy Davis denied the existence of the disconnection policy. This is ridiculous. Every Scientologist knows that this policy exists, and yet the Church blatantly lies about it.

The Scientology Trap

In his letter resigning from Scientology, Paul Haggis wrote:

> *I was shocked. We all know this policy exists. I didn't have to search for verification – I didn't have to look any further than my own home. You might recall that my wife was ordered to disconnect from her parents because of something absolutely trivial they supposedly did twenty-five years ago when they resigned from the church. This is a lovely retired couple, never said a negative word about Scientology to me or anyone else I know – hardly raving maniacs or enemies of the church. In fact, it was they who introduced my wife to Scientology. Although it caused her terrible personal pain, my wife broke off all contact with them.*

When a person decides to leave Scientology's Sea Organization, one of two things happens. Either they are summarily declared a Suppressive Person, and they are denied any connection to others, family and friends, who remain true to the movement, or they are forced to pay a "Freeloader Bill" for all of the courses and training they received while in the Sea Org. This can be as much as $100,000 or more. This despite the fact that they have been underpaid and working like a slave for the movement, often for many years. Paying the cash is the first step to get back into the good graces of the Church and continue the quest for "spiritual enlightenment" as administered in Scientology. The other required steps are even more humiliating.

My personal chosen path, when I left, was to leave the movement without any promise of payment from me to the Sea Org for anything past, present or future. I willingly and happily renounced any opportunity afforded me by my Sea Org handlers to continue my journey up their ladders or across any more of their bridges. Given these circumstances, a Scientologist or Sea Org Member is not permitted to associate with me in any way or on any level, and I accepted my fate.

After I returned from the conference in Germany I started to get that old feeling again, wondering when Scientology would get the kick in the ass I thought it deserved. I read stories on Marty's blog of high-profile Scientologist publicly leaving the movement. A simple thing to say now but until just a few short years ago this was not the case.

Just like Tommy Davis, son of Hollywood actress Anne Archer used to say: A person can leave Scientology (when they are ready to let you go) but there are terms. No part of the terms involves publicly leaving Scientology because they have to kick you out first! The soon-to-be ex-member is forced to stay quiet about any intentions of leaving. Scientology Public at-large don't hear about anyone leaving until they are handed a proper copy of a Suppressive Person Declare against the person leaving. In Scientology world, a Suppressive Person Declare amounts to excommunication.

Suddenly and without prior notice, a member can be in the midst of their fellow members, carrying on as usual, until he or she is handed the uniquely potent and dreadful SP declare. Just like that, all of the person's supposed sins are exposed and mightily condemned to their fellow members. They believe they are condemned to a life without hope of spiritual freedom and are instantly denied any contact with any part of the only life they knew and worked so hard for. This includes any and all contact with family members or friends still in the movement. That is the Scientology disconnection ritual, in a nutshell.

35

SCIENTOLOGY LIES, MARTY AND BLACK DIANETICS

WHILE BROWSING MARTY RATHBUN'S "Moving on up A Little Higher," blog site, I felt encouraged by the stories from people who were publicly leaving the Scientology movement. While each person's story varied according to their individual circumstance, the recurring theme was that they all suffered a crisis of conscience and could no longer deny the obvious.

Several other issues began to irritate me as I read Marty's blog. Some of the people who were publicly leaving the Scientology movement were being corralled by Marty for more "auditing" (Scientology rituals). You know my opinion about auditing and the practice of Scientology rituals in general. Be that as it may, I've learned to be patient with that issue.

I have hung in there and remained friends with some that insist on practicing the Scientology rituals after departure from the movement. In most cases, the reward for my patience was paid to me in spades. Within a maximum of a two-year period, more than

90% of the people that I was able to observe and maintain contact with no longer felt they needed the crutch of auditing or any other Scientology ritual they may have learned and paid dearly for. In my heart, I couldn't ask for a better reward. I learned it took time to unravel and discard the Scientology experience, some longer, others not as long.

People I know who have been involved in activism against Scientology often call when there is "Breaking News" in the Scientology world. Someone informed me that Marty was making denigrating statements about David Mayo and Ray Mithoff. These were the last two people L Ron Hubbard allowed to apply the technology he created for himself. At the time, I actually got pissed off about this.

I'm certain L Ron Hubbard never even heard the name Marty Rathbun or knew of his existence. I say this not to be mean but as a fact. Ever since the 1977 FBI raid against a few of the Church of Scientology locations, L Ron became extremely paranoid about anyone that worked for or was associated with the previous secret service of Scientology. The Guardians Office was the name of the secret service within Scientology. They were the "Eye" organization at the top of the pyramid. The agents who'd gotten caught doing exactly what L Ron wanted were discarded and punished for their incompetence.

L Ron issued orders to his special "Messenger Organization" leaders to get rid of and replace anyone who had gotten caught and prosecuted as a result of the FBI raid. He ordered his messengers to dismantle the Guardians Office completely and recreate it under a different name and organization. He demanded his new secret service organization be staffed with fresh personnel with no connections to the previous GO. The name of the new organization eventually became Office of Special Affairs, OSA for short.

Some of the people who were part of the old Guardians office but were not convicted of doing any criminal activities were ordered gotten rid of as well. David Miscavige was the primary Sea Org Member L Ron used to recreate the old GO by getting rid of and replacing its personnel. Some people could not be gotten rid of because there was no one to replace them. You just don't throw the ex-intelligence personnel out, for your enemy to exploit and use against you. David Miscavige understood this; L Ron didn't and refused to accept anything but the complete eradication of these once faithful followers.

David compromised and decided to hide certain people and their previous connections to the old GO. Marty Rathbun was one of these people from the old GO. Certain agents were one-of-a-kind so were irreplaceable. There was no one person that had a comprehensive working knowledge of the entire intelligence operations of the old Guardians Office.

When I saw from his blog that Marty was now somehow claiming to be superior to the people L Ron trusted with his precious Technology it was enough to make me start writing. Instead of arguing with him and others on his blog I started my own blog in late 2011 and named it Jesse's Place!

My idea was to provide information about the inner workings of Scientology without the Marty Rathbun/Mike Rinder spin. In my opinion, Marty was anything but forthcoming when it came to his rendition of the facts. Mike Rinder was still an L Ron adorer. I decided to give them a hand by reminding them of where they came from.

I posted the following on my blog:

Marty was never known for having anything to do with practicing the precious Scientology Technology as it relates to spiritual advancement. Marty became a high-level player in the inner circle group, but it seems he is hiding the real reason how he got there. I know how and why Marty eventually became part of the inner circle he'd only served before.

Like any job, to be in a position to be referred to as a senior executive you must have a specific skill (credential) that you bring to the table of your peers. I know Scientology demands years of unquestioning service and excellent results with whatever skill the person brings to the table. My specific credential was the supervision of the "Rituals," "Tech," and anything else associated with the application of the Scientology Dogma. This is fully documented in testimony I've given to the courts on both sides of the issue. I've appeared as a Scientology Technical Expert witness on behalf of Scientology. I have also testified as an Expert Witness against Scientology. My testimony has been accepted in courtrooms across America. Right wrong or indifferent understanding Scientology Rituals was my study and path in the movement.

My question to you Marty is this, why are you so shy about your specific credentials as another senior person in all of Scientology? Your actual credentials that earned you a place at the table with your peers wasn't anything involving the "Technology" as given in the red volumes written by L Ron Hubbard, that spot was already taken by a few.

The certified credentials you earned that placed you at the table of your peers involved defending the faith at any cost. For that reason, you have been involved in what can only be commonly described as "Black Operations" designed to ruin lives and leave people on the edge of insanity. The numbers of times you've been ordered to exercise your specific credentials supersede anyone currently involved in the movement who is still breathing.

You literally glided into your high position among your peers by riding the coattails of your sponsor and mentor David Miscavige. You were able to secure your position by always being the one who would execute Miscavige's most secret and criminal assignments. You knew it was a given that he would take all of the credit for any positive result you may have achieved. Because of the methods you were required to employ to succeed at any given task; very few even knew what you were doing. The great works you were able to accomplish are only known by a secret few, on a need-to-know basis.

When it came to responding to Miscavige's demands, you only used two words, yes and sir. Miscavige used you to do things he was too cowardly to attempt himself. You were always so willing to please him. You were not a selfish person. All you ever really wanted was for Miscavige just to smile at you or tell you "good job." It is my opinion that the relationship you had with Miscavige was doomed to fail from the start because of the competition factor. There came a time when L Ron turned on his most trusted "Dirty Deeds" confidants David Miscavige, Pat Broeker, David Mayo....on and on.

While Scientologists and especially Sea Org members are specifically trained to lie skillfully and deceive, another thing they are also trained in is a specialized definition of the word *truth*. I couldn't see how Marty, who touted himself as the new keeper of the precious tech, could survive his lack of honesty in his reporting.

I was able to apply what I'd learned about the application of truth and was able to accomplish getting all of my testimony accepted in courtrooms across America. I appeared as an expert witness in a case involving the death of a Scientology member Lisa McPherson. I'd submitted declarations and affidavits to multiple judges who presided over the Lisa McPherson wrongful death lawsuit.

In Scientology world, the proof of knowledge and understanding of the precious tech is all in the application. According to L Ron, if you apply his precious technology exactly as written you will get the intended result every time. I became more frustrated with Marty. I couldn't for the life of me understand what part of the precious tech he thought he learned and was now applying?

I left the movement in 1992; Lisa McPherson was killed in 1995. WTF would I know about what happened or how it all went down?

In reality, I just used my credentials I learned in Scientology. I learned a unique definition of the word "truth", as defined by L Ron. He defined truth as an exact time, place, form, and event. In Scientology, the practice of lying is a sacrament and is taught and practiced for a dual purpose. In Scientology, lying is expected to be applied liberally when dealing with anyone outside of the movement itself. However, it is strictly forbidden to lie to one another, and this is the dual nature of how truth is practiced in Scientology and the Sea Organization. One of the quickest ways to land in the Scientology jail (RPF) would be to get caught telling a lie about even the simplest of things. To lie to a fellow member, especially a supervisor or senior person was personal suicide.

According to L Ron, when asked to tell the "truth" about something, in essence, it meant being debriefed like a spy agent. All the details are required: What did you see? Not what did you think! Who was there? Where did the event happen? Was it at a party? Was there a meeting? I mean they break it down so that no stone is left unturned. In Scientology, truth is determined solely on a person's ability to observe and report accurately what was observed. Thinking or forming an opinion about what is observed is not part of the process.

I don't think they even notice it among themselves, but there is very little excessive verbal talking in the Sea Organization. Anyone looking in from the outside would think they were all mind readers. When we would talk, it sounded like a different language than the one I speak today. Very few outsiders had a clue of how Sea Org members would be in perfect lock step when working together without a lot of talk. In the Scientology culture, you will get investigated for criminal activity if you talk too much, and this is not a joke.

The definition of truth, as practiced in Scientology, served me well as I battled them in courtrooms. By applying this detailed definition of the truth in my testimony, even a third party (any judge I ever faced) recognized the accuracy and detail of my testimony as coming from one who was there and knows. Telling the truth works with less effort than telling lies.

The Expert Witness

Telling lies is a creative process that's hard to prove when questioned. Telling the truth concerns relating the details of something that happened in the past in most cases, the more accurate the details, the more believable the report. In the Sea Organization we were trained to tell the perfect truth to one another, so we did. I just started telling the perfect truth to those outside of the movement.

L Ron made a visual distinction between "Rituals" or "Technology" he'd developed for the purpose of helping a person; as opposed to the "Rituals" or "Technology" he developed to destroy someone. The rituals L Ron developed that he thought could help a person were issued in red ink. The rituals L Ron developed to destroy a person was issued in either black or green ink. The rituals to destroy a person are the same as the rituals that supposedly help a person. The only difference is, if the intent is to destroy a person then the ritual is done in reverse. In Scientology, this is commonly referred to as Black Dianetics. Only through being demonstrably proficient at the practice of Black Dianetics was Marty Rathbun able to secure a place at the table with his Sea Organization peers. David Miscavige is the only person qualified to mentor and intern another in the application of Black Dianetics. David's mentor was L Ron Hubbard, the source of the madness.

After Marty and his master David Miscavige parted ways, like a jilted lover Marty ran to the press and told his story.

To the casual observer, this story seems to be all about the horror of David Miscavige's destruction of Scientology's good name and intent. Nothing could be further from the truth. When I read the articles what was apparent to me is Marty's expert use of credentials, he learned from his masters.

Marty's story paints David Miscavige as a slaphappy demon. Marty was able to manipulate the journalists who wrote the story; he's been doing that on Scientology's behalf for decades. Please, tell me how Marty was able to persuade these reporters to rewrite history and omit himself and his own personal activity as the trained diehard criminal he is? This is not just my opinion. People who habitually break the laws without regard are called criminals. It just doesn't add up.

A more appropriate story would be about how Marty and whomever else he used to destroy the State of Florida's criminal case for the McPherson murder. Why is Marty still covering for Miscavige even to this day?

At some point, I was David Miscavige's "auditor" which means I practiced and used the rituals on him. David's complete auditing file was available to me when I needed it. This was not the case with Marty's auditing files. I was not allowed to view his auditing files. I remember asking Vicki Aznaran, who was the corporate president of the Religious Technology Center (RTC) what the deal was with Marty's auditing file. She told me the only people that had access to Marty's auditing files were people who had a special security clearance given only by Miscavige. She also told me there was really nothing to see in his files because his auditing records were destroyed the day they are made in most cases due to the nature of the information.

She discouraged me from even inquiring about his auditing files because it would not be good for me to know details of Marty's work. She explained if law enforcement could tie me into those activities it could mean the end of my life as a free man. I went along with her advice.

Now it's clear how Marty earned his credentials and place at the table of his peers. Whatever David told Marty to do he did to the best of his ability and there are little to no records kept substantiating his actual service.

At the time (1982-1986) there were less than ten people that held the distinction of having no records for actual service.

There was also the fact that although it had been seven years earlier, I was still smarting from what Marty and Mike Rinder did to destroy the Lisa McPherson Trust.

36

WHAT ABOUT ME?

I BEGAN TO WRITE THIS STORY after returning from the Scientology Symposium in Hamburg, Germany. I began to post parts of the story on my blog "Jesse's Place" on Google Blogs.

It was during this time that I began to do the research into the Luciferian roots of Scientology as a theology. I hope no one gets the idea I'm some God and the devil fanatic because I'm not, but dead L Ron sure was. I became interested in learning more about this God and devil stuff out of self-defense. I now truly believe what you don't know can kill you dead if it happens to catch you unaware.

I had listened to L Ron taped lectures where he mentioned his association with Alistair Crowley who is probably the most popular Satanist of our times. Crowley referred to himself as the Beast of the Christian Bible. I'd also heard L Ron lecture about being involved with a group called Ordos Templi Orientis. Historically the OTO is one of the oldest groups involved in Luciferian rituals and worship in

America. Interesting stuff and for anyone truly interested in going further down that rabbit hole I recommend you start with Jon Atack's book, *A Piece of Blue Sky*.

I also researched and read information about L Ron's military and medical history. These subjects are more than adequately covered by other authors. Russell Miller's *Bare-Faced Messiah* and Bent Corydon's *Messiah or Madman* are excellent works. I recommend both of these books for anyone who seriously wants to know and understand what Scientology actually is. It is impossible to know what Scientology is while also trying to be a member.

After researching and studying the occult aspects of L Ron I began to write again. I wrote about the final days of the Lisa McPherson Trust.

Within a week of writing that final chapter I began to feel ill. I felt an increasing pain in my back that didn't go away. I tried self-medicating to no avail. After two weeks of this growing pain I found all I could do is lay in bed in curled up in the fetal position. May 16, 2011 was the first time I went to Emergency at the University of Chicago hospital. They performed several tests and informed me they suspected I had the AIDS virus. I was shocked by the news and couldn't think of any way I could have possibly contacted AIDS. I waited until the complete test results came back and was informed that I didn't have the AIDS virus. This was a relief but I was very ill. I still hadn't found out what was wrong with me.

Next, this same doctor diagnosed me as having syphilis or gonorrhea. He said the test to confirm this new diagnosis would take a few days, to come back from the lab, so I waited. I wondered how this could be. I hadn't been in a sexual relationship with anyone for some months. In the meantime, I was given pain medication (hydrocodone) and sent home.

May 26, 2011, I went back to the same emergency hospital in extreme pain. I was informed the test for syphilis and gonorrhea came back both negative. They didn't know what was wrong with me. I went to a different hospital the next day only to just get more pain medication. By this time I had to have the pain medication just to maintain some level of sanity I was in so much pain.

A friend suggested that I go to the John H. Stroger hospital in Chicago because this was supposed to be the best hospital in town. I went there the first time and they did some tests and sent me home with more pain medication. In less than a week I could feel my life slipping away from me. I went back to Cook County and begged them to please find out what was wrong with me. It was then they discovered that I was in stage four non-Hodgkin lymphoma. There were cancer tumors attached to the bones in my spine. I was admitted immediately and was put on a morphine drip. A team of seven doctors began to work on my case.

Within 48 hours of being admitted, I began to receive a nonspecific chemotherapy. At this stage of cancer treatment there were pre-established treatment regimens based on DNA type. For some reason I had an unusual non-standard DNA chromosome that didn't have a specific treatment for that type. One of my doctors talked to my brother and told him it would be wise for the family to prepare for my death. There was no specific cure for the type of cancer I had, but they would try to treat it with general cancer medication they had. My oncologist was a beautiful lady named Shivi, she was from India. She explained to me there was no specific cure for me but there was a possibility I could be cured. I told her as long as there was a chance I was willing to try and fight for my life. I had this conversation with her early in the afternoon.

Later on that evening, after I was alone I laid in that bed and parts of my life seemed come up for inspection. It was strange, like starting a conversation with yourself. As I contemplated my current situation I began to ponder what kind of life I would have even if I survived the cancer. I had learned in addition to having tumors along my spine, I also had tumors in my lungs, on both glands on the sides of my neck and tumors on either side of my nether region.

I thought about what would happen if I just let go. For some reason I was not afraid. If I died, so be it. I was weary of my trials and tribulation of living this life. I felt sad about wasting so much of my life in Scientology only to learn I'd slavishly served a person who thought he was Satan. I thought about who would miss me or who depended on me and the answer I got was no one. I didn't have health insurance, I didn't have a huge savings account either. I didn't want to be a burden to anyone so I decided it would be better for all concerned if I died.

Strangely enough, when I made the decision to die, a peace came over me. It was like I felt like I was somehow wrapped in a warm blanket and it felt good all the way down to my sick bones. I then wondered what time a good time would be to die. I looked at the clock on the wall near my bed and decided to die at five o'clock the following morning. Until then, I'd just quietly lay there a watch a bit of television.

A hard rain began to beat the windows of my hospital room. I could see the lightning flashes. As I lay there I remember getting bored with television. I looked at the clock and it was just after 1am. I thought to myself, it's a long time till 5 am. Why did I pick 5 am? There was no reason to wait till 5 am to die I may as well be dead now.

No sooner than I had that thought I experience the sensation of being lifted out of my hospital bed. I had somehow effortlessly gotten out of the bed and was standing at an unnaturally high height in front of the hospital window. I turned around to look at the bed I'd just sprang from and notice my sick crumpled body lying on the bed with tubes and drips attached to the arms. I hardly recognized that thing that laying on the bed but I didn't care. I was free of that sick body and I began to feel really good. I turned around to look out of the hospital window when I noticed what looked like a dark tunnel with a whitish gold light at the end. I remember thinking to myself, I must be dead.

That's the short simple explanation of what happened when I died a little bit. The next book I write will be about what happened. It's been such an adventure to be allowed to come back to complete certain things that needed to be completed.

Finishing this book was a major goal for me to accomplish. If you're reading this, that means I've succeeded and am living a new life.

APPENDIX 1

LISA MCPHERSON AFFIDAVIT

IN THE CIRCUIT COURT OF THE
THIRTEENTH JUDICIAL CIRCUIT
IN AND FOR HILLSBOROUGH COUNTY,
STATE OF FLORIDA GENERAL CIVIL DIVISION

ESTATE OF LISA McPHERSON, by and through the Personal Representative, DELL LIEBREICH, Plaintiff,

VS.

CHURCH OF SCIENTOLOGY FLAG SERVICE ORGANIZATION, INC.; AFFIDAVIT OF JANIS JOHNSON; ALAIN KARTUZINSKI; JESSE PRINCE and DAVID HOUGHTON Defendants.

Case No. 97-01235 Section "H."

STATE OF FLORIDA:
COUNTY OF HILLSBOROUGH:

BEFORE ME, personally appeared JESSE PRINCE, who, after being duly sworn, deposes and says:

1. I am over 18 years of age and currently reside in the state of Illinois, Cook County. This declaration is of my own personal knowledge, and if called upon to testify to the facts herein I could and would be competently able to testify thereto. My History in Scientology

I was in Scientology for 16 years (1976-92). In July of 1992, I escaped with my wife from Scientology headquarters at Gilman Hot Springs, Ca.

Under duress, my wife and I were forced to return. After intense interrogation and isolation, my wife and I on October 31, 1992, were able to leave Scientology, but only after we were coerced to sign a release containing untrue statements protecting Scientology from legal liability.

I remained silent about my experience in Scientology, since upon leaving I was subjected to routine monitoring by Mike Sutter of the Religious Technology Center, (RTC), and Earl Cooley, Scientology counsel.

In July of 1998, I discovered that others had similar experiences and were courageous enough to speak out against Scientology. I therefore ended my silence so that others would know the truth of what really happens in the inner circles of Scientology.

2. I am intimately familiar with the organization, movement, beliefs, practices and technologies of Scientology. I served in the highest ranks of Scientology, including second in command of the Religious Technology Center (RTC), the most senior body of Scientology.

APPENDIX 1

3. Beginning in March of 1983 and until the spring of 1987, I held the position of "Deputy Inspector General, External". In this position, I was one of the three members of the Board of Directors of RTC while David Miscavige was on its Board of Trustees.

4. In the position of "Deputy Inspector General, External", I was in charge of supervising all activities in every aspect of Scientology, i.e., supervising senior management structure of the "mother church", Church of Scientology International, CSI.

In the hierarchy of all of Scientology, I was only two steps removed from L. Ron Hubbard. Mr. Hubbard gave his orders to David Miscavige, who in turn gave them to me to supervise, delegate and enforce their execution. Corporately speaking, Vicki Aznaran, the President of RTC, and I were accountable and reported only to David Miscavige and L. Ron Hubbard. RTC gave CSI the license to use Dianetics and Scientology technologies.

5. Moreover, I was in charge of the Trademark Integrity Secretary, (TMI Sec), Jim Mooney, who had authority over the senior management of CSI called the Watchdog Committee. This Committee has complete authority over the different sectors of all of Scientology. The members of this committee are comprised of senior management officials who oversee and control the management of the following: FLAG SERVICE ORGANIZATION,(FSO); World Institute of Scientology Enterprises, (WISE); Scientology Missions International,(SMI); Reserves, the person responsible for the management and supervision of all bank accounts and revenues; Golden Era Productions, (GOLD);Flag Land Base,(FLB); Sea Org, (SO); Celebrity Center

International, (CC Into); and Office of Special Affairs, (OSA), which handles all the legal and intelligence functions of Scientology.

6. Some of my specific duties as Deputy Inspector General, External, included supervising all litigation by or against any Scientology organization, intelligence and covert operations brought against perceived or imagined "enemies", trademark registrations, and the licensing of trademarks to other Scientology corporations to create the false impression of "corporate integrity".

I was also in charge of the "Celeb Project," which ran all auditing of Scientology celebrities, such as John Travolta, Priscilla Presley, Kristi Alley, Anne Archer, and Chick Corea to name a few. I was also the auditor for David Miscavige and his wife, Shelly.

I was the course instructor for all of the auditing courses for Alain Kartuzinski and his Cramming Officer for Class 10, 11, and 12, 12 being the highest level an auditor can reach.

7. I first became involved with Scientology in September 1976, in San Francisco. In late 1976, I joined the elite Scientology paramilitary organization known as the Sea Organization, also known as the "Sea Org" or the acronym "SO". Sea Organization personnel are authorized to take over and control Scientology organizations and to demote or promote personnel including chief executives, move bank accounts, and run the corporation as if SO personnel were employees or representatives of that corporation.

The power of the SO is not only over the purported religious Scientology organizations but also prevails over the secular organizations such as WISE

APPENDIX 1

or Bridge Publications. The Sea Org's pervasive authority is possible because the only personnel allowed into executive positions in these organizations are those who are in full agreement that the Sea Organization is the commanding organization.

8. Before I was recruited into the Religious Technology Center (RTC) in 1982, most of my experience was with Scientology technical material; the actual codified auditing and administrative techniques used within the organization.

This gave me considerable time to become familiar with these technical materials, most of which was written by Scientology founder L. Ron Hubbard.

My knowledge and expertise of the technologies prompted my promotion to a technical position at RTC.

9. In the fall of 1982, L. Ron Hubbard issued an order to find the best Supervisor/Cramming Officer in all of Scientology and bring that person to Golden Era Productions (GOLD) to correct and train the senior executive management structure of the Scientology Empire around the world.

A Supervisor in Scientology is analogous to a teacher in a classroom. A Cramming Officer is responsible for the correction of individuals who have difficulty in executing the techniques of Dianetics and Scientology or otherwise following the dogma of L. Ron Hubbard to the letter.

Mike Eldridge, a personal emissary of L. Ron Hubbard, in charge of conducting the search to find the most qualified person to serve as Supervisor/Cramming Officer, recommended me to David Miscavige, who ultimately approved my appointment. I was transferred to, lived and worked in what is known as "Golden Era Studios, "near Hemet, California. It is also known as "Gold" or simply "The Base", where senior management of Scientology is headquartered.

10. By Scientology standards, I was a very highly trained auditor and case supervisor. An auditor in Scientology is a trained practitioner of the pseudo-scientific methodology of psychological counseling commonly referred to as "The Tech," as dictated and written by Scientology founder L Ron Hubbard.

A case supervisor is also a trained auditor who reads the "auditing" records of every counseling session performed by an auditor to ensure "The Tech" was applied exactly.

In Scientology, there are 12 levels of auditor and case supervisor classification, each level being "higher" than the next. In this system, I was certified as a Class 9 Auditor and a certified Class 9 Case Supervisor.

11. In my capacity as Deputy Inspector General, External, I traveled to the U.S. and outside of the U.S. on behalf of RTC. I traveled to Germany, Italy, Australia, United Kingdom, Denmark, Mexico, and Canada. These trips were designed to put together an infrastructure that would interface with RTC for the purpose of trademark enforcement.

I was personally chosen by David Miscavige over Vicki Aznaran to speak on behalf of RTC to a worldwide audience via satellite to warn them that RTC holds the trademarks of Scientology and eradicates all those who violate "The Tech" or infringe on trademarks.

APPENDIX 1

12. I became familiar with the trademark laws of the various countries in which I traveled. I interviewed and retained law firms, and put personnel in place that would report to RTC and be our site representatives. I testified as an expert witness on Scientology technology on behalf of RTC in federal court in Los Angeles in an RICO action with RTC as the plaintiff in 1985.

In 1983, on orders from L. Ron Hubbard, I brought into existence within RTC a unit called "The Tech Unit." The Tech Unit had the responsibility of inspecting PC files a/k/a Pre-Clear files, (counseling files), in all Scientology organizations to ensure "The Tech" was being applied 100% according to the standard tech.

13. When Hubbard died in 1986, there was a power struggle in Scientology for the next 18 or so months that resulted in Hubbard's closest and most powerful aide (Pat Broeker) being removed from Scientology. Total power was taken over by David Miscavige, who purged the organization of anyone who was friendly with Broeker.

In mid-1987, because I did not want to participate in Miscavige's power struggle to become the head of Scientology, I was forcefully removed from my position and put under armed guard at Happy Valley, located deep in the desert behind the Soboba Indian Reservation. It is my belief that my undated resignation, which I signed when appointed to the Board, was then dated and used to make it appear that I had resigned, when I had not.

Practices of Scientology:

13. From time to time, based on orders that I received from David Miscavige, I would order others

to engage in illegal activities against perceived enemies of Scientology. These activities included, but were not limited to, wire-tapping and document destruction. For example, on or about April, 1983, I was present at a meeting which took place in Los Angeles, California, at a Scientology office called Author Services, Inc. (ASI), a for-profit company and the "literary agency" for Hubbard, run by David Miscavige.

There is no real corporate structure among the many Scientology corporations. ASI was the meeting place where various Scientology corporations went to receive orders.

Present at this meeting was David Miscavige, then the Chairman of the Board of ASI, Vicki Aznaran, Deputy Inspector General of RTC, Marc Yeager, Commanding officer of CSI, and Lyman Spurlock, who was "Director of Client Affairs" for ASI. Mr. Miscavige expressed concern at this meeting that there might possibly be a raid on Scientology by the IRS.

At that time, none of the churches of Scientology had received tax-exempt status. At this meeting, David Miscavige announced to the group that the destruction and alteration of documents to protect Scientology was in progress. One principal reason why tax-exempt status had not been granted was the IRS's position that Scientology founder, L. Ron Hubbard (LRH), was actually the managing agent of Scientology in complete disregard of the corporate structure of Scientology.

We knew this to be a fact, but also knew that it violated IRS rules and thus had to be hidden. There was concern that the IRS would obtain the hundreds

APPENDIX 1

of daily, weekly and monthly LRH orders written by Hubbard and distributed throughout Scientology. These orders were commonly referred to in Scientology as "advices" to avoid the appearance that Hubbard was actually running Scientology. In fact, Hubbard was running Scientology.

The principal concern expressed at this meeting was that the LRH orders or "advices" would be used to name Hubbard as the managing agent of Scientology. Because of an already existing fear that an LRH "advice" might fall into the wrong hands, these orders from him were written in a way that we could deny it was from him. His name was not on them. He was never cited in the dispatch except in the third person. There was no signature and a salutation in reply was never more than "Dear Sir."

The routing at the top referred to him merely as "###", (three pound signs), while his closest aides, Pat and Annie Broeker, were referred to as "* ", (an asterisk). However, if a person (or agency) got enough of these, there would be little doubt that we were in touch with Hubbard (via ASI) and that he was telling us and each corporation what to do to make him more money.

14. David Miscavige specifically ordered destruction of any documents in ASI's possession, which would implicate Hubbard as managing agent of Scientology. He stated that under his directive the LRH orders or "advices" were being collected and transferred by truck to a Riverside County recycling plant where the documents were to be "pulped."

This method of destruction was considered to be better than shredding. I was also put in charge of purging the remainder of the LRH orders, i.e.

"Advices". This was to include "advices" that were located in Church of Scientology of California (CSC); Church of Scientology International (CSI); and RTC.

15. Several weeks after the April, 1983 meeting, I attended another meeting at the ASI offices concerning the continuing destruction of Scientology corporate documentation. In attendance at this meeting were David Miscavige, Lyman Spurlock, Vicki Aznaran, Norman Starkey, Marty Rathbun, and Scientology attorney, Earl Cooley. At this meeting, Miscavige, for the first time, stated that Scientology had been ordered by a court to produce various documents concerning a former Scientology member, Lawrence Wollersheim, who had a lawsuit pending in Los Angeles against the Church of Scientology of California. The court had ordered Scientology to produce Wollersheim's entire Pre-Clear file.

16. A "Pre-Clear" file is one of the several files kept on members. The Pre-Clear file is the file that includes all written records of all "confessionals' done by the member. This means that it includes not only the most self-damaging material, but it also reflects every problem the person might have had with the organization, including complaints. This Pre-Clear file grows with the person's tenure in Scientology.

17. Mr. Wollersheim's Pre-Clear file was several thousand pages in length and stood as high as a six-foot tall man. Initially at this meeting, it was decided that Mr. Wollersheim's Pre-Clear file would be redacted and culled of any evidence or documentation, which might assist Wollershiem in his lawsuit against CSC.

There was also concern that the materials known as Clear, OT I, OT II, OT III and NED for OT's

Appendix 1

(NOTS) would be open to public inspection if Wollersheim's files were produced as ordered. Scientologists are taught that a person could catch pneumonia and die if that person is prematurely exposed to these "upper level" materials without first having taken many hours of preparatory auditing.

18. Wollersheim's Pre-Clear file was purged of any incriminating evidence against Scientology based on a direct order from Miscavige in the presence of Scientology's lead trial counsel, Earl Cooley of Boston, Massachusetts. Mr. Cooley thereafter represented to the court that the purged file was indeed the entire PC File of Mr. Wollershiem. Ultimately, approximately 50 pages were produced pursuant to the court order.

21. Later, I was informed that a second court order was issued to produce Wollersheim's entire file. Faced with the prospect of having to produce the entire file, Miscavige gave orders that the entire file simply be destroyed by being pulped.

22. Pursuant to Miscavige's orders, I ordered Rick Aznaran to take Wollersheim's Pre-Clear files to the recycling plant in Riverside to be pulped. Several hours after I gave the order to have Wollersheim's Pre-Clear files destroyed, Rick Aznaran returned and confirmed that the records had been pulped and even showed me a small bottle of pulped material. "Here's what's left," he said.

23. Members of Scientology are induced to confess to acts that, if not outright criminal, are embarrassing or possibly destructive to the person's job, marriage or profession. For example, shoplifting, adultery, masturbation, homosexuality, drug abuse, or any other potentially embarrassing or illegal matters are

recorded. Members are urged to write down these compromising facts in their own handwriting, under the guise that it is a "religious confessional" for the member's good.

The truth is that these "confessions" are kept to blackmail and extort members should they dare to speak out against Scientology. Members are also coerced to sign documents that are self-damaging in order to protect Scientology in case they dare to leave its control and speak the damaging truth. I know all this to be true because I watched this done to others; I did it to others, and it was done to me.

24. I have personally witnessed executive decisions directed to members instructing them to "end cycle", i.e., die. I have personally read written instructions by Ray Mithoff concerning the following individuals:

Diane Morrison, a personal friend of mine. She had cancer. Radiation treatment is forbidden by Scientology. She was instructed by Ray Mithoff to "end cycle." Her husband, Shawn Morrison, was ordered by Ray Mithoff to transport her off of the Scientology property at Gilman Hot springs, California, to her mother's house so that she would not die on Scientology property.

Ted Cormier, a personal friend of mine. He had Parkinson's disease. He was ordered to leave Gilman Hot Springs and go directly to Flag for NOTS 34, auditing to cure his cancer. When this failed, Ray Mithoff sent him orders in his Pre-Clear folder for him to "end cycle." He died.

25. I have personally reviewed a video of a television interview with Roxanne Friend, a former Scientologist. She had cancer, which could have been successfully treated. She was kidnaped in California

APPENDIX 1

and taken across the country in a motor home to FLAG in Clearwater where she was held against her will, which prevented her from getting cancer treatment. After she had escaped, she gave this interview that I observed on a television talk show. She disclosed that she was beyond treatment because of this delay and subsequently died. Based on my experience in Scientology, her statements ring true.

My Experience with Isolation:

26. In 1973, Hubbard announced to the Scientology world that he had solved the problem of how to handle a person in a "psychotic break". Hubbard stated that this was a "technical breakthrough" which possibly ranks with the major discoveries of the twentieth century. He further said his discovery means the last reason to have Psychiatry around is gone. He went on to say the key is what caused the person to introspect before the psychotic break.

During my tenure in Scientology, I have observed four instances of people having a psychotic break. In each case the person was sleep deprived; each had been told their job performance was inadequate, and each person was subjected to Scientology ethics.

27. I am familiar with the practice of "Isolation," also known as "baby watch" as practiced by Scientology and I have participated in the "handling "of one Scientologist that was ordered to "Isolation". No one volunteers to go into Isolation.

I have seen with my own eyes how a person is driven to the point of having a "psychotic break" and the subsequent brutality of treatment the person then receives as a result of the handlers following strict Scientology methods.

28. In the four instances of Isolation I observed, the person was locked in a room with at least two other people guarding the exit door. The people that watch the person in a psychotic break are not allowed to talk to the person at all. They are only allowed to physically restrain the person. The reason there are people guarding the exit door is that the person wants to leave and attempts to leave time after time. By their own policy, the person in a psychotic break is not allowed to leave until the Case Supervisor allows it.

Here is a direct quote from Scientology technical "Introspection Rundown, Additional Step": "Dear Joe. What can you guarantee me if you are let out of Isolation?" If the person's reply shows continued irresponsibility toward other dynamics or fixation on one dynamic to the exclusion of others damaged, the C/S (Case Supervisor) must inform the person of his continued Isolation and why. Example: "Dear Joe. I'm sorry but no go on coming out of isolation yet..."

29. In 1987, I was at a place called Happy Valley, located behind the Soboba Indian Reservation in California. Happy Valley is where the Scientology Rehabilitation Project Force, RPF, is located. It is a prison /slave labor camp for Scientologists who no longer ascribe totally to the doctrine of Scientology. I, along with six other Sea Org members, was ordered to do an "isolation watch" on another Sea Org member who was having a psychotic break.

Prior to having the psychotic break the person was very normal. She had been deprived of sleep for many days due to a deadline she was ordered to meet on her job. She was sent to "Ethics" and was constantly humiliated and degraded for making errors and for falling asleep at her workstation. When she was given

APPENDIX 1

to me to watch, she was on her hands and knees and literally barking like a dog.

She thought she was L. Ron Hubbard. It was at this time that I learned how forced feeding was done and the extent of restraint we all had to enforce on a young woman barely 5 feet tall. I was horrified at just how close she was to losing her life due to the "help" we were being ordered to give her.

Even though she was now being allowed to sleep, she could not sleep and have been up for nearly four days. She was in a very agitated and violent state.

She would scream for hours until she could scream no more. She fought to escape and mutilated herself in the process. Finally, a doctor was called in, and it took four people plus the doctor to hold her down to give her a shot to make her go to sleep.

30. A major part of the trauma a person experiences in Scientology's "isolation" treatment is the person's struggle to get away or to get out of the room they are being confined in. The young woman I had to "isolation watch" had numerous injuries as a result of her beating on the walls and the door trying to get away. She would drift in and out of her psychotic state.

I was informed by the security guard watching over us all that her family was desperately trying to find her and during the times when she was "okay" I had to let her call her mother after I told her what to say. I held a separate phone while she talked to her family and when things started to get "weird" I would end the conversation. She would tell her mother that she was okay and would be home soon.

During this time, she became very upset with me because I made her see a doctor she did not know and who was not allowed to talk to her while he was giving her shots. She physically attacked me on more than one occasion. This was a public relations nightmare for Scientology, and this is why she was told to lie to her family about what was really going on with her.

This went on for two months. After she seemed stable for a week and completed the "Introspection Rundown" she was made to sign a release form which in essence said Scientology was not responsible for what had happened to her and she was quickly sent home.

31. If I had not forcibly made her drink water, I am positive that based upon my own observations she would have died.

32. The people who are selected to watch a person in a psychotic break are trained to make a person physically comply with orders and demands.

Controlling a person physically is taught in Scientology in its Training Routine Courses. As an example, in what is called "Training Routine 7, High School Indoctrination" the Scientology student is trained never to be stopped by a Pre-Clear. No matter what the person in "Isolation" does or says, they are not allowed to leave until the C/S says they can.

My Involvement in the case of Lisa McPherson:

33. I have been retained as an expert witness and trial consultant in the case of Lisa McPherson since Nov, 1998. In Dec, 1998, Scientology representative Glenn Stilo brought Lisa McPherson's Pre Clear files to the office of Ken Dandar by order of this court for inspection. Glenn Stilo and I knew each other when I was in Scientology.

APPENDIX 1

At that time, Glenn was fully aware that I was present at Mr. Dandar's Office and that I was there inspecting Lisa McPherson's auditing files. I have also reviewed the "caretaker logs" of Lisa McPherson at the Fort Harrison Hotel and her Ethics File.

34. It is obvious from these files that Lisa McPherson complained that auditing and Scientology were not working for her in 1995 and that she wanted to leave and return to Texas. Her "stats" were down, i.e., her production and income at AMC Publishing.

As a result, she was placed in Ethics at her work where the records revealed that she was constantly doing "amends" and writing "O/W's", overts and withholds, which resulted in less time to obtain adequate sleep which further, in my own observations, leads to psychotic breaks. L. Ron Hubbard confirms this in his own writings, "Introspection Rundown Additional Steps."

35. FLAG at the Ft. Harrison Hotel is "the mecca of technical perfection" according to Scientology. I can attest that it is a high crime in Scientology to alter or ignore the tech. It is also a high crime to lose or omit vital information from any PC folder, including "caretaker logs." The Lisa McPherson "caretaker logs" are missing substantial day-to-day portions, in particular, the last three and one-half days of her Isolation.

This is no accident. Records of this magnitude are not lost. Based on my experience, these missing records were intentionally destroyed to conceal material matters damaging to Scientology. Hubbard explicitly writes in CS SERIES 97 and CS SERIES 98 "omissions from folders and complete loss of folders is a very serious matter...." If proven, expulsion from Scientology is mandatory.

36. I have been asked to address the issue of whether or not Lisa McPherson would have consented to her own isolation prior to experiencing a psychotic break. Without question, no Scientologist, except a Class 4 auditor or above, would have prior knowledge of how someone would be treated who is declared to be PTS Type III: "Potential Trouble Source" who is experiencing a psychotic break.

Only those auditors would have the knowledge that "Isolation" is implemented or the details of "Isolation" for those who are PTS Type III. In reviewing the Scientology records of Lisa McPherson, she was not an auditor and would therefore never have acquired the knowledge prior to becoming PTS Type III to consent to be held against her will in isolation.

37. In Scientology technical bulletin "Search and Discovery" under the subtitle "Handling Type III", L. Ron Hubbard wrote, "But there will always be some failures as the insane sometimes withdraw into rigid unawareness as a final defense, sometimes can't be kept alive and sometimes are too hectic and distraught to ever become quiet, the extremes of too quiet and never quiet have a number of psychiatric names such as "catatonia" (withdrawn totally) and "manic" (too hectic)."

38. Following the dogma of L. Ron Hubbard to the letter is the highest priority for a person practicing Scientology. In a Scientology policy letter called "Keeping Scientology Working," L. Ron Hubbard says, "The proper instruction attitude is, 'You're here so you're a Scientologist. Now we are going to make

APPENDIX 1

you into an expert auditor no matter what happens. We'd rather have you dead than incapable."

39. In terms of the report and control of RTC, it is required by any and all Scientology organizations to report directly to RTC any extreme deviations from "standard tech". For example, it would be considered a deviation when a Scientology Pre-Clear, (a person that has paid for auditing services from Scientology), has left Scientology and threatens to sue.

Other examples would include a Pre-Clear, who is not getting the expected results or one who has had a psychotic break (PTS Type III). Once the RTC Tech Unit completed a review of a Pre-Clear folder, it would be sent back via the Office of the Senior Case Supervisor International (located in Church of Scientology International) to ensure compliance with orders and correction as deemed necessary by the RTC Tech Unit.

CSI receives updated status reports and without question would have received updated status reports on the Isolation of Lisa McPherson and her deteriorating medical condition because RTC has an on-site representative at FLAG. These reports would be composed and sent up the line to Ray Mithoff at RTC by the Senior Case Supervisor, Alain Kartuzinski. Ray Mithoff would then take the report to RTC. The Office of Special Affairs, OSA, locally and internationally, would be informed of the Isolation as well.

Marty Rathbun, Inspector General Ethics, is over all the legal affairs of every case and situation in Scientology and would also have knowledge of a PTS Type III in Isolation.

40. The above reporting procedure is still practiced in the Scientology conglomerate today. For example, in the attached "D/Inspector General Office," published by Religious Technology Center and copyrighted in 1997, it compels reporting directly to RTC any listed situation, such as "any person who acts PTS Type III." This is all done in order to help RTC "locate and eradicate any suppression (i.e., a threat) and thereby make sure that Scientology keeps working." Lisa McPherson was deemed PTS Type III and therefore was such a threat.

41. RTC receives all reports on situations involving Isolation for guidance from RTC to the Senior Case Supervisor, Sr. C/S. RTC then reports the matter to Sr. C/S INT, i.e., International, office for further investigation. Senior C/S INT then reports back to the RTC Reports Officer. Ray Mithoff is the Senior C/S INT at CSI, the mother church.

Ray Mithoff, Marty Rathbun, and David Miscavige, as they have done on other occasions within my personal knowledge, meet and discuss various options available to Scientology on how to deal with a public relations flap. No one else has the authority to do so. Lisa McPherson was such a public relations flap to Scientology since she took her clothes off in public and was placed in Isolation.

42. In records I have reviewed provided by FLAG in this case concerning Lisa McPherson; she had previously complained that Scientology was not working for her, and her stats were down. Based on my own experience and Scientology procedures and protocol, these three individuals would have met and discussed on several occasions what to do with Lisa since she was not improving in Isolation. It is

APPENDIX 1

important to know that Scientology has no prohibition on members seeking emergency medical treatment as stated in HCOB Physically ILL PCs and Pre-OTs, 12-3-69, which mandates a medical cure before auditing, where Hubbard states "if we already know he is ill we should call in the doctor." page 328 of Volume 8 of the Technical Bulletins.

43. Yet, from the available records, it is apparent to me that these three individuals: Mithoff, Rathbun, and Miscavige, had no option other than to permit her to die in Isolation rather than take her to the hospital for emergency medical treatment and risk embarrassing questions from the attending physicians, press, and authorities with likely claims of imprisonment and abuse being made by Lisa McPherson upon her recovery. This is true because in Scientology it is never an option to be held accountable.

Contrary to their own policy that "THE CORRECT ACTION ON AN INSANE PATIENT IS A FULL SEARCHING CLINICAL EXAMINATION BY A COMPETENT MEDICAL DOCTOR." Page 327, Volume 8 of the Technical Bulletins, Scientology decided in Lisa's case, through these three individuals acting through FLAG, not to follow this particular policy and let her die.

Scientology provides an option called "end cycle" which is permitting and ordering the person to die. It is obvious to me that the decision was to permit Lisa McPherson to die rather than face an extreme public relations flap by taking her to the local emergency room in her morbid condition as described in the "caretaker logs."

44. Based on my personal experience and expertise in Scientology, I have formed the following opinion: Lisa McPherson was held against her will in Isolation and when she did not respond to Scientology technical handling, FLAG, on orders from David Miscavige, Ray Mithoff, and Marty Rathbun sat mute and watched her die after she no longer had the strength to fight for her freedom. Her death was no accident. It was the chosen option to minimize a public relations flap.

45. I declare under penalty of perjury under the laws of the State of Florida that the foregoing is true and correct.

JESSE PRINCE

SWORN TO AND SUBSCRIBED before me at
Tampa, Hillsborough County, Florida, this ___ day of August, 1999.

Appendix 2

MSH Affidavit

Harold J. McElhinny (Bar No. 66781)
Rachel Krevans (Bar No. 116421)
Stephen P. Freccero (Bar No. 131093)
Ronald P. Flynn (Bar No. 184 186)
Jason A. Crotty (Bar No. 196036)
MORRISON & FOERSTER LLP
425 Market Street
San Francisco, California 94105-2482
Telephone: (415) 268-7000 Facsimile: (415) 268-7522

Jana G. Gold (Bar No. 154246)
MORRISON & FOERSTER LLP
755 Page Mill Road Palo Alto, California 94304-1018
Telephone: (650) 8 13-5600
Facsimile: (650) 494-0792

Attorneys for Defendant
DENNIS ERLICH

UNITED STATES DISTRICT COURT
NORTHERN DISTRICT OF CALIFORNIA
SAN JOSE DIVISION

RELIGIOUS TECHNOLOGY CENTER,
a California non-profit corporation; and
BRIDGE PUBLICATIONS, INC.,
a California non-profit corporation,
Plaintiffs,

v.

DENNIS ERLICH, an individual,
Defendant
AND RELATED COUNTERCLAIMS.
No. C-95-20091 RMW (EAI)

Date: N/A
Tie: N/A
Ctm: Hon. Ronald M. Whyte

DECLARATION OF JESSE PRINCE IN
SUPPORT OF MR. ERLICH'S MOTION FOR
RECONSIDERATION OF SEPTEMBER 30, 1998
SUMMARY JUDGMENT ORDER

I, Jesse Prince, declare as follows:

1. This declaration is of my own personal knowledge and if called upon to testify to the facts herein I could and would be competently able to testify thereto.

2. I was in Scientology for 16 years (1976 - 92) and served in the highest ranks, including as the second in command of the Religious Technology Center ("RTC"). Because of this experience, I am intimately familiar with the Scientology organizations, the Scientology movement, and the beliefs of Scientology. At that time, my position was "Deputy Inspector

APPENDIX 2

General, External," I was in charge of all activities inside and outside the Scientology organization. This included being in charge of all litigation by or against any Scientology organization, intelligence (e.g. spying and covert operations) against perceived "enemies" (ranging from critics to media to the courts), trademark registration, and the licensing of trademarks to other Scientology organizations.

3. I first became involved with Scientology in September 1976, in San Francisco. In late 1976, I joined the elite Scientology paramilitary organization known as the Sea Organization, also known as the "Sea Org" or "SO." The Sea Organization is the organization that actually controls the Scientology empire. SO personnel are authorized to take over and control any Scientology organization. This is also true of the nominally secular organizations, such as Bridge Publications. The control by SO is possible because all the executives in these organizations are selected for their agreement that the SO is the commanding organization. This weeding out process guarantees there will be nobody to resist the SO's management. In this manner SO can control the entire Scientology empire.

4. Before I was recruited into RTC in 1982, most of my Scientology experience was with technical material; the codified methods and techniques used within the Scientology organizations. During these years, I became intimately familiar with the technical material of Scientology, most of which was written by Scientology founder L. Ron Hubbard. It was that familiarity that prompted my promotion to a technical position at RTC.

5. When I moved to RTC, I was transferred to and lived and worked at what is known as "Golden Era Studios," near Hemet, California. It is also known as "Gold" or simply "the base." RTC's presence at Gold was known to all at the base, but was kept hidden from others, to try to make it appear that Gold was merely a video production studio. In reality, the studio is a front for the top of Scientology's actual power structure. (The security system at Gold is elaborate; it includes motion detectors, buried sensors, high-speed cameras, night cameras; motorcycles guards, and barbed wire fences). RTC was, at that time, the most powerful organization within Scientology. All RTC members were also Sea Org members, as were all at the base.

6, L. Ron Hubbard died in 1986. His widow was Mary Sue Hubbard, who was by then an elderly and fragile woman. David Miscavige, then, as now, the leader of Scientology, had Mary Sue Hubbard watched at her home and received daily reports as to her condition and activities. Mary Sue Hubbard was under constant surveillance by the Church of Scientology and Miscavige.

7. A number of weeks after L. Ron Hubbard's death, I was present at a meeting where David Miscavige and a group of 12-17 other Scientologists coerced Mary Sue Hubbard into relinquishing her legal rights to the Scientology writings of the recently-deceased L. Ron Hubbard. I participated in that meeting in my capacity as a high-level member of RTC and Sea Org. The day before this meeting, David Miscavige told me and a group of other senior Scientology executives that he wanted a group, including me, to go over to Mary Sue Hubbard's

APPENDIX 2

home in Los Angeles in order to get Mary Sue Hubbard to sign an agreement relinquishing her claims to L. Ron Hubbard's estate. Miscavige said he wanted a group to go the house because he wanted, in his words, a "show of force" and that the group would stay at Mary Sue Hubbard's house until the agreement was signed. The next day the meeting did take place at Mary Sue Hubbard's home. The group that went to her house, including myself, went over with the intent to overwhelm Mary Sue Hubbard and get her to sign an agreement. That was something we had openly discussed and was the purpose and intention of our going over there. The meeting lasted about 3 hours, from about 12:30 to 3:30 in the afternoon. I was personally present at this meeting, along with a number of Scientology officers and officials, including David Miscavige, Norman Starkey, Lymon Spurlock, Marty Rathbun, Vicki Aznaran, Mark Yeager, Ray Mithoff, and Mark Ingber. I believe that Warren McShane was also present, as well as a Scientology lawyer, Earl Cooley. At the end of the meeting Mary Sue Hubbard was forced to sign an agreement in which she transferred her rights to L. Ron Hubbard's works to various Scientology entities. Those works included copyrights, trademarks, bank accounts, and other property - anything of value related to the Scientology fortune. In "exchange" Mary Sue was compensated with a monetary amount. I believe it was $100,000. Diana, Suzette, and Arthur Hubbard, the children of L. Ron also received a monetary amount. I believe those amounts to be $50,000 each. All of those amounts, individually and in total, were trivial in relation to the value of the L. Ron Hubbard fortune, which I understand was then valued at between $200 and $400 million, possibly more. David Miscavige also personally informed me that he obtained similar agreements from L. Ron Hubbard's other children, outside the Hubbard family.

8. Based on my personal observations at this meeting, Mary Sue Hubbard did not make the transaction voluntarily. At the time of the meeting, Mary Sue Hubbard appeared elderly, in her late 60s or early 70s, and seemed obviously sickly and was overdressed in that she was wrapped in clothes. She remained seated throughout the whole meeting. Based on my observations, including her appearance, mannerism and some of the things she said, she did not seem altogether coherent. At times she seemed to rant or speak non-sequitors. At the beginning of the meeting, Mary Sue Hubbard was introduced to everyone in the group and told their positions in Scientology, and things were cordial. When David Miscavige asked Mary Sue Hubbard to sign an agreement things changed. Mary Sue Hubbard stated that she would not sign the agreement proposed by Miscavige because she did not agree with it. She told everyone that she did not trust Miscavige and felt he was destructive to Scientology. She made reference to Miscavige as a "deceptive, power-hungry person" bent on taking over everything and said she was not going to go along with it. However, Mary Sue Hubbard was confronted by Miscavige and 12-17 others, including myself. Most of the others, including myself, were large men who wore the paramilitary uniforms of the Sea Org. David Miscavige screamed at her to sign the document and screamed that she would sign the document Miscavige also told her that:

Appendix 2

"Everything that L. Ron Hubbard did, he did for the church. We are the church, not you. Therefore everything is staying right here with us." Miscavige also told her that the persons who were there would stay until she did sign the agreement. The combination of Miscavige screaming at her, sometimes very close to her face, and the rest of us browbeating her, was an intimidating and coercive environment, particularly for a frail and elderly woman. There was an implicit threat that she and her family would be subject to various Scientology sanctions such as "auditing," "ethics," or "sec checking" involving long interrogations if she did not comply with the demands to sign the documents. Mary Sue Hubbard was told that the group would stay there no matter how long it took, and it could either be done the easy way or the hard way. During the entire proceeding, Mary Sue Hubbard was never left alone; she was always in the presence of Scientology members bent on getting her to sign the legal documents that would strip her of her legal interest in L. Ron Hubbard's Scientology works.

9. A Scientology lawyer, I believe it was Earl Cooley, was at this meeting, but he did not advise Mary Sue Hubbard of her legal rights. At no time during the process was Mary Sue Hubbard advised of her legal rights, either community property rights or her inheritance rights. Mary Sue Hubbard had no personal counsel present at this meeting. The only directions given by the Scientology lawyer was that the agreement would make things better for Scientology and Mary Sue Hubbard was told where to sign the documents.

10. I was informed by David Miscavige that although Mary Sue Hubbard and L. Ron Hubbard had been separated and had not talked for a long time, she was saddened by the death of her husband. Miscavige told me he would use this to his advantage. Also, before the meeting took place, Ray Mithoff told me, in the presence of David Miscavige, that he couldn't wait to tell Mary Sue Hubbard that L. Ron had not asked about her before his death. Mithoff seemed anxious for Mary Sue Hubbard to ask him about this and appeared gleeful at the opportunity to tell her this. Near the end of the meeting, Mary Sue Hubbard did in fact ask if L. Ron Hubbard had said anything about her or had asked about her before he died. Ray Mithoff then told her that Hubbard had not even mentioned her name. At that point, after the hours of browbeating, the screaming by Miscavige, which was sometimes done very close to her face, the implicit threats, the emotional turmoil, and the general coerciveness of the situation, Mary Sue Hubbard became silent, bowed her head and proceeded to sign anything Miscavige and his minions put before her. I saw her sign multiple documents and she did not seem to pay any attention to them she just signed them. She then said words to the effect that you got what you want, now you leave.

11. I do not believe that either Mary Sue Hubbard or her family knew that the L. Ron Hubbard estate was worth between $200 and $400 million. I base this on the fact that neither Mary Sue or any of L. Ron Hubbard's children were on the Board of Directors of any of the umbrella corporations of Scientology, such as Author Services, Inc., RTC, CST or CSRT. Because of my position within the organization, I

APPENDIX 2

know that it was the policy of the corporations to keep the financial information secret. Under the coercive conditions she was put under and the information she was given, Mary Sue Hubbard did not knowingly or voluntarily relinquish her claims to the L. Ron Hubbard estate. I do not believe that Mary Sue Hubbard would have signed the agreement had she been advised or her legal rights and provided additional information, particularly information regarding the value of the L. Ron Hubbard Scientology fortune. It is also my belief, based on what I saw happen at this meeting, the Mary Sue Hubbard felt very threatened by David Miscavige and the rest of us. Mary Sue Hubbard was allowed to read the documents, but because of her actions and words that day, I do not believe she understood what she was reading. I regret that I had any part in this and am saddened because I realize now that this was destructive and wrong.

12. I left Scientology on October 31, 1992. From the time Mary Sue Hubbard got out of jail, which I believe was 1981, until the time that I left my post at RTC, Mary Sue Hubbard was cared for around the clock by two Scientologists, Neville and Leslie Potter. The Potter's provided a detailed report to Norman Starkey, a Trustee of RTC, and David Miscavige, also a Trustee, every day on Mrs. Hubbard's activities, even including trips to go shopping. Because Starkey and Miscavige were trustees for RTC, RTC was always acutely aware of Mrs. Hubbard's whereabouts, and always would have been able to produce her if needed for a deposition. I declare, under penalty of perjury under the laws of the United States of

America that the foregoing is true and correct. Signed this 17th day of March, 1999 at Boulder, Colorado.

Printed in Poland
by Amazon Fulfillment
Poland Sp. z o.o., Wrocław